COMMUNICATIONS WORKERS OF AMERICA

Also by Thomas R. Brooks
Toil and Trouble
Picket Lines and Bargaining Tables
Walls Come Tumbling Down

COMMUNICATIONS WORKERS OF AMERICA

The Story of a Union

THOMAS R. BROOKS

MASON / CHARTER   NEW YORK 1977

Published simultaneously in Canada by George J. McLeod, Limited, Toronto.

Cataloging in Publication Data

Brooks, Thomas R
  Communications Workers of America

  Bibliography: p.
  Includes index.
  1. Communications Workers of America—History.
1. Title.
HD6515.T7B76   331.88′11′3840973   77–8650
ISBN 0–88405–585–X

TO
JOSEPH A. BEIRNE
February 16, 1911—September 2, 1974

CONTENTS

PREFACE

William Cobbett, ploughman, pamphleteer and an English radical of the early 1800s, once wrote, "To come to the true history of a country you must read its laws; you must read books treating of its usages and customs in former times; and you must particularly inform yourself as to prices of labor and of food." In a modern republic, a pluralistic democracy, I would add that you must also treat of its institutions, especially those created by its working people. Do workers have the right to strike? To organize? To bargain collectively with their employers? To participate in their country's political life through their unions as well as through their political parties? The answers to such questions tell much about the true history of a modern industrial society.

Ever since the industrial revolution began workers have banded together to improve their lot. Today, collective bargaining is an enormously complicated process, touching upon nearly every facet of industrial life, ranging from the procedures through which a worker may file a grievance against his foreman, to the control of work assignments, to the uses of huge welfare funds. In short, collective bargaining gives working men and women some say about the conditions of their employment—it opens up democracy in industry. This is acknowledged in public policy as approved by Congress. The law guarantees workers the right to organize, to choose their representatives, to strike and to bargain collectively with their respective employers. The law, however, not only guarantees industrial democracy through collective bargaining, it also insists that unions *be* democratic. No other institution within our society is required by law to adhere to a bill of rights. American workers are not only free to join a union but they are also free to exercise their rights as individuals within the union—to speak, to elect officers and to make policy.

Trade unionism, however, is not limited to what takes place behind plant gates or within union meeting halls. The terms of employment, conditions of work, welfare benefits and the like are subject to government regulations of increasing complexity. To protect their rights under law as well as gains won through bargaining, trade unionists engage in political action. Unions encourage their members—and other citizens—to register and vote. They also raise money through voluntary contributions in order to support political candidates. And, perhaps more important, unions are a powerful peoples' lobby, pressing for progressive social change within the legislative halls of the nation. Social security, unemployment insurance, Medicare, public housing, anti-discrimination laws, and public education are among organized labor's many achievements. Through their unions, workers have enlarged economic, political and social democracy. To know a trade union's history is to know more about how our democracy works.

This history is the story of the making of an unusual union, one that reaches into more American communities than any other—The Communications Workers of America, AFL-CIO. Its 575,000 members live in 10,000 communities and are organized in 900 local unions scattered across fifty states. Those members are employed as switchboard operators, installers, clerks, cable splicers, linemen, engineers, laboratory technicians, directory salespersons, secretaries, data processors, news gatherers, as well as in a broad range of other job classifications within communications and related industries. A little more than half of its members are women; all work at the very heart of our complex industrial society where vast corporations employ thousands in the production of goods and services.

CWA is an industrial union with a jurisdiction, in the words of its Constitution, embracing "all communications work and . . . the persons engaged therein." The union has been portrayed as a prototype white collar and/or professional organization, the union of the future as well as the union that automation made. CWA members do work in a technologically advanced industry and tend, figuratively perhaps in these modish times, to wear white collars. Still, it is not by these characteristics alone that the eleventh largest union in America is distinguished from its brother and sister unions. CWA members work for telephone operating companies, equipment manufacturers and related firms throughout the U.S. They are to be found in large towns as well as small in every state. Some work alone, climbing lofty poles in lonely hamlets or installing dial telephones in individual homes; others work in large groups, side by side on a factory bench or seated in rows before complicated exchange panels. N. R. Danielian, the biographer of Ma Bell, observed in 1939, "The characteristic thing about Bell System employment is that it is spread throughout the United States, reaching into all of the large cities and most of the counties. In this respect it differs from industrial concerns which employ large numbers of people concentrated in the comparatively few localities where their plants operate." And so it is for the union. The full extent of CWA's potential may be imagined when one considers that ninety percent of all U.S. households have telephones installed which are serviced by telephone workers.

There is more than just a spread of membership to the CWA story, for the union is justly proud of its reputation as a "community-minded union" and it works hard at maintaining that reputation. Its members are encouraged to participate—and do so—in community affairs, working with the Boy Scouts, joining community chest drives, and engaging in volunteer social work of all kinds. Each local union has a community services committee with standing orders to carry out innovative as well as traditional community programs. The late Joseph A. Beirne, a founder and president until shortly before his death in 1974, not only served as chairman of the AFL-CIO's Community Services Committee but was also the first labor leader ever elected president of the United Community Funds and Councils of America, now the United Way of America. CWA president Glenn E. Watts, who came out of the Washington, D.C. local union, has been active in District of Columbia community affairs for over thirty years and currently serves as Secretary to the United Way of America. Community participation for CWA members involves a wide-range of activity, from drug/alcoholic programs to day-care centers and senior citizens' clubs. That range sums up CWA involvement with America.

CWA has a unique birthright and, as a consequence of the technological character of the communications industry, has had to pioneer the development of new techniques to resolve the conflicts of labor and management. Without yielding the fundamental right to strike, it has become far more selective than most unions in the use of the strike weapon. There is, too, a lively internal life; democracy flourishes within the union at all levels. The union has succeeded remarkably in relating the needs of its members to the broad interests of the community and, more directly, with those of the public directly affected by the outcome of its negotiations. Without yielding its integrity, the union has been realistic about its relationships with management. CWA, on the whole, has welcomed change and inventiveness and flexibility.

Unlike Topsy, however, the union did not "just grow," nor did it spring full-blown, all wise, from an industrial Jupiter's forehead. While telephone workers may have started their union with some advantages other workers did not enjoy, nonetheless, they had lessons to learn, birthpangs to suffer, and obstacles to overcome. Mistakes were made and some ways of doing things had to be unlearned or re-shaped to fit new circumstances. There were confrontations with employers and conflicts within the union leadership. CWA, as it is today, evolved out of these struggles.

It would be impossible within the scope of one book to do full justice to the union and all its members. Each local has its own story to tell, each member, an anecdote. Every picket line has contributed its measure to the trials and tribulations of change. Grievances, committee meetings, negotiations—countless threads are woven into the rich tapestry of the union's history. Still, there is a pattern of development and it is the concern of this work to trace that pattern, a process of development that saw telephone workers transforming a collection of independent organizations into a truly national union.

Joseph Beirne, president of CWA for so many of its formative years, once observed, "American trade unions have contributed much to the history of our country. Perhaps their most important contribution has been the creation of ferment which precedes progress." But he also thought it odd that "while living in a world of ferment" American trade unions were "relatively quiescent." He, therefore, expressed greater concern for "the dynamics" of trade unionism than for trade unionism itself. "If we fully utilize labor's creative intelligence," he argued, "we can help make not only America but the entire free world a more interesting, a more satisfactory, a more wholesome environment for our children." There is a sense in which that task can never be finished; this book, then, is the story of some men and women who have contributed to its unravelling and who, therefore, have moved us still another step along the arduous road of human progress.

THOMAS R. BROOKS

ACKNOWLEDGMENTS

I want to thank the members and officers of the Communications Workers of America, AFL-CIO, for the opportunity to write this history. It was a most enjoyable and memorable experience. A great number of people contributed directly and indirectly to my fund of knowledge about the union and I wish I could record them all. I am grateful for their willingness to share their experiences, insights and information about the union's past. I am, however, solely responsible for the uses of the material offered as well as for the opinions and work of these pages.

Specifically, I would like to thank: Henry Fleisher, who introduced me to the union; Glenn E. Watts and Louis B. Knecht, who most graciously opened doors that might have otherwise been closed; D. L. McCowen, William Smallwood and William Dunn, who shared their past and helped to bring it alive for me; and Lee White, who provided leads and insights without which I would have been hopelessly lost.

As always Knox Berger, my agent, deserves the best for his invaluable assistance; Nancy Davis, for her editorial guidance; and my wife, Harriet, for her patience.

I
ORIGINS

Few unions in America admit to having been born of a company union, even though countless local unions owe an unacknowledged debt to employer efforts at setting up employee associations to further management policies. The Communications Workers of America is one exception. On one August afternoon in 1950, CWA president Joseph A. Beirne told a group of senators, who were examining labor-management relations in the Bell telephone system, "the beginnings of national organization in the telephone industry were not frowned upon by the Bell System." Today, the lineal descendant of those "beginnings," the Communications Workers of America, is widely considered to be among the most progressive and forward-looking unions in the country, and is certainly not among the least militant.

Before we can understand this union changeling we must consider its origins. What brings a union's rank-and-file together initially is the choice of employment. Work then shapes character; the history of a craft, an industry or even a firm leaves its stamp on those engaged in its productive activities. While working people share much in common one can distinguish between electricians and plumbers, auto and steel workers, garment and telephone workers. Their respective unions, too, differ in elan, style, character. Today, CWA members are found working for a variety of firms within the communications industry and related fields. Yet we must open our account with an analysis and description of the Bell System, for that is where most CWA members work and where the union's history began.

The Bell System encompasses American Telephone and Telegraph Company (AT&T), the largest corporation in the world. In 1976, its assets were $86,716,989 with operating revenues of $32.8 billion. AT&T wholly owns fifteen operating companies, controls majority interest in five others and maintains substantial minority interest in four additional operating companies. The operating companies provide telephone service within states or regions as, say, Indiana Bell Telephone Company does for the Hoosier State or as Pacific Telephone and Telegraph Company does on the West Coast. AT&T operates long-distance lines, while manufacturing, installation and maintenance of telephone equipment is performed by a subsidiary, Western Electric Company. AT&T and Western jointly own Bell Telephone

Laboratories, the research source for all types of electronic communications systems.

A. A. Berle, Jr., a member of President Franklin D. Roosevelt's Brain Trust and a noted corporation law expert, called AT&T "the only real American monopoly." The Bell System's $56.1 billion investment in plant in 1970 represented ninety-five percent of the total investment for the industry. It operates about eighty-four percent of all the telephones in the United States, or roughly 100 million. AT&T is technically a holding company, and this, along with the continued existence of the independent telephone companies, keeps the Bell System clear of Federal anti-trust actions.* Still, the facts of life being what they are, this exemption does not appreciably lessen the economic power and thrust of the telephone giant. Its financial connections alone interlock to the tune of $242 billion with sixty-three major corporations. AT&T shareholders numbered 2,898,000 in 1976, the largest constituency, as such, in the country. And with 776,170 employees, excluding Western Electric, the Bell System is the nation's largest private employer.

"Ma Bell" projects a friendly image, as cheering as the operator's cheerful, "May I help you?" AT&T's "associated" companies are said to be autonomous. "In the conduct of business," Walter S. Gifford, AT&T president and board chairman 1925–1948, once said, "responsibility is decentralized so that the man on the spot can act rapidly and effectively." In a court brief, AT&T attorneys put it in even stronger terms: "no such interference or control has ever been exercised by the American Company [over Illinois Bell and presumably over the other associated companies], nor contemplated by the officers of either company." And, further, "the distinction between the corporations is as clearly marked as to property, money, records, accounts, and other details of corporate affairs, as if the American Company were not a stockholder at all." Yet, from March 7, 1876, the day a bespectacled clerk in the U.S. Patent Office assigned Number 174,465 to a patent sought by a Scot immigrant, Alexander Graham Bell, the name of the telephone game has been "control."

The Bostonian founders of the Bell System exercised control by licensing the use of telephone equipment patented by Bell. Later, through the acquisition of licensee stock, they converted franchise operators into "associated companies." Wall Street banking interests wrested control from the Boston group during the 1920s, a corporate struggle that allowed the emergence of what K. B. Thayer, AT&T president from 1919 to 1925, termed "self-

---

*Economist D.H. Robertson gives the best definition of a holding company: "An arrangement under which the whole or a majority of the stock of the existing companies is taken over by and held in the name of a new separate company, which may or may not also directly acquire properties of its own, and where shares are distributed among the shareholders of the original company."

continuing" management. But the basic system evolved long before this process was completed. By 1890, the 1920 AT&T annual report stated that "the organization [of the company] embodied the essential elements . . . of the Bell System of the present, that is: central control—a central advisory staff—a central laboratory of development and research—a central department to promote progress in operating technique—a central source of supply of standarized material—local operating companies and a national network of lines connecting them. . . . With all the complications of varying state legislation and supervision it has made possible the operation of the System through scores of companies as an homogeneous whole."

"The Bell System is really a new sort of thing. It is a publicly owned, privately managed institution," Walter S. Gifford, then first vice president of AT&T, informed the Bell System Educational Conference in August 1924. Bell management, at various times, has enthused over being an "integrated system," or "one organic whole" generating what Gifford termed as "a sense of trusteeship on the part of the management." This trusteeship, Gifford asserted before Federal Communications Commission hearings on March 17, 1936, was exercised on behalf of investors, employees and customers in equal measure:

Q. Mr. Gifford, do you recognize in your capacity and your position as an executive of the Telephone Company is one of stewardship in the interests of the employees, I take it, as well as the investors and the patrons, is that correct?
A. Yes, sir.
Q. And I take it that you feel that your responsibility and your loyalty is divided as nearly equal as it may be to the three parties in interest?
A. Yes, sir.

A system that can be autonomous, or an organic whole at will, is ingenious indeed. "It was a very clever pudding to invent," as the White Knight told Alice. Still, the test of a trusteeship lies in how well it is administered and this, as we shall see, was something else again when it came to Bell System dealings with its employees. The System has always prided itself on the quality of its service, and, by extension, on the quality of its employees. And, to be a telephone employee meant something special in most communities. As Elizabeth Beardsley Butler found in her classic 1907–1908 survey of Pittsburgh working women, "Telephone and telegraph work, like 'clerking,' is socially desirable, and by reason of this, claims the American girl." Working conditions, too, were considered superior. "In its lunch rooms and rest rooms," a Pittsburgh observer noted a few years later, "its kitchen where tea and coffee are served free of charge and odorless cooking is permitted; its fortnight vacation with pay, its sick benefits, pensions and medical service, the Central District Telephone Company has adopted many of the welfare features in which the Heinz plant led [H. J. Heinz, the canning company, was a progressive employer of the day]; but in common with the national social policy of the Bell System it has introduced a more modern note in its physical examinations, its scientific study of workroom environment, and of work processes." As an example, the observer added, the telephone company had developed "a one-day-of-rest-in-seven schedule in its continuous operations, years in advance of the steel companies."

Arnold Bennett, the English novelist, caught the atmosphere of telephone work in a visit to a New York City telephone exchange: "A murmuring sound, as of an infinity of scholars in a prim school conning their lessons, and a long row of young women seated in a dim radiance of a long row of precisely similar stools, before a long apparatus of holes and pegs and pieces of elastic cord, all extremely intent: that was the first broad impression. One saw at once that none of these young women had a single moment to spare; they were all involved in the tremendous machine, a part of it, keeping pace with it and in it, and not daring to take their eyes off it for an instant, lest they should sign against it. What they were droning about it was impossible to guess; for if one stationed oneself close to any particular rapt young woman, she seemed to utter no sound, but simply and without ceasing continued to peg and unpeg holes at random among the thousands of holes before her, apparently in obedience to the signaling of faint, tiny lights that in thousands continually expired and were rekindled. (It was so that these tiny lights should be distinguishable that the illumination of the secret and finely appointed chamber was kept dim.) Throughout the whole length of the apparatus the colored elastic cords to which the pegs were attached kept crossing one another in fantastic patterns . . .

"I learned that even the lowest beginner earned five dollars a week. It was just the sum I was paying for a pair of clean sheets every night at a grand hotel. And that salary rose to six, seven, eight, eleven, and even fourteen dollars for supervisors, who, however, had to stand on their feet seven and a half hours a day, as shopgirls do for ten hours a day; and that in general the girls had thirty minutes for lunch and a day off every week, and that the company supplied them gratuitously with tea, coffee, sugar, couches, newspapers, armchairs, and fresh air, of which last fifty fresh cubic feet were pumped in for every operator every minute.

" 'Naturally,' I was told, 'the discipline is strict. There are test wires . . . We can check the "time elements" . . . We keep a record of every call. They'll take a dollar a week less in an outside place—for instance, a hotel . . . Their average stay here is thirty months.' . . . Imagine quitting that convent with its guaranteed fresh air and its couches and sugar and so on, for the rough hazards and promiscuities of a hotel! On the other hand, imagine not quitting it!"

Nelle B. Curry, a field investigator for the U.S. Commission on Industrial

Relations, reported in 1915, "I was told by the girls that the telephone company paid more than any other line that the same girl might go into. This I believe to be true, based not only upon my present investigations, but from observation and inquiry into the wage rate of department stores and factories." Of the seven "typical" cities Miss Curry studied, Madison, Wisconsin paid the least with switchboard operators starting at fifty cents for a nine-hour day with an hour off for lunch for beginners ($13 a month), to $1.20 a day ($31.20 a month) for experienced workers. In Nashville, beginners worked two weeks *without pay* then earned $22.50 a month for a year-and-a-half before rising to $35 a month. Switchboard operators in other cities were paid a bit better—$20 to $40 a month in Kansas City; $7 to $10.50 a week in Salt Lake City; and $1.10 a day ($26.80 a month) to $1.80 a day ($46.80 a month) in Los Angeles. Chicago's scale started at twelve cents an hour ($26 a month), rising to twenty cents an hour ($43.50 a month) after four years and hit a high of twenty-three cents an hour ($50 a month) after seven years of service. But the average length of service in Chicago was a bare two years and six months, which left most of the operators with earnings of sixteen cents an hour, or $35 a month. Food prices, admittedly, were low, but not so low as to make telephone wages munificent. Chuck roasts cost sixteen cents a pound; bread, seven cents; butter thirty-five cents; potatoes fifteen cents; pork chops twenty cents, and coffee thirty cents a pound in 1915. Yet one young woman, living in a rooming house with another operator, told Miss Curry that after the rent and grocery bills were paid, "there is nothing left." As for clothes, she remarked, "Oh, I just don't have any."

Miss Curry worked up the following minimum monthly budget for a telephone operator:

Rent	$12.00
Food (50¢ per day)	15.00
Carfare (10¢ per day)	2.50
Laundry (where she does part of it herself)	2.50
Clothes	13.00
Amusements and recreation	2.50
Newspapers and magazines	.50
Incidentals (toilet articles, church, gifts, etc.)	2.00
Emergency fund (insurance, sickness, medical attention, dentistry, unemployment	5.00
	$55.00

"It is doubtful," Miss Curry added, "if the amount in the foregoing suggested budget for board and room would allow the girl to a room to herself in sanitary surroundings, with proper bathing facilities, in such a place as would guarantee at least the most ordinary facilities for social intercourse such as receiving visitors, all of which I deem highly important to the enjoyment of normal existence."

Most of the telephone operators interviewed by Miss Curry "declared that they would quit the telephone service if they could secure other employment at the same wages." Nonetheless, telephone company managers informed the indefatigible Miss Curry that they had "no trouble in securing the best material for the work—the brightest and freshest of young girls seem to be keen for the work. They say that the girls like the excitement of the work and the mystery element appeals to them." Miss Curry found the spirit of the new operators—average ages ran from sixteen to twenty-five —"generally good and optimistic, especially during the first year of service." The necessity of constant restraint when confronted by uncharitable, insulting, harshly critical and *unseen* patrons, however, exacted a toll. Miss Curry found operators feeling isolated, evidencing "a shy, recluse spirit." Moreover, they worked in an industry with no future for them: "A few . . . may become supervisors at an increased wage; for the rest there is nothing in view but the same day-in and day-out grind at the board until the limit of their expectations—a salary of $40 or $45 a month in the far distant future—is reached, but as a general rule, they have dropped out of the ranks long before that goal is attained." Younger girls were preferred recruits for telephone work, Miss Curry reported. "They are most likely to live at home. They are keener for the work, livelier in spirit, more alert to discipline. They enter with more eagerness and zest into the excitement that the character of the work affords. They worry less. They are physically more able to stand the strain. So it is that, year by year, there is drawn into the service of the telephone companies an army of girls in their years of adolescence . . ."

With heads held high and full of hopes, the young women flocked to work in the new telephone exchanges. "On entering one of these rooms," the perceptive Miss Curry observed, "one sees from eighty to 100 young women seated beside each other on high chairs opposite a keyboard which extends in the form of a semi-circle around the three sides of the room. The position of the operator in regard to the keyboard is the same as if she were seated at a table, except that the divisions are so narrow that if the operators were to place their arms akimbo they would touch each other." On going to work, the operator puts on a headset, a metal and rubber contrivance, with a plugging cord attached, that connects her for the day with the switchboard. "A light flashes before [the operator] indicating a call from a certain number. Instantly the operator takes up a plug, inserts it in the office below the light, which extinguishes the light, pulls a little lever and says, 'Number, please.' The subscriber gives the number, say, 'Twenty-four eighty-five East.' She repeats the number, placing the office prefix in the proper place and spelling the number out thus: 'East 2-4-8-5.' At the same time she picks up the corresponding plug and inserts it in the 'multiple' or upper portion of the board, then pulls the lever which rings the number called. As soon as she inserts the plug, a corresponding light burns until the party called answers. If the party doesn't answer immediately, the operator, after a period of fifteen seconds (she guesses at the time), opens the lever again and says to the party calling, 'I'm trying to get your party.' Then she waits another fifteen seconds—I say 'waits,' but in the meantime she may be attending to two or three other calls. She opens the lever and says, 'Please repeat your number and I will ring them again.' This is called 'reporting on the call.' This is repeated until the party called answers or until 120 seconds have passed, when she opens her lever again and says, 'East 2–4–8–5 doesn't answer.'"

The making and severing of connections is what operating is all about, whether "untrunked calls," as above, or "trunked calls", which involve the service of another operator. Each operator was responsible, initially, for the section before her, which, if exceptionally busy, may only have had five or ten lines, or if not, over 100 lines (or subscribers). Less efficient operators were placed between older and more experienced hands who were expected to watch the board of the middle operator as well as their own and to help if calls came in too fast. But the outside operator in each section of three was the middle operator of the next group, and so on along the entire exchange, creating a series of teams to effect speed and economy of service. Miss Butler of the *Pittsburgh Survey* reports that operators maintained a rate of 250 to 350 calls an hour. A Canadian Royal Commission, in 1907, reported that Toronto operators averaged 287.6 calls an hour. Miss Curry found operators handling 200 to 250 calls an hour, or an average of three to four calls each minute.

Supervisors constantly stalked behind the operators to see to it that no one lagged. "It is a mistaken idea to suppose that, in the daily work of the operator, there are periods of relaxation which compensate for the high pressure hours," Miss Curry stated. Relief periods were rigidly confined to five, ten or, at best, fifteen minutes for each shift and were granted, "not as a matter of right but as a privilege," by the supervisors. "The management expects you to be just a machine," a Los Angeles operator told Miss Curry. Another said that being "poked in the back and told to hurry when you are working as fast as you can is not very soothing to the nerves." Operators, another explained, "are not allowed to speak one word to each other—not allowed to turn their heads—not even allowed to smile, nor to fold hands, nor cross feet, nor even to lean back in their chairs." Operators were literally pinioned for hours, facing flickering lights, compelled to listen in meekness and humility to insults and complaints from irascible subscribers, plugging in and plugging out hundreds of calls with a thousand nervous muscular motions of the body, while a supervisor walked back and forth, urging alertness at the least sign of laxity or impatience. Secret monitors listened, recording all errors and deviations from the rules. "Slow answers," "slow disconnects [over ten seconds]," or an "unanswered flash," were punished by requiring the offender to work certain undesirable hours for a stated period. A Los Angeles operator, for example, was assigned a week's night work at the regular day rate of pay for a single "unanswered flash." No wonder Miss Curry was prompted to observe, "There is possibly no woman in any industry whose remissness is more instantly checked by the incisive action of an overseer than the telephone operator."

"Telephone work makes nervous wrecks of all the girls that stay in it," a Chicago operator complained. While telephone management righteously claimed, "we only know our present requirements are not detrimental," operators told a different story. "Nervous collapses at the switchboard are of frequent occurrence," Miss Curry informed the Commission on Industrial Relations. "Hysterical attacks, where the operator, after reaching the limit of nerve endurance, throws up her hands, screams and faints at her work, are said to occur quite frequently during the busiest periods and most frequently during the summer days."

As a consequence, few women remained on the job for long. Miss Curry reported that "a vast majority of the girls leave the service after about two years." A high turnover characterized telephone operating even as late as 1946 when the findings of the CWA Research and Statistics Department showed that 55.7 percent of all traffic employees had two years *or less* service, and only 24.1 percent of the group had completed five years or more of service. (This, it should be noted, was in sharp contrast to the plant work force of which 57.6 percent had been employed for five years or more.) As Miss Curry noted, telephone management preferred "younger girls," and for good economic reasons. Bell interviewers visited the homes of young prospective employees, ostensibly to check on parental attitudes to the odd night hours beginners must work but in reality because young women living with their parents might be expected to work for what one trade unionist called, "pin money." More to the point, as Miss Curry noted with some asperity, that while full efficiency as an operator could be reached by an ordinary intelligent girl in a period of from six months to a year, maximum wages, as in Chicago, were not paid until much later. "The company profits enormously by withholding the difference between the wages paid the girls and the amount which they actually earn on the basis of efficiency," she concluded. After the introduction of the Bell pension system in 1913, the turnover in employment not only diminished employee's chances of collecting benefits but also *saved* the system money. Out of every 100 women entering the service between the ages of fifteen to twenty-five, only six to seven would expect to receive a pension.

The constant turnover, too, helped to prevent the women in the industry from organizing to improve their lot. A 1908 investigation into the telephone industry by the Department of Commerce and Labor found that "practically no organization exists among telephone operators . . . In the larger cities the attitude of the local managers is severely antagonistic to local organization among operators." Miss Curry reported to the Industrial Commission that this finding had been "amply substantiated in my field investigations." She added, "The officials of the telephone companies give many reasons why they think it is undesirable for their employees to organize, the principal one being that the telephone is a necessary public utility; that any interference with its functions would work great hardship upon the subscribing public; that the first duty of such a company is to the public; that strikes and other obstructive measures, which might follow organization, could not be tolerated in such an industry, and, finally, that clearly *a labor organization composed of telephone girls would be an irresponsible body.*" (My italics.)

That telephone management felt the same way at all about *any* unionization was obfuscated by the segregation of women in the industry. Bell hiring practices quickly sorted out the work force by sex: operators and clerical workers must be women; plant craftsmen were always men. Bell claimed that extensive experimentation had proved women better operators. Most of those experiments, such as they were, were conducted very early on; the very earliest operators had been men. Since one suspects that Bell deliberately sought out young women who would quit after a year or two—as one manager told Miss Curry, "We prefer girls of naturally nervous temperaments"—one must take those experiments with a large dosage of salt. All one can say with surety is that Bell opposed unionization with every bit of managerial skill and muscle at its command.

One may pass over the propaganda of concern for either the public, subscribers or employees. A hard-nosed concern for profitability, the maintenance of dividend payments—these concerns were behind the system's labor relations decisions. To give an example drawn from the *Pittsburgh Survey:* The electricians' local union in 1907 established a scale of $3.25 a nine-hour day for journeymen after a quicky strike of twelve hours. The union permitted no specialization on such work as installing telephones, requiring a skilled mechanic to do this work. But Bell, which employed 225 men, forced an open shop on its employees and, while it paid $3.50 a day for cable splicers, it paid $1.50 to $2.75 a day for installers. Bell reduced minimum wages by subdividing the work and grading the pay accordingly. Again, this represented a considerable saving for the company.

During this early period, whatever unionization took place was accomplished by the International Brotherhood of Electrical Workers (IBEW) along craft lines and on a local by local basis. The first decades of this century were not a good time for American workers or their trade unions although there was considerable ferment in the land. The 1904 recession and a major employer counter-offensive undercut the American Federation of Labor's (AFL) organization efforts. Nonetheless, the IBEW managed to establish a precarious toehold in the industry. What happened, apparently, was that IBEW journeymen found work as linemen and cable splicers with various telephone companies, held on to their union cards and organized. The first formal agreement so far discovered was achieved in 1898 with the New Telephone Company in Indianapolis. According to an account in the *IBEW Journal,* it provided for a nine-hour day and "price and one-half for overwork." The correspondent who reported the agreement called the company "the grandest enterprise . . . Management seems to be perfect . . . employ the best labor and have the best of work done."

Sporadic strikes broke out—400 men struck in St. Louis for $3 a day and stayed out eight weeks in the summer of 1898—before the walkout collapsed. Telephone workers went out in Cleveland, in 1899; New Jersey and Buffalo, in 1900, and in Wheeling, Terre Haute, Chicago, Akron and Detroit, the following year. Many of the strikes were violent and marked by the employment of detectives and imported strikebreakers, according to contemporary accounts in the *IBEW Journal.* Stable locals, however, were established in Chicago and in the state of Montana, and remain so to this day. But these units were exceptions. The IBEW sought to counter the growth of corporate power with some kind of joint action. A western conference of locals was organized in 1903 to bargain with the Pacific Company up and down the West Coast. Southern locals came together in an effort to bargain with Southern Bell. In 1906, a bitter strike ensued which lasted for sixteen weeks. Injunctions and professional "plug-uglies" were deployed against unionists during a 1907 strike in Wheeling, West Virginia.

Whatever successes the IBEW enjoyed were scored, by and large, with the independent telephone companies. Acquisition by Bell, however, invariably eroded even these minor gains. Very little organization took place among the operators, then as now, the bulk of telephone employment. As of 1909, a United States government survey could only locate five unions of telephone operators. These were federal local unions directly affiliated with the American Federation of Labor and outside the IBEW. The report found some of these local unions "more like social clubs than trade unions."

Unionization of women workers was rare at the time. The organization of the needle trades in 1909 and 1910 was the first major outbreak of trade unionism within a predominantly female work force. The famed "uprising of the twenty thousand," a walkout of shirtwaist workers that ran from November 22, 1909 to February 15, 1910, was the "Largest strike of women ever known in the United States" and it marked the real beginning of the International Ladies' Garment Workers' Union. That strike, Samuel Gompers informed delegates to the 1910 St. Louis AFL convention, "brought to the consciousness of the nation a recognition of certain features looming up in its social development. These are the extent to which women are taking up with industrial life, their consequent tendency to stand together in the struggle to protect their common interests as wage earners, the readiness of people in all classes to approve of trade union methods on behalf of working women, and the capacity of women as strikers to suffer, to do, and to dare in support of their rights."

That capacity was soon tested in Boston when telephone operators went out on strike in 1913 to preserve their organization, the first permanent local of telephone operators in the country which had been founded the year before. It was a sublocal of a linemen's IBEW local in Boston, and this was the form the organization of operators then took. Similiar sublocals quickly sprang up in other Massachusetts cities and towns. But the women were dissatisfied with what they considered "second-class citizenship" and pushed for full recognition of their rights. The IBEW, perhaps responding to the consciousness referred to in Gompers' speech, agreed to a compromise. Operator locals were chartered directly but paid only a per capita one-half of the men's per capita and, consequently, had only one-half of the voting strength of the men's locals at IBEW conventions.

This arrangement reflected fears within the IBEW that should telephone operators take to unionism the women would become so numerous within the organization that they would outvote the men and therefore control it. As an IBEW executive board report in 1918 phrased it, "We think there can be no rule of ethics or human rights which requires men handling the sting of electricity to submit forever to the rule of telephone operators in their methods and conditions of work because they have tried that arrangement for a while."

Numerically, though perhaps not otherwise, there was some foundation for this fear. Telephone operators were a rapidly growing class of workers, rising in number from 19,000 in 1900 to 98,000 in 1910 and to 190,000 by 1920. Electricians were not much larger in number—51,000 in 1900, barely 108,000 in 1910 and 192,000 in 1920. In 1919, the IBEW convention in New Orleans established an autonomous department for the telephone operators' locals. The Telephone Operators Department, headed by Julia O'Connor, claimed a membership of 20,000 organized in 200 local unions throughout the country.

It was a beginning, but the aftermath of World War I and the growth of corporate power would abort these early efforts of telephone workers to create an organization of their own.

II

Paternalism Rampant

World War I raised trade unionists' hopes for recognition. America entered the war on April 6, 1917 to make the world "safe for democracy." In the fall of that troubled year, President Woodrow Wilson made his first trip out of Washington since American entry to Buffalo, New York, where, on November 12, he became the first president of the U.S. to address a labor convention. Accompanied by his wife and a cordon of soldiers, President Wilson entered the American Federation of Labor convention hall to be introduced to the delegates by AFL president Samuel Gompers with a "thrill of pride."

The Presidential presence was tantamount to official recognition of organized labor. The federation had supported the President's efforts to keep the country out of the European conflict. President Wilson came to Buffalo to plead for labor's continued support of a country at war and for his ultimate goal of a "just peace." He came, too, for practical reasons, seeking uninterrupted production of war materials. "Nobody," the President declared, "has a right to stop the processes of labor until all the methods of conciliation and settlement have been exhausted."

While the President spelled out for the AFL delegates the details of wartime labor relations, he laid the cornerstone for what has since become public policy for labor: "We must," he said, "do what we have declared our purpose to do, see that the conditions of labor are not rendered more onerous by the war, but also that we shall see to it that the instrumentalities by which the conditions of labor are improved are not blocked or checked."

The fruits of that policy were soon evident. While the war engendered trade-union growth, concomitant with war-stimulated economic gains, the roots of labor's progress were to be found in the reform wave that crested in 1912 and subsequently became Wilsonian. The Clayton Anti-Trust Act, adopted in 1914, forbade the use of injunctions in labor disputes unless a court decided that one was necessary to prevent irreparable damage to property. (A loophole that anti-labor judges walked through with impunity, but at least a step in the right direction.) "The labor of a human being," Congress declared in the Act, "is not a commodity or article of commerce."

After his election in 1912, President Wilson appointed William B. Wil-

12

son, a Democratic congressman from Pennsylvania and a former secretary-treasurer of the United Mine Workers, Secretary of Labor. President Wilson also established the Federal Mediation and Conciliation Service, another important milestone in the development of our public policy towards organized labor.

For the first time, labor was represented on a host of public and regulatory bodies, ranging from the Advisory Council of National Defense to fuel, food, emergency construction and war industries boards. A War Labor Board, charged with the mediation and conciliation of disputes in war-connected industries, was established in April 1918. The policies framed by this board later became the basis for much of the New Deal legislation in labor relations and the basis of public policy toward labor in all subsequent administrations. The board and other government agencies, under President Wilson, implicitly recognized the right of workers to bargain collectively through representatives of their own choosing.

As a consequence, from 1917 to 1920, unions expanded with a balloon-like rapidity. The meat cutters and butcher workmen, as an instance, grew from a tiny organization of 10,000 to a respectable 85,000-member trade union. The railway clerks bounded from 7,000 to over 71,000 members. The electrical workers, *including telephone workers*, grew from 42,000 to 131,000. The American Federation of Labor (AFL), jumped from slightly more than two-million in 1916 to twice that number in 1920.

"Democracy is infectious," the *New Republic* proclaimed in a 1917 editorial of the "war to end war". "It is now as certain as anything human can be that the war . . . will dissolve into democratic revolutions the world over." Surely, America would not be exempt for there was a promise of a new era for labor. In May 1919, President Wilson cabled from Paris to a special session of Congress, calling for "a new organization of industry," a "genuine democratization of industry," and a "cooperation and partnership based upon a real community of interest and participation in control." A special mention was made of the rights of workers to share "in some organic way in every decision" that affected their welfare.

Telephone workers were among those workers who expected a change for the better. Telephone operators had served their country well in the Women's Signal Corps. The IBEW had established a modest beachhead of 20,000 within the industry. The federal takeover, under a wartime grant of authority to the President, of the telegraph and telephone systems at midnight on July 31, 1918, not only combined the wire services but, in effect, added the unionized strength of the telegraphers to that of the telephone workers.

Union hopes were further raised by the precedents set by the wartime nationalization of the railroads the year before (December 1917). While the railroads were under federal operation during and after World War I, three national adjustment boards were established, representing management and the rail unions, to settle grievances. Subsequently, the Esch-Cummins Act of 1920 created a Railroad Labor Board, with three members each from the companies, the employees and the public, which continued to implement the policies established by the government under its wartime rule, even though the railroads were returned to private ownership. The Labor Board was replaced by a Board of Mediation in 1926 and by a National Railroad Adjustment Board in 1934, which finally guaranteed the right of rail employees to organize and bargain collectively through representatives of their own choosing. The communications industry, however, would be successful in forcing its employees down another path altogether.

Unfortunately for union hopes, President Wilson placed the telegraph and telephone services under the administration of Postmaster-General Albert S. Burleson, who was not sympathetic to union organization. He dodged the issue of union recognition by insisting that negotiations be conducted through the Wage Commission of the Wire Control Board. Julia O'Connor, the IBEW leader of telephone operators, was forced out as a member of the commission. In her letter of resignation, she declared that, "to retain membership would amount to a serious betrayal of the rights and interests of my fellow workers." The commission, she said, was consistent in only one respect—in its "hostility to the organized telephone and telegraph workers."

Communications workers, however, fought back gallantly. In the spring of 1919, over 3,000 telephone operators at ninety exchanges in Massachusetts, New Hampshire and Maine walked out on a strike that completely tied up telephone services in the region. Mrs. Mary E. June, Miss May Mahoney and Miss Birdie Powers of the Boston Operators Committee and Miss Helen Moran of Lowell, representing strikers outside the Boston District, made up the IBEW strike committee leading the strike. The greater number of the 12,000 cable splicers, testroom men and other workers belonging to the New England Joint Council of Electrical Workers joined the walkout. In an action comparable to the breaking of the famed Boston police strike in the fall of 1919, telephone management recruited Harvard and Massachusetts Institute of Technology students to man struck telephone exchanges. Twenty Harvard students, who had to be taken back to the Harvard Yard in police wagons, said that they had taken switchboard positions for "a little excitement." When strikebreakers were taken to nearby hotels to be fed, the Cooks and Waiters Union declared that none of its 2,000 members would serve scabs. The Cooks and Waiters also pledged $28,000, their total funds, for use if necessary to win the strike. The IBEW threatened a nationwide walkout to back its demand that the Postmaster-General recognize the telephone employees' union.

The New England Strike forced Postmaster-General Burleson, as he put it, to act "for these telephone girls myself," and to place their demands for a wage "adjustment" before William R. Driver, the general manager of the New England Telephone Company. Following negotiations with the striking employees, Burleson added, the Wire Board would review Driver's subsequent recommendations. The battle soon shifted to the South where members of the Commercial Telegraphers Union walked out to protest the discharge of some 300 Bell Telephone workers for union activity. On June 7, 1919, the telegraphers called for a nation-wide strike of its 25,000 members working for Western Union and AT&T. The strike was set for a week later; on June 12, the IBEW joined the struggle. Some 30,000 to 75,000 more communications workers were expected to walk out in the battle for union recognition. The nation-wide strike was postponed; though various groups walked out when Postmaster-General Burleson appeared to capitulate. Later, it was called off at the request of President Wilson.

On June 14, 1919 Postmaster-General Burleson issued a directive that seemingly resolved the matter:

Employees of telephone companies shall have the right to bargain as individuals or collectively through committees of their representatives chosen by them to act for them. Where prior to Government control a company dealt with representatives chosen by the employees to act for them who were not in the employ of the company, they shall hereafter do so. The telephone companies shall designate one or more officials who shall be authorized to deal with such individuals or representatives in matters of better conditions of labor, hours of employment, compensation, or grievances, and such matters must be taken up for consideration within 5 days after presentation.

Such employees shall have the right to organize or to affiliate with organizations that seem to them best calculated to serve their interests, and no employee shall be discharged, demoted, or otherwise discriminated against because of membership in any such organization, as prescribed in Bulletin No. 9, issued by me, dated October 2, 1918.

In case of dismissal, demotion, or undesirable transfer of employees where no real cause is shown by the company for said dismissal, demotion or undesirable transfer, it shall be considered that discrimination was practiced, and upon such finding the employee shall be reinstated to former position with full pay for time lost or shall be reimbursed for any loss sustained by reason of demotion or transfer.

Inability or refusal to perform the regular work or position occupied by them, excessive use of intoxicants, dishonesty, incivility to subscribers or the public shall be considered sufficient cause for removal.

Where requests or demands are now pending, the telephone companies shall immediately proceed to negotiate a settlement.

All telephone companies are hereby requested to comply strictly with the requirement of this order, and failure to do so on the part of any official will result in disciplinary action.

Two days after Postmaster-General Burleson issued his directive, AT&T issued one of its own. The corporation announced that an American Bell Association was to be organized among its employees. On the next day, June 17, F. H. Bethell, first vice president of the New York Telephone Company, gave the press some more information about the proposed Association. The plan, he said, was to organize groups in each city with a central body in New York. Employees were to be formed into what might be described as chapters, to be governed by a body chosen from all the chapters. Bethell said no dues were to be charged and that there would be no charge to members for halls or other places of meeting. Officials of the company, he added, would address the workers from time to time to increase their efficiency and their morale.

The nation's telegraph and telephone wires were returned to their respective owners on August 1, 1919 with what many felt was an excessive gratitude on the part of the government. The United States had assumed all the obligations of the wire companies but allowed the businesses to be run by the officers of the company. In arguing for the original takeover, administration officials not only emphasized "the indispensable importance of continuity of these lines during war times" but also, in the testimony before the House of Navy Secretary Josephus Daniels, expressed the hope that acquisition would be "a permanent policy." Questioned by congressmen, Daniels added, "If you wish my views, I would say it ought to last forever."

Postmaster-General Burleson recommended that "the telegraph and telephone should be made part of our Postal Service, reminding his hearers that the first telegraph service in the country had been constructed, maintained and operated by the government throughout the administration of President John Tyler (1841–1845) down to 1847. Nonetheless, the wire services were returned and the communications companies came out of it with their rates raised by nearly $50 million a year and with a check of over $13 million from the U.S. Treasury to cover their "deficits." As N. Danielian wryly put it in his history, *AT&T. The Story of Industrial Conquest,* "The Bell System benefited handsomely from this largess."

While some of this largess no doubt went to pay for halls and meeting places for the association, it is not otherwise apparent that Bell employees benefited overly much from their government's generosity. During the week of December 13, 1919, cited as typical by a study of the telephone industry by New York State Industrial Commission's Bureau of Women, more than half the operators received a basic wage of less than $16, while actual earnings, including pay for overtime, reached a peak of $15 to $18 a week. Bureau chief Miss Nelle Swartz pointed out that during the study, "the company raised the wages of New York City operators $3 a week and $2 a week for upstate operators, making the minimum wage for New York City

$15 and the maximum, $23. The bureau feels, however, that since an operator reached her maximum wage, which in New York is $23, and for upstate ranges from $17 to $19, after six years of service, the rate is still too low and that the rate of promotion is too slow, to be an incentive for an operator to remain with the company."

Operators worked eight hours a day, six days a week, earning thirty-one to forty-eight cents an hour. (Split-trick operators worked a seven hour day.) In 1919, average hourly earnings in manufacturing were 52.9 cents an hour and 70.6 cents in unionized jobs. Average annual earnings in the telephone industry in 1919 were $844. Bell employed 209,860 people, and there were 190,000 telephone operators in the country that year. The cost of living had risen sharply during the war, and a one pound loaf of bread, selling for 7.3 cents in 1916, sold for ten cents in 1919. Chuck roasts were selling for twenty-seven cents a pound; butter, 67.8 cents; eggs, 62.8 cents a dozen; potatoes, thirty-eight cents a pound; coffee, 43.3 cents, and sugar, at 56.5 cents a pound. So, telephone operators were not exactly among the affluent of 1919.

Telephone operators worked hard for their money. According to the engineering department of the New York Telephone Company, an operator, after two years with the company, must carry a theoretical load of 230 units an hour. The Women's Bureau study found that fifty percent of the operators had been with the company less than that length of time. Two percent of the operators, incidentally, worked a seven day week. The bureau study also showed that the youthful age of the operators, mostly between sixteen and twenty-three, "makes them peculiarly susceptible to strain and injury."

Miss Nelle Wooding, a retired CWA representative, went to work for the telephone company in Dallas, Texas, as a student operator in 1914 at a salary of $20 a month. "I was just a teenager," she recalled, "and I didn't have an advanced education, and that was just about the best job I was able to find." Wages were not high generally, according to Miss Wooding, but operator wages were "among the lowest wages paid anywhere other than laundry workers and dime-store employees." Miss Wooding's experience was fairly typical for beginners at the time. Supervisors watched operators "like a hawk," she remembered. "The companies always had a procedure of making observations, and they made what they called 'speed of answer tests.' They'd have someone with a stop watch throwing in calls, and if they weren't answered within ten seconds—that was the time allotted—it was a slow answer.

"They did train well in those days," Miss Wooding's reminiscences continued. "They needed to because everything was manual, and it was much more—well, I shouldn't say more complicated than it is now. But for one thing they paid more attention to the articulation of the operators. We had hours of drilling on how to pronounce the digits. They had a special way: you were to trill your 'r' in the 'three,' and you were to say the figure two as though it was 'tue,' like t-u-e for Tuesday, and that sort of thing . . . We had a huge manual of instructions that we had to read, some of which I can almost quote yet: 'Skill is not mere speed, but rather the quiet, easy execution,' and so on, which was all very good, but it took time."

Student operators, then, were given four weeks of training, working dummy boards in a school room before assignment on an exchange. Miss Wooding worked from one in the afternoon to ten-thirty in the evening, with an hour off for supper. She was paid an additional five dollars a month for working the late hours, and at the end of her first year, earned a salary of $30 a month, or $1 a day. Texas had a law prohibiting women from working over fifty-four hours a week. "We usually worked every other Sunday," Miss Wooding remembered. "The force was divided just about half and half and one half would work one Sunday and one the next. And in the week prior to the Sunday we were to work, we were given a weekday off. But then we got a mayor here in Dallas . . . an attorney for the telephone company. And he said, 'You don't have to give those people a day off.' Of course, I'm not quoting him verbatim, but this is what it resulted in. He said, 'The law says you can't work over fifty-four hours in a calendar week, but Sunday's the beginning of a new week. So, they can work Monday through Saturday, straight through Sunday, and on till Friday of the next week if necessary, and still not violate the law.' So that's what we began to do. We would work ten and twelve days without a day off. It was just another example of exploiting the workers, it seemed to me. The telephone company was always smart enough to obey the letter of the law, but the spirit was mutilated many times."

Discontent continued to percolate among telephone workers throughout the decade. Over 5,000 women operators and 1,000 male employees struck telephone exchanges in northern and central California mid summer, 1919. Jamestown, New York, went without telephone service when ninety operators walked out in sympathy with twenty linemen. And the IBEW locals on the Pacific coast were virtually destroyed by a strike in February 1920 when workers struck against an ultimatum that all employees had to join a company union. Shortly before the strike, it was revealed that many officials of the IBEW locals were also officers of the Pacific Company Association. As IBEW president J. P. Noonan later reported, "Our members were induced by these men whom they trusted, to accept the company's proposition and betrayed their fellow workmen by acting as strikebreakers."

The IBEW had organized along its main line of strength, the craft of its members. This enabled the union to make inroads into the Bell System as IBEW members took jobs with the company. But the craft approach opened the union to the divide and conquer tactics of the industry. Mechanical workers, as an instance, were induced to break-away from the IBEW in New England; only much later did they discover that their new organization, the International Brotherhood of Telephone Workers, was a front for the New England Bell Telephone Corporation. The craft unions were able to survive in the electrical construction and allied industries largely because when once organized the craftsmen were often stronger than the individual firms in the business. When confronted with a giant nationwide corporation, however, craft unionism was inadequate to the task of organizing. The AFL, inferentially at least, recognized this when its 1920 Montreal convention authorized "a nationwide campaign to organize all the telephone operators." State federations, city bodies and volunteer organizers, the *New York Times* reported, "are to take to the field at once in the campaign." The action was necessary, declared the AFL delegates, because of the "oppressive anti-labor policy of the Bell Telephone Company and its associated companies."

The drive, however, never got off the mark. In the 1920s, the unions were unable to hold their own in the face of a big business, anti-labor onslaught, nor were they able to until the federal government had assured workers of their rights to bargain collectively and to freely choose a representative of their own.

"During the war period," AT&T solemnly informed its stockholders in its 1919 annual report, "the officers of the companies have been impressed ... with the desirability of the adoption of some practical plan which would assure a closer and more informal contact between the managing officials and the other employees than is readily afforded by the regular channels of administrative organization. In these abnormal times when new problems are continually being presented not only to every department of the company but to every individual employee, as well as to every managing official, it has seemed more than ever essential to formulate some plan which would give to the management of the companies a more intimate knowledge and appreciation of the personal problems of the individual employee, his relation to the company's organization and his contribution to its success, and which would give to the employees generally a clearer and more general understanding of the policies and principles governing the administration of the business. It has been deemed wise to go further than this and give to those employees who desired it, an opportunity to discuss collectively as well as individually, their relation to the business."

What the company did not tell the stockholders, nor for that matter, the public or its employees, was that corporate management had decided to join a major business effort to head off unionization, not only with the Bell System but throughout the land. AT&T did not originate the idea of organizing its employees on the basis of "a harmony of interests," as "partners in production," into associations, or, company unions. That idea developed out of what might be termed "corporate welfarism." By 1910, or even earlier in some instances, America's giant corporations had become far too cumbersome for the traditional boss-worker relationship of an earlier day and possible yet for the small firm. Industrialists, too, had dropped the crude domineering attitude, once expressed by railroad financier Jay Gould —"I can hire one half of the working class to kill the other half"—though retaining in a somewhat more sophisticated manner the sense of *noblesse oblige* once formulated by George F. Baer, president of the Philadelphia and Reading Railroad Company: "The rights and interests of the laboring man will be protected and cared for, not by the labor agitators, but by the Christian men to whom God in His infinite wisdom has given the control of the property interests of the country."

This obligation to look after the interests of the working man was given a new formulation by George W. Perkins, chairman of the Finance Committee of U.S. Steel and a Morgan partner. (Significantly, Morgan had an interest in AT&T, too.) Competition, Perkins held, had become "too disturbing to be tolerated. Cooperation must be the order of the day." The corporation, he declared, must "people-ize" modern industry. Profit-sharing, social insurance, and pensions were to be the cement of the new order. With the encouragement of Perkins, a pension plan was developed for U.S. Steel in 1910 and—was it coincidental given the Morgan interest in AT&T? —discussed within the Bell System the same year. The Bell Employees' Benefit Plan was adopted by the parent company on October 15, 1912, and AT&T's announcement in its 1912 annual report contained more than an echo of the Perkin's philosophy of corporate responsibility: "Employers buy and employees sell service. Perfect service is only to be found when fidelity and loyalty are reciprocal in employer and employee. It is this relationship that brings satisfaction and success to both. The intent and purpose of the employer, in establishing a plan of benefits, is to give tangible expression to the reciprocity which means faithful and loyal service on the part of the employee, with protection from all the ordinary misfortune to which he is liable; reciprocity which means mutual regard for one another's interest and welfare."

But the provision of benefits, especially when capriciously denied (Bell System employees daring to strike lost *all* their service credits when rehired), did not suffice to head off worker organization. To accomplish this, the Bell System drew on the Rockefeller experience with employee representation plans in the Colorado Fuel & Iron Company and the Standard Oil concerns. In 1914, the Colorado Fuel and Iron management, with assistance from the National Guard, brutally crushed a miners' strike, raking with machine-gun fire a tent colony at the edge of the southern Colorado coal fields and setting the tents afire as women and children huddled in hastily dug trenches. Three workers were murdered while ostensibly under arrest and under guard; eleven children and two women were found suffocated or burned to death in one pit.

The brutality of the Ludlow massacre shocked the nation and upset the Rockefellers, who claimed no knowledge of the events leading up to the disaster. John D. Rockefeller hired Ivy Lee, a superb publicist, to undo the bad publicity given to the Rockefeller name by the tragic events in Colorado. W. L. Mackenzie King, former Minister of Labor for Canada, was asked to work out some means of fostering amicable relations between capital and labor. After the suppression of the strikers, the Colorado Fuel and Iron Company unveiled a plan for improved employee relations. The so-called Colorado Industrial Representative Plan, or, more popularly, the Rockefeller Plan, was a fruit of Mackenzie King's labors. It called for the election of a joint committee on industrial cooperation and conciliation, to be composed of representatives of the company and of the employees. The individual worker was to have the right to appeal grievances from local officials and to send representatives to the joint committee. According to John D. Rockefeller, in an article ghosted by Ivy Lee, the plan "brings men and managers together, facilitates the study of their common problems, and it should promote an understanding of their mutual interests."

While the Rockefeller Plan worked less than perfectly at Colorado Fuel and Iron, it did fend off unionization. The United Mine Workers would not come back until 1933, and within the Standard Oil companies, unions made little or no headway for years. This lesson was not lost on employers who feared the growth of the unions which was so evident during World War I. So, as the 1920s began, there was an openness among corporate managements to Rockefeller proselytizing of the Colorado Plan. In 1919, at the suggestion of A. C. Bedford, president of Colorado Fuel and Iron, and Owen D. Young of General Electric, the presidents and industrial relations executives of ten (later twelve) corporations formed a Special Conference Committee to promote "harmonious relations" with employees, to pool information and to develop policy.* Or, in less genteel fashion, to bust unions by heading them off.

Employee representation, AT&T Vice President, E. K. Hall, informed his audience at an American Management Association Representation Conference held in Philadelphia, December 1 and 2, 1927, "is a new and additional form of organization in industry. Its adoption constitutes recognition of certain things not previously recognized or fully appreciated by

*The twelve were: AT&T, U.S. Steel Corporation, Bethelehem Steel Corporation, General Electric Company, General Motors Corporation, U.S. Rubber Company, Standard Oil of New Jersey, E. I. du Pont de Nemours and Company, Goodyear Tire and Rubber Company, International Harvester Company, Westinghouse Electric and Manufacturing Company, and Irving Trust Company.

management. First, the normal or the military form of organization in industry is not adequate for promoting, developing and maintaining the best relations between management and men as individuals. Second, the worker is entitled to a better status in the industry than that of being a mere servant or a mere contractor. Third, the worker ought to be considered and treated as a part of the organization just as much as an employee who happens to carry the title of supervisor. Fourth, as a part of the organization, as a part of the industry, the worker is entitled to confer with responsible representatives of the management concerning his own relations to the business and everything involved in that relation. Fifth, he is entitled to know and ought to know something about the plans and the procedure, the practices and the objectives of the industry itself, and he is entitled to have a chance to do this and to ask these questions without seeming impertinent or feeling embarrassed or being told that it is none of his business. As a matter of fact, management assumes responsibility for taking the initiative in telling employees about these things. Sixth, where size prevents this contact between representatives of the managing employees and all the members of the general working forces, then an orderly method to accomplish these ends is for the general forces to confer with management through representatives, through people whom they select, their own side partners, people who are more or less working under the same conditions they are working under in the business."

This, of course, was the velvet gloving an iron and manipulative hand. The Bell System, as in Atlanta, did not hesitate to fire militant workers. When a group of desperate Arkansas operators walked off the job in a protest over wages and working conditions, the company fired every one and brought in operators from all over its territory and from as far afield as Dallas, Texas. According to Miss Wooding, the out-of-town force was kept on until an entirely new set of operators had been trained. The out-of-towners were paid expenses and their hometown salary, which in most cases was better than the salary paid the local women. Management people were also sent in as chaperones. The visitors were, of course, strikebreakers, but as Miss Wooding put it, "they didn't think of it in those terms . . . it was just a ball."

Miss Wooding described it as "one of the most unjust things I've ever heard of . . . the company probably spent ten times as much money on that thing as it would have cost them to give those girls a decent wage. But they knew if they gave a good wage rate there, everybody else would clamor for it. So to keep wages down, and particularly to crush any idea of a union having any authority, the sky was the limit on expense."

The Bell System employees were extensively organized—by management. Two talks given by Bell officials before the 1927 American Management Association Conference on employee representation were revealing, both in content and title. The first, "Technique of Holding Council or Committee Meetings: Male Manual Workers Predominating," given by Harold B. Porter, general plant manager, Bell Telephone Company of Pennsylvania, and the second, "Technique . . . Where Female and Often Young Workers Predominate," by Howard L. Fitch, General Traffic Manager for the Pennsylvania Company. "Picture to yourselves," Mr. Fitch said, "a group of some 3,000 young women, mostly ranging from eighteen to twenty-five years of age. Scattered through this group are a few hundred older ones who, though in the minority, are the backbone of the department. These 3,000 are located in thirty-nine central offices throughout the city having anywhere from five employees in the smallest to 280 in the largest office. There are twenty-two separate council committees representing these employees with a total of 114 representatives. About half of the committees represent a single large central office. The other committees represent a group of from two to five smaller offices."

Joint conferences were held once a month, presided over by the administrative heads of each of the seven Philadelphia districts. Mr. Fitch stated that it was the company's belief that "if employee representatives considerably outnumber management representatives in a joint conference, the employee representatives feel more confidence in discussing controversial questions. Our ratio is generally about two to one." Employees were encouraged by suitable election procedure "to select the type of person who will effectively represent the general employee body—a thoughtful, intelligent person who has the courage of her convictions and some facility in expressing her views." Group discussion is encouraged by the chairman framing his questions "so as to give no clue to his ideas on the subject." The chairman, too, "should help a representative to develop her case by supplying information she may lack, or by suggesting additional reasons favorable to the employees' proposal." Both employees and management were allowed to introduce any subject they wished; Mr. Fitch, however, observed that "many broad subjects which are of interest to the male part of the telephone organization do not interest all of our group, because their direct application is not obvious." Still, no matter how unusual a proposal or how contrary to tradition or at variance with written routines, the chairman should welcome it "as an indication of what is on the mind of the employee body. One never knows [whether or not] some change, easily made, will contribute greatly to the employees' satisfaction in their work."

Organization on the male side was not appreciably different. In Philadelphia, according to Harold B. Porter, there were nine committees, with about forty-two employee committeemen, representing approximately 1,850 employees or about one representative to every forty-four. Various vocations were represented, such as janitors, installation, cable-splicing and repair forces, clerical, engineering, motor vehicle and supplies. Employees were encouraged to elect "only those who are 'simon pure' employees and not in some border line class between management and employee." To avoid individual complaints to the representative committees, foremen were encouraged to be "both big brother and boss to his people," a tactic that apparently worked, for Porter reported that he had practically eliminated individual complaints, a decided tendency when the committees were first formed. Group questions were discussed at the joint conferences "covering wages, carfare, working practices, improvements in tools and methods, accident prevention, etc.," as well as "general reviews of business conditions, company programs, accident prevention, thrift, company policies, possibility of increasing revenue by employee effort, etc."

"All questions are decided by getting the facts," Porter asserted. "No change in our working practices governing carfare, vacations, hours of work, etc. is made without full discussion with the employee committees and gaining their agreement." Meetings were chaired by management, but an effort was made to "Make them [employees] feel they are a part of the works in their proper sphere." Employee committeemen were encouraged to bring members of their groups as visitors to the joint conferences. And committee members were taken on tours of Bell facilities, the company rest home for girls, the warehouse of the Western Electric Company, the accounting department, and so on. "This stimulates company interest, discussion, and also adds to their prestige and the knowledge of their business." Management, Porter declared, is open to discuss any matter, believing that "it is better to discuss wages . . . in the committees than on street corners or in the storerooms." Above all, Porter concluded, "Management must be absolutely sincere . . . Your heart must be in it for the benefit and good it will do your own people."

That, of course, is how management viewed employee representation. How the workers did was something else again. T. E. Webb, a former lineman, cable splicer and later north Texas CWA director, belonged to an employee association in San Antonio, chaired by a construction foreman. "Every time we had a chapter meeting," Webb has recalled, "you could bet that there would be supervisors there. You can readily see that there was never anything, in my opinion, in a constructive way that went on in those meetings because a lot of guys were reluctant to even open up and talk about their grievances with supervisors present." Al DiProspere, a former lineman and CWA area director for east Missouri, Arkansas and Illinois, said, "I found out that this meeting [of the employees association] was an arena to gather favor with the supervisors and foremen who were always in attendance."

Fred D. Waldeck, who once worked in the plant and maintenance unit of Western Electric in Philadelphia and later became an assistant to the executive vice president of CWA, viewed the employee representation plan as a means "whereby the Company would designate a person to be the spokesman for the group. And if they were to change some policy or something of that sort, they would call that individual in and say, 'This is what we are going to do. Thanks for coming in and listening. Go back to the job.' . . . I guess they felt it would promote some kind of harmony and better relationship between the brass and the employees if somebody would come out of the unit and was *told* what the company was going to do." And William J. Walsh, who started working with Ohio Bell in 1930—just after graduating from high school in Cleveland—as an installer, but "actually, more or less, just a grunt, helping the older fellows." He recalls that they had two or three social events a year, "and once in a while you'd have a so-called membership meeting, but if anybody talked about anything other than about the pencil sharpener [that] needed replacing or was dull, why, there [were] some reprisals very shortly thereafter. A guy that was working in a location that was nearby his home found himself transferred to the opposite end of Cleveland, fifteen miles away from home . . ."*

During the 1920s, the Bell System constructed an ideology and a way of constraining their employees and of harnessing their energies for the expansion of the corporate enterprise. They were not alone in this. The so-called American Plan, which coupled employee associationism with outright union busting, had a devastating effect on the American labor movement. Union membership in the entire nation, according to Leo Wolman, peaked at 5,047,800 in 1920; by 1923, it was driven down to 3.6 million, and, in 1933, down to 2.9 million. According to a 1933 survey of the National Industrial Conference Board, workers covered by employee representation plans, excluding the railroads, numbered 932,270, the equivalent of 74.4 percent of the estimated American Federation of Labor membership in manufacturing and mining. On the eve of the passage of the Wagner Labor Act in 1935, a Bureau of Labor Statistics survey found that 78.5 percent of telephone employees were in an employee association of one sort or another. Only three Bell companies reported dealing with independent unions as well and these three employed about 16.2 percent of the System's total labor force.

The System did indeed flourish. During the 1920s, Bell workers strung 50,000 miles of wire, twice that laid since the founding of the company. Operating revenues jumped from $448.233 million in 1920 to $1,094,883 billion by 1930, and the number of Bell employees rose from 231,316 to a peak of 324,343 over the same period. Declared dividends nearly quadrupled, $40 million to $156.625 million, while total wages and salaries barely

*Car ownership was not as common among workers as it is now and the worker involved in Walsh's anecdote had to travel to and from work by streetcar, taking transfers, which took three hours a day.

doubled, $263.729 million to $534.468 million. Average annual earnings of telephone workers rose, too, but not on such a grand scale, from $980 a year in 1920 to $1,497 in 1930. The system, then, seemingly worked: Yet, cataclysmic events would soon give it a shaking and change it beyond all recognition.

III

Go Thou, and Be Independent

During the summer of 1929, stock prices rose to new and giddy heights. As novelist F. Scott Fitzgerald later observed, "Life was like the race in *Alice in Wonderland,* there was a prize for everyone." On the New York Stock Exchange, brokers traded four and five million shares a day. A lover seeking advice wrote, "I find your column interesting and need advice. I have saved $4,000 which I want to invest for a better income. Do you think I might buy stock?" Blue chip stocks bubbled up and up and up; barbers clipped coupons as well as hair, and waiters leaned solicitously over tables to catch the latest tips as much as to take orders. Westinghouse went from 151 to 286; General Electric, from 268 to 396, and U.S. Steel soared from 165 to 396. Even as sober a stock as American Telephone and Telegraph Company, riding firmly on a nine dollar dividend, rose from 209 to 304. John J. Raskob, an ally of the Du Ponts on the General Motors board of directors and Al Smith's choice as chairman of the Democratic National Committee, wrote an article that summer for the *Ladies Home Journal,* hortatorily entitled, "Everybody Ought to be Rich."

When the stock market crashed, a five-day fall from capitalist grace that started on Black Thursday, October 24, and ended the following Tuesday, October 29, Americans were stunned. As an observer noted of the people who gathered outside the Stock Exchange on Wall Street that fateful Thursday, their expressions showed "not so much suffering as a sort of horrified incredulity." As well they might, for solid blue-chip stocks were tumbling as so many leaves were doing in the October wind. By the time Wall Street was able to take a weary breather a few weeks later, the stocks listed on the New York Stock Exchange had fallen over forty percent in value—a paper loss of $26 billion. But the puncture of inflated values not only brought down ballooning stock prices, it tipped the industrial and market basket precariously roped on below. National income, which had topped $87.8 billion in 1929, plummeted to $40.2 billion in 1932. Gross private domestic investment at $15.8 billion in 1929 dropped to $1.3 billion in 1932. The Federal Reserve Board's index of manufacturing production slid from 110 in 1929 to fifty-seven in 1932. Wage payments collapsed from $51.1 billion in 1929 to $29.5 billion in 1933. Unemployment rose—over four million in

27

1930, double that a year later, twelve million in 1932, hitting a peak of nearly thirteen million in 1933. While the nation's babbitts passed the economic graveyard whistling "Happy Days Are Here Again," American Federation of Labor president, William Green, informed a 1930 congressional committee that in Detroit "the men are sitting in the parks all day long and all night long, hundreds and thousands of them, muttering to themselves, out of work, seeking work."

For telephone workers, the 1929 crash and its depressing aftermath came as a double shock. Communications people, naturally, shared the pervasive apprehension common to all Americans. If you had a job, you did not jeopardize it, not with willing workers lined up by the thousand outside plant gates. Craft-proud men swept floors, clinging to their jobs on any terms as the specter of unemployment haunted the nation. Clarence Good, later in life CWA's Southern California Area Director, who was "fortunate enough to stay on the payroll," remembers: "I went into the engineering department as a cable-splicer's helper, then to trimming trees, and finally, in the depths of the depression, to a janitor." And though he tried to find other employment, "there just wasn't anything. I came to the realization I was lucky at that time to just have a job even as a janitor." As fearful as that experience undoubtedly was, it might have proved bearable had Ma Bell remained the friendly, maternal old gal portrayed in company propaganda. Excepting operators, who were subjected to a subtle forced turnover practice ("In those days," Mrs. Norma Naughton, now retired as chairwoman of Branch 127 Federation of Long Lines Telephone Workers, NFTW, recently recalled, "When you were married, you no longer could work for the telephone company."), telephone employees were encouraged to think of themselves as special, secure in their jobs.

"The telephone employee," Good says, "was different from any other employee in any other industry. Supposedly he was a cut above the steel worker or the auto worker, any of the others who were then in unions or were becoming unionized. And I guess all of us liked to hear that sort of thing."

Even "boomers," those peripatetic installers and linemen who "floated from place to place," and, according to James Mahady, "had a bad reputation," were encouraged to think of themselves as somehow unique. "They had no roots," Mahady, CWA's Louisiana director, explains. "They had no homes; they were just living in camp cars, or they were living in the cheapest habitations that the company could find to house them." As CWA vice president James M. Massey recalls his life as an installer, "We Western installers were kicked around all over the country. The first thirteen years of my married life I never owned a stick of furniture." Sardonically, yet with a touch of pride Massey adds, "At that time everybody was Ma Bell's children."

The Bell System became one of the first among America's corporation giants to engage in human engineering, the sociology of manipulation. Sociologist Elton Mayo and his Harvard Department of Industrial Research colleagues were brought in the late 1920s to the Hawthorne Works, a Western Electric manufacturing plant in Chicago. The sociologists initiated a series of experiments that were to last more than nine years. The most famous of these experiments took place in the relay test room, where five women worked at assembling pieces of telephone equipment. They were subjected to an extraordinary range of tests—lights were turned up and turned down; rest periods were given and taken away, and even lunches were denied. Paradoxically, whether cosseted or cruelly driven, the women increased their output steadily. Neither adversity or good fortune affected production. Then Mayo came up with the deceptively simple, brilliant answer: It was the experiment itself that was the determining factor. Workers hitherto ignored were now recognized, given attention and it did not matter so far as productivity was concerned whether management dangled the carrot or flicked the the whip, both were forms of recognition. This led Mayo, and the management of Western Electric, to experiment with "a new method of human control"—walking counselors ready at any moment to stop and listen to a harassed worker. A counselor described the process: "In the case of the downgraded employee . . . her focus of attention shifts from alleged inequities, transfer and downgrading grievances, etc . . . to her unhappy home life; then, when she returns to her original grievance, things do not look so bad."

Concretely, this meant management did not have to do anything about the grievance, treat its employees as equals, or worry about unions. Touted as a science as a consequence of the Hawthorne experiments, human relations became for the Bell System a process of indoctrination. One sees this in a memorandum prepared at a 1929 Bell System wage conference and sent to all presidents of the operating companies describing the stages of an employee's progression:

> In the early stages of the schedules, wage progress should be sufficiently rapid to stimulate and hold the employee's interest through a *period of orientation and learning.*
>
> *A period of developing skill and technique* follows, and wage schedules should give adequate recognition to demonstrated improvement in the quantity and quality of production and progress in business capabilities and other requirements of the job.
>
> Then there is *a period of seasoning in the broader aspects of the job—a period in which the factors underlying wage progress should include more consideration of the employee's attitude and activities in connection with public relations, personnel relations, and the other policies and ideals of the business.*
>
> (My italics.)

The goal, of course, was the "happy worker."

Burleigh Gardner, a researcher at Hawthorne and a leading management consultant, phrased it this way: "The more satisfied [the worker] is, the greater will be his self-esteem, the more content he will be, and therefore more efficient in what he is doing." It is, as Daniel Bell acidly noted, "A fitting description not of human, but of 'cow' sociology."

The Bell System seasoning often contained a sting. An old-timer recalls walking the streets of New Orleans, heading for a job with a telephone in hand and smoking a cigarette, being stopped by an elderly gentleman, who asked if the company permitted smoking by its employees. The answer was at that time, no, and the inquisitor took the worker's name and reported the incident to a vice president of the local company. Luckily, the worker was not fired outright though he was reprimanded. As James Mahady, who tells the anecdote, adds, "It gives you an idea how dominating management was. They set the morals, and they set habits, and everything else they could set. They'd dominate the life of the telephone worker completely."

The sting was clothed in a blanket of security. "The Bell System," N. Danielian observed in his great study, "has cultivated the 'white-collar' psychology among its workers; and with employee welfare and benefit schemes, it has taken the edge off the psychology of self-help."

We forget, for example, how recent pension coverage is. Most workers were protected for the first time in 1937 when the Social Security Act became effective. (The first check, however, was not paid out until 1941.) Bell employees were an exception, being covered by a pension plan as well as the right to compensation in cases of industrial accidents from 1912 on. As a 1952 study, prepared for the Joint Congressional Committee on the Economic Report by the National Planning Association, noted, "A little over fifteen years ago there were only about nine million persons, less than fifteen percent of those employed, with this [retirement] protection. Coverage was very uneven, *ranging from virtually 100 percent in the communications industry* to virtually nothing in retail trade or agriculture." But Ma Bell treated pensions much as the donkey's master did the carrot and the stick; it was not a worker's right or resource but a management tool. It was often withheld for arbitrary reasons. An Indianapolis operator, in 1939, came down with a terminal illness and her doctor told her she had to quit work. With twenty-two years of service, she was entitled to a disability pension of $30 a month, or so she thought. She applied, but the telephone company turned her application down on the grounds that her husband was working—and even more outrageously, not even for the system but at the Bendix plant!

Significantly, the system's use, or misuse, of pension benefits as a carrot/stick foreshadowed AT&T's depression labor relations policies. Its 1915 annual report stated that "we believe it is no more than simple justice that the men and women who devote their lives to the telephone service should be assured of some income when they are sick or come to old age . . . *If justice demands this, its cost is a fair charge against the business, and we so regard it.* "

In the mid-twenties, however, there was a change in policy, succinctly described in the 1937 FCC investigation: "Whereas in 1912 pension expenditures were justified as a reward for fidelity and loyalty of the employees to the companies, and in 1915 the payments were held to be a fair charge against the business on the grounds of social justice, in the year 1924 a new philosophy was evolved as to the function and purpose of the plan. In June of 1924, M.B. Jones, president of the New England company, wrote E.K. Hall, vice president of the American company, that he believed the plan could be utilized to a far greater extent than was then done for clearing the decks of people who had not reached the retirement age, but who were pensionable and whose places it would be well to fill with younger people." In 1934, FCC investigators reported "the view that the primary function of the pension plan was to eliminate from the ranks long-service employees who were under-productive and were inefficient in the performance of their duties, was stated in unequivocal terms in testimony prepared by the American company for use in the Tri-State Telephone and Telegraph Company rate case." On September 3, 1936, E.F. Carter, vice president of the American company, attested to the FCC investigators, "The purpose of the retirement plan of the Bell System is to further the efficient and economical operation of the business."

Bell employees, nonetheless, saw in their employment a haven as the economy began to go to pieces in 1929. At the end of that year, the system employed 454,500 workers; of this number, 364,000 were in the telephone system and 85,000 engaged by Western Electric in manufacturing, with the balance at work within various subsidiaries. By all accounts, 1929 was a banner year for the Bell System. Telephone stations in service had increased to 15,414,005 on December 31, 1929, nearly 900,000 more than the year previous. The average number of telephone conversations mounted to over 64 million a day, five million over the year before. Total revenues climbed to an all time high, $1.115 billion, a hefty $112 million boost over 1928. Forecasts were Hooverian in their optimism, but with more foundation than that given to the President. Bell-owned telephone stations increased by 268,000 in 1930; the average number of daily telephone calls was in excess of a million over the 1929 average. Total revenues zoomed upwards by $37 million to reach a 1930 top of $1.152 billion. Perhaps no other company in America was in a better position to weather the economic catastrophe than flourishing Ma Bell, or, one must add, to make a contribution to the shoring up of the economy by keeping people employed. Yet, at the very highest levels of telephone business activity in 1930, a year when plant investment was expanded by $372 million, Bell management sharply curtailed employment by firing 60,000 loyal employees.

"The real shock of my life came when I was laid off in April of 1931," says Robert Pollock of CWA District 6. "I felt I was an unusually good telephone man," he adds. But neither that nor his employment with the company since his graduation from the West Technical High School of Cleveland, Ohio, in 1926, saved him from the layoff ax. "When your paycheck was coming on Friday," Thomas C. Ryan, Ohio director of CWA District 4, remembers, "you didn't know whether you were getting the pink slip or not. And every Friday was known as Black Friday." Layoffs intensified in 1931 through 1933 when the system's total employment dropped to a 270,660 low. More than a third of the total Bell System labor force had been fired. Western Electric alone discharged seventy-five percent of its work force, dropping to a plant-force low of 18,446 in 1933. "On Friday afternoon," Arthur B. LeFevre, retired vice president of CWA District 5, recalls, "at four forty-five, the boss would come around and speak to somebody quietly, and the substance of the conversation was, 'We have to let you go. Will you get your things together? You'll be finished at five o'clock.' "

A fifteen minute notice is all they ever got from good old maternal Ma Bell. The brunt of the layoffs fell on Bell employees earning less than $4,000 a year. The number of Bell System employees receiving below $1,000 a year dropped from 128,242 to 48,286, a reduction of 80,000. Of this number, 74,000 were women, and 6,000 were men. Of 170,749 employees in 1929 receiving from $1,000 to $2,000 a year, 49,300 were laid off, and most of these were women. The decline was not pronounced among "experienced operators"—roughly a loss of 34,000—and "operators in training"—some 31,000 were laid off. Among the hard-hit were "line and station men," who dropped in number from 23,833 in 1929 to 7,294 in 1924, and "cable and conduit men," who were cut back from 12,221 to 1,665. The company attributed the cutbacks to the depression and adverse business conditions. There was a decline in telephone business, yet, according to the FCC, "Different indices of volume of business indicate declines of eight to sixteen percent in 1934 as compared with 1929; company stations declined by about twelve percent, gross revenues by about sixteen percent, and average number of daily calls by eight percent; whereas the number of Bell Telephone System employees diminished by thirty-one percent." As the FCC investigators pointed out, "It cannot be said, therefore, that the reduction of traffic is the primary cause for the falling off of employment."

Ma Bell's layoffs were among the first, if not the first, victims of automation. The real reason for the layoffs, FCC investigators concluded, "seems to be the introduction of automatic or dial central office equipment." Between December 31, 1929 and 1934, the number of dial offices more than doubled, increasing from 433 to 924, and the number of dial telephones increased from 4,014,153 to 6,320,823, roughly forty-seven percent of the system's total number of telephones. Danielian estimates that the displacement of labor from this cause alone is close to 20,000 workers. To support a fantastic expansion of telephone plant investment—$372 million in 1930 —management increased shareholdings from 13.322 million shares in 1929 to 18.663 million shares in 1935, an increase of paid-in capital guaranteed, so to speak, by the assurance of a $9 dividend. To maintain the dividend, layoffs were extended and the speed-up introduced. The work week was cut from six days to five, then to four and three days. Workers were sent home with no pay on what were called "lack of work days." The reduction in the work week amounted to a pay reduction of 16.67 percent.

During the 1920s, the operators' average hourly work load varied between 139.1 and 142.5 calls at manual exchanges, and hovered around 105 or so units at dial exchanges. Dial exchange loads were increased in 1930 to 128.4 units and rose upwards thereafter. Where the average load per hour per operator on all exchanges combined was 139.7 in 1930, performance was souped up to 150.3 units per hour in 1931, 163.2 units in 1932 and 172.0 units in 1933. In 1931, the chief engineer of AT&T estimated that each unit of load added to the average performance of operators meant a saving of $1 million a year to the system. Even after the telephone business recovered, topping and surpassing the peak of 1933, employment in the Bell System at the end of 1937 was twenty-seven percent less than in 1929, and Western Electric's labor force was still half of its '29 strength. At the time Ma Bell fired 70,000 from traffic jobs she increased her total annual dividend payments by $52 million a year, from $116 million in 1929 to $168 million in 1935; so much for Mr. Gifford's notion of "stewardship." As Danielian phrased the impact of Bell System's depression policies, "Every dollar of dividends per share received during the depression was at the expense of leaving at least 18,000 people on the relief rolls."

Management's patent unfairness added to the shock of the depression layoffs. There were no seniority provisions, no negotiations, no consultations with the employees. When an engineer from the Milwaukee plant department spoke up for his fellows at a meeting with management and protested the layoffs, suggesting that work might be shared among all the men, or, at least, more notice be given, the manager replied, "I hear everything you say, and the question of part timing, the company has decided, would not meet our requirements. However, on the business of more notice for people who will be laid off, that seems to make some sense, and so I'm giving *you* notice now. You will be laid off next Friday."

Mrs. Naughton recalls that when they started to layoff long-distance operators at 32 Sixth Avenue in New York City, "they came along hit and miss and [it was] largely a matter of favoritism, which employees would go and which would stay. And I saw girls dismissed with eighteen- and twenty-

years service, and girls kept on who had only been there a couple of years."
Older, allegedly less efficient workers were fired; younger, supposedly more
efficient and vigorous workers were retained. That the latter were paid less
than the former for the same work did not go unnoticed by their fellow
workers, though, ostensibly, the company, as Thomas C. Ryan, recalled,
"got into such things as trying to determine what your economic conditions
were, whether you had a wife working, whether or not you owned property,
and they were so far *wrong.*"

Some, naturally, returned to work for the Bell System as the country
worked its way out of the trough of the depression. Significantly, most, if
not all, of the men and women who were to shape the destiny of worker-
organization within the telephone industry were of that generation of telephone workers hardest hit by the depression years, those who had been
demoted and laid-off. Robert Pollock spoke for them when he said, "When
I came back to work for the telephone company, I guess I had two ideas
in mind. One was that I never was going to go through anything like that
again if I could help it. So I was interested in job security. And two, I felt
that my being laid-off was unwarranted and unjustified, and I didn't think
that ought to happen again."

Throughout the country, more and more workers were of the same mind.
Three times as many workers struck in 1933 as in 1932, 812,000 as against
243,000, and many more would do so in 1934. Increasingly, the sole issue
became union recognition. The Norris-LaGuardia Act of 1932 freed unionists of crippling federal court injunctions against boycotts, picketing and
strike action. Yellow-dog contracts—a pledge, signed by an employee when
hired, not to join a union—were no longer enforceable in federal courts.
Sections 7a and 7b of the National Industrial Recovery Act guaranteed the
right to collective bargaining. Franklin D. Roosevelt encouraged hopes of
economic recovery through industrial self-government, and the famed Blue
Eagle of the NRA blazoned forth on sound trucks invading the coalfields
of Kentucky, West Virginia, Pennsylvania, and Illinois as well as the garment centers of New York, Philadelphia, Cleveland, and Chicago, carrying
the message, "The President wants *you* to organize!" Auto workers, rubber
workers, steel workers, truck drivers, longshoremen, and electrical workers
thronged to the unions.

Communications workers were not immune nor isolated from this ferment as management believed and fervidly hoped. A surprising number of
the early founders and leaders of the CWA were the sons or daughters
of unionists; some even had experience as union members. John Crull was
the son of a carpenters' union's business agent, and started his working
life as an apprenticed carpenter and a member of his father's union.
D.L. McCowen's father was a blacksmith and belonged to the Horseshoer's
union. T.E. Webb's dad was a coal miner, active in the United Mine

Workers. All of Mrs. Marie (DeMartini) Bruce's relatives were members of one union or another, and her brother-in-law was a Teamster. Ruth Wiencek's father was a member of the Industrial Workers of the World, a bindlestiff following the harvest as well as a woodworker; in his youth he was a socialist, later becoming an anarchist. William Dunn's grandfather was a molder and his father, an Operating Engineer. Joseph Beirne, Robert Pollock and Mrs. Helen Carmody were all children of railroad workers, who were loyal members of their respective trade unions. One should not make too much of this for these people were widely scattered and certainly held no common, coherent ideology or philosophy. Beirne's brother and sister were members of unions in the 1920s but, like the others above, Joe Beirne was not and for the same reason, "Because there was no union in the Bell System." And like most of the early leaders of the CWA, as Beirne has said, "I had no real attachment; I was not out there with any kind of deep burning desire to create a union." Yet, these men and women were open to new ideas, and in the 1930s, that of organization was very much in the air.

Gingerly, a few people, here and there within the Bell System, began exploring the question of organization. As John Crull, a Kansas installer, repairman and transmission inspector before becoming a union activist and a CWA executive vice president, put it, "A few secret meetings were held. Nothing much came of them for a while." The telephone business began to pick up in 1935; Bell operating revenues climbed towards the 1929 peak, reaching $934.371 million in 1935 and exceeding $1 billion a year later. In December 1936, the system granted its first general wage increase since the start of the depression. The telephone business pickup reflected a general improvement in the economy. Congress, in part, because the Supreme Court found the NRA unconstitutional and, in part, because of the general recovery, came under increasing pressure to formulate a labor policy for the country. In July 1935, Congress passed the National Labor Relations Act, known familiarly as the Wagner Labor Act after Senator Robert F. Wagner, Democrat of New York, the father of the bill. Correctly characterized as organized labor's Magna Carta, the act prohibited employers from committing such unfair labor practices as firing union activists, spying on employees or refusing to bargain. It guaranteed workers the right to bargain collectively and to freely choose their own representatives. It also created an agency, the National Labor Relations Board, to enforce the act. Bell management, naturally, opposed its passage, and representatives from several system employee associations were gulled into testifying against it. John Risser, an Iowa installer who later became state CWA director, then a chairman of an employee group, remembers a district plant superintendent calling him, "asking if I would write to my Congressman to discourage him from voting for the Wagner Act, and asked me to call various guys and ask them to do the same thing." Risser evaded the issue, letting the matter drop. But representatives from the employee associations in Long Lines, New England telephone operators, and Northwestern Bell plant groups, traveled to Washington to oppose the Wagner Act. Along with a spokesman from one of the New York Telephone Company associations, they objected in particular to provisions that outlawed financial assistance from employers to labor organizations.

The reasons for employer opposition to the Wagner Labor Act were soon apparent. John L. Lewis founded the Committee—later Congress—of Industrial Organizations in 1935, breaking away from the American Federation of Labor a year later. Industrial unions flourished in the mass production industries where none existed a few short years before. Soon over a million workers were enrolled in infant CIO unions; the AFL flourished too. In 1937, the federation had a membership of 2.8 million to the CIO's 1.5 million. By 1941, the AFL had a membership of 4.5 million; the CIO, 2.8 million. As Walter Galenson concluded in his study of AFL and CIO rivalry, "The expansion of trade unionism from 1936 to 1941 had one overriding characteristic: it extended the power of labor into new and strategic sectors of the economy."

For Ma Bell, the new law created uncertainty. Would the CIO "invade" the telephone field? What would their employees do? Should Bell management sever financial aid to its employee associations? Mrs. Naughton remembers: "Of course, AT&T and all the big industries fought it, and it was taken to the Supreme Court. But in the meantime a number of us in the New York [long lines] office were meeting together secretly and discussing ways in which we could get the people at 32 Sixth Avenue organized." Elsewhere, notably in Ohio, Illinois and the southwest, there were covert rebellions against management domination of the employee associations. D.L. McCowen, CWA District 6 vice president, then a tool line repairman in suburban Fort Worth, Texas, remembers campaigning for the election of Andy Anderson as chapter chairman against the management nominee. He was elected by one vote, the edge being provided by the suburban bloc. As McCowen quickly added, the company immediately created a separate suburban chapter and designated a chairman. "We didn't even elect anybody," McCowen says, the division plant superintendent "pointed his finger at me and says, 'You can be secretary-treasurer. That's an office in a labor union.'" McCowen thought that pretty funny. "I chuckle about it. That was my first office, even though it was not a labor union at all."

When the Wagner Act was held constitutional by the Supreme Court in April, 1937, the Bell System companies officially severed their relationships with the employee associations. T.E. Webb, now retired as North Texas CWA director, recalls a meeting after the Supreme Court's Wagner decision at which the district plant superintendent explained the company's position.

"Well, we have no objection. The law says this, and we got to abide by the law. We're hopeful you boys will go along with whatever you think is right. We'd hate to see some Bolshevik or anarchist organization come in here and you become a part of that." John Crull claimed, "Although I never saw the money—and never had anything to do with it—I'm told that the company gave to each of the chapter chairmen $200, in the western Missouri and Kansas area as well as over in the eastern Missouri and Arkansas and down into Oklahoma and down into Texas. The company gave them the money while it was still legal for them to do it. The suggestion was made that they use that money however they saw fit to set themselves up an organization of their own." A.B. Herrington, subsequently public relations director of CWA and then an official in the newly-formed Illinois plant craftsmen's union, once said that between the time the Wagner Act was passed and signed by the President, when it was legal to do such things, officials of the Illinois Bell Telephone Company helped the plant craftsmen write their constitution and gave the new union $1,000 to start out on. William J. Walsh, formerly CWA community relations director, remembers going back to work in 1936 with Ohio Bell after a four year layoff, and being greeted by a district plant supervisor, who leaned back in his chair and said, "Well, there've been a few changes since you left, Bill. One of them is we've now got a union, and, boy, I'm proud. We've got 100 percent membership." And as Walsh added, "It is as true today as it was then or it ever has been: management makes union members, in various different ways, either by over-supervision, under-supervision, or just being obnoxious in the matter of power."

Whatever management's expectations, they were no longer dealing with a tractable labor force. Joseph Beirne has succinctly summed up what a good many people were then beginning to feel: "I *resented* intellectually, I guess, what was successful in 1935 and 1934, with the management of an industry subtly telling us all how to think. And it finally dawned on me that this was exactly what had been happening during the years I worked in that company. And when it dawned, I just resented somebody trying to use the power of their position and the fears that were there of holding a job in the depression years, using all of that to sort of brainwash and capture people." So, all over the country, telephone people began to organize for themselves, taking what amounted to a company gift and turning it to their own account, refashioning it, to suit their own purposes and needs.

It was an extraordinarily complicated, difficult and long drawn-out process. Organizing, say, for the International Brotherhood of Electrical Workers or as a CIO union, was not practicable. Clarence Good still remembers the day an IBEW organizer was thrown bodily out of a southern California telephone building by the employees. Mrs. Helen W. Berthalot, CWA legislative representative and in the 1930's a Michigan operator, reminds us,

"At that period of time, our kids were scared to death of the union." While a majority of the Bell System employees, in the words of Frank Lonergan, a CWA charter member and a division vice president, were "still too timid or still steeped too deeply in Bell System tradition to want any outside established union representing them, they *were* willing and seriously thinking of an independent union of their own." So, for anyone seriously interested in an organization of communications workers in the late 1930s there was only one place, one direction to go; that is, into the emerging so-called independent associations or unions. That was the only game in Ma Bell's ballpark.

Among the various Bell System employee representation plan associations undergoing the transformation to post–Wagner Act independence, perhaps the most militant were those in the southwest. When it came to choosing a name, they did not equivocate with the soft sounding "Employee Association" or "Employee Federation," but forthrightly declared themselves the Southwestern Telephone Workers Union. A small thing, but a heady decision with the company presence still very much behind the scenes. The STWU was the first of the incipient telephone unions to organize telephone workers outside the Bell System, a significant step forward towards true independence and unionism.*

What the company wanted at the start was clear. As John Crull phrased it, management said, "We have always got along very well together in the old employees' association. There's no reason why we couldn't continue those same harmonious relationships." This, for example, meant that in 1938, Southwestern Bell proposed bargaining area by area within the four departments—plant, accounting, commercial and traffic. But the chairmen of the four plant department unions began to consult with one another, taking advantage of their accessibility to the toll test rooms. According to Crull, the test-board man even linked up all the area chairmen on a "conference call." Copies of allegedly different proposed contracts were also exchanged. Crull recalls, "As strange as it might be, those contracts were *word for word*—indicating the strong influence of the company." The only difference in words were between Oklahoma-Texas where the unlocated construction man "carried" his wife with him, and Missouri-Kansas where the man's wife "traveled" with him. "They just don't use the word "travel" in Texas and Oklahoma," Crull explained. "A man 'carries' his wife with him."

While there was some dissatisfaction over the contract, it was, as D.L. McCowen put it, "presented" to the independent unions. "Really,"

---

*According to John Crull, the first group of independent telephone workers organized by what would become the CWA were employees of the Middle States Utilities Company, a group centered in the small towns of Kansas to the northeast of Kansas City.

McCowen adds, "there was no bargaining that took place." Nonetheless, the "presentation," as it were, accelerated the process of coming together. The plant chairmen—Arthur Fortner, Oklahoma; D.L. McCowen, northwest Texas; Pat Newman, west Missouri, and J.J. "Jake" Schacht, east Missouri-Arkansas—met in Galveston, there deciding to call a meeting in Oklahoma City, during the summer of 1938. In St. Louis, a group thought they ought to have "something concrete" to offer to the projected Oklahoma City meeting "to get something going." J.J. Schact, Bud Powers, a construction man and Madge Murphy, a traffic representative, met with Dean Eberly of St. Louis University Law School and asked him to draw up a constitution that would comply with the Wagner Act. They brought that document with them to Oklahoma City.

Meanwhile, illustrating the vagaries of history, Erwin Cotter, a cable splicer and a local plant chairman in Oklahoma City, had come up with a charter for a corporation of telephone workers. Cotter, as it happened, got into an argument with a union man over whether or not he was a member of a real union. "It couldn't be much of a union," the man said, "I'll bet you don't even have a charter." When Cotter repeated this to his brother Everett, a lawyer, Everett Cotter said, "Don't worry about that. I can get you a charter."*

McCowen has described what happened at Oklahoma City, "We put Jake Schact's constitution and Erwin's charter together and formed the union." Much of the first meeting, he adds, "was spent in discussing whether or not Jake's group should be reimbursed for the $300 they spent for the constitution and whether or not we should give Erwin or his brother the five or $25, whatever it was, it cost to get the charter. . . . That was a demonstration of some of the thinking at the time about money."

Although McCowen now takes a wry view of that first meeting—"We were ill-advised to form a corporation as such, but the facts are that's what we did"—it was a vital first step. Dues were set at ten cents a month. The executive board consisted of the sixteen departmental chairmen, four from each area, four from each department. Arthur Fortner was elected president; J.J. Schact, vice president; Beulah Hamilton, secretary, and L.W. Powers, treasurer. Elected area chairmen were D.L. McCowen, Texas plant; Lena Trimble, east Missouri-Arkansas traffic; Madge Murphy, southwest traffic; Mary Walker, Oklahoma traffic; and Nancy Franks, west Missouri-Kansas traffic. J.J. Schacht subsequently became president, and D.L. McCowen, vice president. William Bastian, an arthritis victim on a disability pension, was hired as an office manager, maintaining the union

---

*There are two versions of this anecdote John Crull's and D.L. McCowen's. Both agree that Cotter was at work in a manhole when this discussion took place, but Crull reports the conversation as being with an organizer from the Oil Workers; McCowen says the man was an IBEW member.

office in his home for a time. Collective bargaining, however, remained an "iffy" proposition. As Miss Nelle Wooding notes, there was "a terrible hodgepodge to start with, and we fell into it and had to just work out of it as best we could." In 1939, the Dallas local won a dollar increase for the operators. "A dollar wasn't much," Miss Wooding remarks, "but it looked big to us because we got it ourselves." A small, confused beginning, but the union was on its way.

The southwest experience parallels that of others throughout the Bell System. In Cleveland, young Turks began taking over the old ERP plant locals, eventually "capturing" all six. Charles West was elected Illinois Joint Plant Council president, running on the slogan, "Down with company stooges! Up with real representatives of the employees." According to Paul E. Griffith, later the first president of the National Federation of Telephone Workers, "With the full knowledge and approval of the company, we proceeded voluntarily to purify our organization, if that is the word . . . We set up our own office. We hired a young man to be our full-time secretary. We increased our dues structure and we tried to operate as we thought an independent organization should." Annie Benscoter, Rose Sensibauch and Katherine Dugan set out to organize "the whole state of Illinois," operators all together. "They gave us the cards," recalls Miss June McDonald, then a Chicago telephone operator, "We signed people up." Even with the covert backing of the company, it was hard going. "You would try and get your trade around and get off a four-day weekend," Miss McDonald explains. "Then you had Friday, Saturday, and Sunday to get on a bus and go down-state to Peoria or Springfield or Quincy or Hannibal and Decatur. You would hit the towns that you could, and . . . this was how we organized the state. By bus and sleeping in people's homes, you know. This was how we did it."

The Long Lines people in New York opened a small office, and began reaching out across the country. Western Electric employees, too, started to pull together a national organization. George DuVal of the Kearny Plant explored the possibilities of organizing on a metropolitan basis with Louis Junker of Western Electric Distributing House (Sales) and Joseph Beirne, already head of the New York local. Ernest Weaver organized the Western Electric based Association of Equipment Workers, and Joseph Beirne went traveling for the sales group. "We started with the hat," Beirne liked to recall, it being a mark of the new independence. "My trip around the country in a Greyhound bus was just financed from one stop to the next stop. I'd come from one stop, and I had nothing left, and we'd pass the hat. And whatever we got out of the hat, why, that would tell me what city I could go to next."

Inexorably, the pressures for change built up. Officers of the Illinois Joint Plant Council, in the words of the Council historian, came to believe "that it was almost hopeless to even attempt to change anything that was national in scope [as, for example, the Bell System pension plan] . . . it was obvious that a national organization of employees was necessary to cope with this and other systemwide problems." And, in Ohio, Thomas Twigg was preaching amalgamation, urging the need for a national organization of telephone workers. Born in Wales in 1893, the son of a coal miner, Twigg became a sailor at thirteen and later liked to recall how, as a youth on shore leave, he once led a parade of striking workmen. The colorful Welshman had been an amateur boxer, a diamond miner in the Kimberley fields of South Africa; he had been wounded while serving in the Royal Navy during World War I, and he was an able debater, who "could deflate the wildest ideas imaginable in such a manner that though the speaker would admit his error, it was without a sting and resulting hurt pride." He had hired on with Ohio Bell in Cleveland as a splicer's helper in 1921, becoming active in the employees' association a decade later. By the mid 1930s, he was saying, "The plan of representation has been outgrown, and we must have something better, something more vital, and not a pink tea party."

IV

An Idea Is Born

When the United States Supreme Court on April 12, 1937 upheld the constitutionality of the Wagner Labor Act, AT&T corporate officers decided to comply with the new labor relations law. Employee representation plans, company unions in any guise, were now clearly illegal. Nonetheless, Bell System management wanted little or nothing to do with unions either affiliated with the established American Federation of Labor or with the newly emerging Congress of Industrial Organizations. It was devoutly hoped that the old "satisfactory" relationships with the employee associations would somehow be carried over to the "new" employee groups or to the independent unions springing up throughout the system. Here and there, however, legitimate unions, chiefly the International Brotherhood of Electrical Workers, were charging under National Labor Relations Board procedures that the new telephone workers' organizations were "company dominated." This raised a serious question: What were the criteria of true independence?

Increasingly, it appeared that one essential criterion was the formation of a national organization. The need to discuss certain national issues, pensions and collective bargaining, the fending off of IBEW and other "outsiders," the rise of a new leadership were other factors giving impetus to the coming together of the Bell System's independent employee organizations. While these considerations were percolating among telephone workers all over the nation, giving rise to much discussion, it was the Ohio Federation that acted. At the instigation of the Federation's forty-six-year-old president Thomas Twigg, the Ohio group sent out a call to a conference to be held in St. Louis, Missouri, at the Hotel Statler on December 16 and 17, 1937. The invitation was limited to groups from AT&T associated companies because, as Kenneth M. Blount, then secretary of the Ohio Federation, has recalled, "Twigg felt that the associated companies had problems different from the Western Electric manufacturing organizations." Twenty-nine delegates from seventeen groups, representing 80,027 employees, came to St. Louis to debate the future of telephone-worker organization. Of these, the Southwestern Telephone Workers' Union, covering all departments (plant, traffic, commercial, accounting, engineering),

42

with 19,000 members was the largest; next came the Long Lines Association with 9,400 members; United Telephone Organization downstate New York plant, 9,353 members; the Ohio Federation, 7,000 members; International Brotherhood of Telephone Workers, New England (except Connecticut), plant, 6,800; Pennsylvania Plant Employees, 5,212, and the Illinois Joint Plant Council, with 4,350 members. The International Brotherhood of Telephone Workers of New England was the largest plant group represented and the Michigan Traffic Employees' Federation, with 2,557 members, the largest traffic organization.

The eight women and twenty-one men gathered at the Hotel Statler in St. Louis were embarking on an untraveled road for telephone people. There were fears, suspicions and a wariness induced by years of Bell System indoctrination. As a witnesses retrospective account describes it, "The press and organizations of employers had colored the labor movement until many of those arriving for a first meeting wondered whether they were to find some red beards and convenient soap boxes. . . . They wondered what motives other representatives might have. They wondered what the boss back home thought of their activity in an organization that might become a labor union." A regional parochialism intruded, creating ethnic and religious distrust. Paul Griffith recalls being asked, "Don't they have anybody but Irish employees back there [in the East]?" In Illinois, Griffith added, "The names of officers might vary from Peterson to O'Malley and Fox to Cerminaro. Therefore, it was a trifle of a surprise to attend National meetings and hear the large number of Irish names when the roll was called." (Later, Griffith would be asked about Joseph Beirne, "Do you think he would be priest-ridden?")*Some Easterners, according to Jacob J. Schacht, "thought of our people as a bunch of hoosiers and that the Indians were still running around on horseback, especially out in Oklahoma [and] down in Texas. They couldn't visualize people, you know, being civilized yet."

The St. Louis conference might have simply disintegrated in a welter of mutual distrust had it not been for Thomas Twigg. In his opening remarks, he pointedly noted that his organization (the Ohio Federation) had just gone through "quite a war," a reference to attacks on the independence of telephone worker organizations by AFL and CIO unions, and stressed that his members were convinced that outside control was undesirable. Yet, as the conference proceedings report stated, "They were very much interested in a national employee organization and thought that such an organization

---

*Griffith's reply is of interest: "I replied, 'Of course he's influenced by his priest, but to what degree I can't say. What is really bothering you and a number of other officers is, in the event you elect Beirne as vice president, would he be a stooge of the Bishop of New Jersey or something of this sort?' Answering my own question, I said, 'I don't know . . . but if you don't believe that he could handle a job without influence from his church, why, vote accordingly, that's all I can say.' "

should be formed for many reasons, including the necessity of influencing legislation affecting telephone workers." (Twigg was named permanent chairman of the conference, and Mrs. Theresa Donahey from Ohio Traffic was appointed secretary.) While Twigg was considered an advocate of a strong national organization, he carefully ensured that all sides of the question were amply debated. Earl Hill of Pennsylvania was asked to submit an organizational plan that, in essence, called for an "exchange of information," for the "Coordination of Activities of Mutual Interest," and for "Mutual Protection and Development." This sparked a discussion of the purpose and scope of the proposed national organization. Someone remarked that since the Ohio group had called the conference, it must have a plan to offer. Twigg allowed as to how this was the case, and an outline for a constitution was passed out among the delegates. The Ohioans proposed a "national independent labor organization," providing for "common counsel and united action" on employment problems as well as for legislation action.

This provoked, in the words of the proceedings, "a definitely unfavorable reaction disclosing two lines of thought:"

> (a) One line of thought, as very capably expressed by Mr. [Kendall T.] Stevens of the Northwestern Bell Association, was definitely and vehemently opposed to any form of National Organization other than a very loosely knit type. Such an organization, he stated, could act as a clearing house for dissemination of news-bulletins, ideas, and exchange of organization structures, working-agreements, etc.
>
> (b) The other line of thought, as eloquently advanced by Mr. [Jerry J.] Coughlin representing the New England Bell Employees (excepting Connecticut), scoffed at Mr. Stevens' ideas, calling it a 'pink tea' affair and unworthy of the slightest consideration by his constituents. He proposed a 'real' organization with teeth, and officers in whom some genuine authority would be vested.

There was a good deal of discussion from the floor with a large number of the delegates expressing the fear that their individual organizations would eventually lose their separate identities. An effort was made to break the deadlock between the warring factions, "East vs West," by appointing a constitutional committee to draft a compromise. Chaired by Earl Hill, the committee—Paul E. Griffith (Illinois plant), R. Bagg (Connecticut), R. L. Spaulding (Long Lines), Donahey (Ohio Traffic), and Helen Ward (District of Columbia Traffic)—came up with a proposal for a "rather loosely-knit type of national organization," which was turned down "decisively." Twigg threatened to resign as chairman, "because it was evident that the meeting had failed to accomplish its objective . . . the fact that many representatives would not even accept such a simple document, even for discussion by their members, showed them to be without sufficient initiative to even be a representative of an afternoon sewing circle." Twigg, however, was asked to reconsider his threat, which he did. The first effort of telephone workers to get together nationally had reached an impasse, or so it appeared.

Paul E. Griffith has assessed the forces at that first meeting rather accurately. "I would divide them somewhat as follows: advocates of a strong national organization were perhaps ten percent of the delegates. Those who wanted a moderately strong federation of some kind, with authority to function on items which were authorized by the members—you might call it a moderate organization—probably about eighty percent of those present. The other ten percent either wanted nothing at all, or they wanted what was sneeringly referred to as a 'clearing house,' where statistics on wages and working conditions would be compiled and made available to other member organizations." This constellation of forces would remain roughly constant through the founding of the National Federation of Telephone Workers. Indeed, the only action taken at the St. Louis meeting was the approval of a questionnaire to be sent to each delegate. Yet, the concerns reflected in the questionnaire went beyond those implicit in a mere collection and dissemination of statistics. For this reason perhaps, the delegates ultimately decided to continue their efforts. Whether he had intimations of mortality (Twigg would not live to see his dream of a national organization become a reality; he died on March 8, 1939), or felt that his advocacy of a strong organization would hurt his cause if he continued chairing national conferences, Twigg, in effect, stepped aside and put forward Paul E. Griffith, a moderate from Illinois. As Griffith recollected the event many years later, over lunch on the last day of the St. Louis meeting, Twigg told him, "Paul, everytime I get up to the podium, I see fear in the eyes of ninety percent of the delegates present. And, every time I start to speak, I see that look of fear reappear in their eyes. They are really scared." While Twigg thought the situation all but hopeless, he expressed his belief that Griffith might possibly hold the factions together until some kind of trust developed. He suggested, therefore, that Griffith ask for the floor when the convention reconvened to state his belief that some progress had been made and to invite the delegates to another meeting in Chicago. Griffith agreed to do so, and the delegates at St. Louis concluded their deliberations by agreeing that the contacts made should not be lost, discussion should be encouraged "back home" and that a second meeting should be held before the next summer. Griffith, who extended the invitation, was named chairman. L. A. Polabykian, president of Illinois Accounting, was named secretary for the Chicago and New Orleans conferences. He died a few years later of throat cancer.

When the group met again, June 15–17, 1938, at the Allerton Hotel in Chicago, its size had been augmented. Seventy-three delegates, fifty-two men and twenty-one women, came, representing thirty-one Bell System employee groups with a combined membership of 141,231. Who made that decision—and when—is not clear. Some of the delegates from newly-represented plant and traffic organizations complained that they had not received invitations to the first gathering. But the crucial decision was to invite delegates from Western Electric installation, manufacturing and sales groups. It was a recognition of the oneness of Ma Bell, a mark of the new militants. Many Bell employees believed that the associated companies were somehow truly independent of AT&T, that Bell System policy was not all of a piece but somehow decentralized. It was a view carefully cultivated by the company, a sophisticated divide-and-conquer paternalism. As Joseph Beirne once explained this "caste system" operating among Bell people: "A plant man looked at a traffic girl with suspicion, and the traffic girl looked at the plant man with the same suspicion . . . Within the plant, the inside man looks upon the outside man with skepticism. The clerical people in accounting and commercial, they have always been taught that they are much superior to so-called production workers. The Long Lines people look at the operating company people as people who are below them . . . and Western Electric was the second cousin of the whole Bell System; we were the 'weirdos' . . ." To have invited the weirdos to take part in the Chicago conference was a critical step, the first move towards one union for all telephone workers and, ultimately, towards national bargaining with Ma Bell.

The forces at work at the St. Louis meeting were active in Chicago. It was not only a larger meeting but, as Griffith, the elected chairman, recalled, it was "much more animated as well, and the people were more sure of themselves than they had been in the beginning. Some really great speeches were made." There was broader agreement among the delegates on the need for a national organization, and fewer reservations even among the moderates. As F. Seith, secretary of the Ohio Federation of Telephone Workers, informed the delegates, "The IBEW has a National Board of Strategy, which is on the lookout for possibilities to enter the telephone field. If they can enter and dominate one, they will have established a precedent. This is one of the reasons why we *must* have a national organization." H. A. Schultz, secretary-treasurer of the Southern California United Brotherhood of Telephone Workers, agreed and to the cheers of the delegates declared, "We are really looked upon just as company unions, and until we can get a national organization so that we can spread propaganda throughout the nation, we will never be able to get out of our own particular little locality. We represent the highest type of labor in the country and we will be isolated until such time as we organize and can put a finger on congressmen and senators. Until that time, we will be at the mercy of unfair and unscrupulous politicians."

Of gravest concern to the delegates was the pressure then building up against recognition of independent unions by the National Labor Relations Board. The *bona fides* of the Wisconsin Independent Union of Telephone Operators were under challenge by the IBEW at the time of the Chicago convention. As the *New York Journal of Commerce* on May 27, 1938, put it, "Decisions of the National Labor Relations Board in the pending Humble Refining and Wisconsin Telephone cases should settle definitely the question as to whether any of the independent unions formed after the Wagner Act decision of the Supreme Court can survive. The board already has disestablished dozens of such unions in recent months. Moreover, the trial examiner's intermediate report in both of the cases cited, favored abolition of the organizations on the sole grounds that some members were also associated with the old employee representation plan. Members of both independent unions pay dues and finance all activities independently of the company. Therefore, some observers feel that if the board cannot sustain the legality of the Humble and Telephone employees' organization, it will not approve any." As it turned out a year later the NLRB dismissed the "company union" charges in the Wisconsin case, but the delegates in Chicago feared the contrary and believed that establishing a national organization would help to set to rest similar challenges. So, it was with relief and unanimity that they voted "aye" on a motion made by a slender, intense, beetle-browed young man from the National Association of Western Electric Employees (Sales), Joseph Beirne, during the afternoon session on the first day, that "a national organization be formed."

But the Beirne motion left open the questions as to what kind of organization telephone workers ought to have. Chairman Griffith was authorized to appoint a committee to draft a constitution. He named R. L. Spaulding, chairman of the Long Lines Association; E. R. Hackett, president of the Chicago Area Illinois Bell Telephone Commercial Employees Association; D. L. McCowen, area chairman of the Texas plant, South Western Telephone Workers' Union; J. J. Schacht, president, STWU; R. McNair, suburban division president, Illinois Bell Telephone (Plant) Employees Association; K. T. Stevens, president of Northwestern Bell Telephone Employees' Association (Plant); Bert Horth, state council chairman of Wisconsin Bell Plant Employees' Association, and Miss Eunice Russell, president of the Association of Clerical Employees of the Chesapeake & Potomac Telephone Company of Baltimore City. Before the constitutional committee retired to deliberate, the delegates, on a motion by Beirne, heard exponents of the three basic views on organization.

Kenneth Stevens spoke for the so-called "loose" types of organization: "I believe we have something to preserve now. Each of us has a job to do to preserve our present working conditions and keep our present organizations intact. We have a very happy situation with our management that should not be jeopardized by the doubtful benefits of a so-called 'strong' organization.

"Let us take it easy at first and not be too hasty. Let us work together and learn to cooperate with and assist one another. A simple majority can take care of everything at the present time.

"Various member organizations can be furnished with a mailing list for the exchange of information. This is sufficent, as we need no one to help us run our own affairs. The officers elected or appointed here can call meetings when necessary. Let us walk before we run."

L. H. James, president of the Illinois Plant Association, then rose to defend the so-called middle-of-the-road course:

"There are, of course, bound to be several different opinions on any important subject and this is no exception. Instead of the two possible extremes, I prefer the happy medium or the middle of the road course.

"We do need a national organization of a more substantial nature than merely a committee. There are real reasons for it which I will undertake to mention. In the first place, I think our members will speedily lose interest in and refuse to support a 'loose' type. In the second place, we all work in an industry in which the problems are pretty much the same the country over. We are all telephone people with a standard type business and similar job requirements. That puts us on a common footing to start with.

"It is obvious that there are many problems that are of interest to all and that they must be handled on a national basis for any degree of success. For example, take the pension plan. Most of us have found out from experience, that it is too much for us to handle on a local basis in our individual organizations.

"There are many problems that are of importance to more than one section of the country and we must, therefore, have an organization sufficiently well set up and financed to be capable of caring for these things. This might well include keeping an eye on unfavorable legislation."

Finally, Tom Twigg put the case for a strong organization:

"What Ohio wants is a strong organization. We have had four types in Ohio, each one stronger than the other. There are several individual groups headed up under a State Federation. Each group keeps its own autonomy in all matters of interest and concern to that group alone. Collective bargaining is done by the state group.

"In a national organization, each member organization would keep its autonomy in the same way, with the national officers or board to care for national problems, such as the pension plan already mentioned, and to observe the legislation being passed in Washington.

"In addition to this, the national organization should help others to get better organized. Many member organizations do not know the requirements of an independent union and would welcome advice from a full time member or committee who would go out and visit all organizations.

"There may be organizations represented here which could not stand up without the protection of the laws of the land. What about the time when Washington is in the hands of reactionists and the Wagner Act is amended or done away with? How many of us could then stand up? Those are the things to consider."

The delegates, however, were not about to consider such far-reaching questions. They drafted a constitution, but not a very satisfactory one. The delegates, for example, thumbed down an effort by R.W. Long of Illinois Accounting and D.L. McCowen and his fellow Southwesterners for open membership to any worker organization "within the telephone industry," limiting membership instead to those "within the Bell System"—this despite an argument advanced by L.W. Powers of Southwestern, who pointed out that "should we exclude independent telephone employees from membership, the NLRB may claim we do not have a labor union as is required by law." In any event, the delegates could not bring themselves to approve the constitution wholeheartedly; a motion to accept the constitution as tentative finally carried but with the proviso that no one ratify it until after another meeting.

There were few changes in the composition of the group (fifty-four men, seventeen women representing thirty-one organizations with a combined membership of 144,998) as it reassembled in New Orleans, November 14 to 17, 1938, at the St. Charles Hotel. Among the new voices were Pansy M. Harris, the executive head of the Telephone Traffic Employees' League of Southern California, and W.J. McPherson, Chairman of the Pacific Plant Council. The debate over constitutional revisions at New Orleans was a good deal more acrimonious, although Chairman Griffith recalls that "the former sarcastic strong union advocates were subdued. They knew, I think, that they were strictly in the minority, and further, that if they persisted, there just wouldn't be any national organization whatsoever." Griffith's point is borne out by the willingness of such strong organization advocates as Joseph Beirne to go along with the "autonomy" clause in the constitution. Beirne moved the insertion of the autonomy clause, which declared affiliates "forever autonomous and . . . free from interference in the conduct of their internal affairs," and accepted the amendment proposed by T.F. Murphy of the New England Brotherhood of Telephone Workers that "this principle shall remain forever inviolate."

Even though the autonomy clause became the *bête noir* of those who soon assumed leadership of the National Federation of Telephone Workers, it was clear at New Orleans that this was the price to be paid for the formation of a national organization with at least some structure having elected officers (admittedly part-time), finances, and, significantly, with membership open "to independent labor organizations within the telephone industry." As the Ohio leaders put it in a subsequent issue of the *Federation Bulletin*, "The New Orleans convention is now history, and the Ohio delegation is satisfied that the new National Constitution is definitely and basically a reasonable and substantial document. For a while it seemed as if the adoption of a weak structure would cause Ohio to wash its hands of any attempts toward a national organization. Today, however, matters are different . . ."

Those who favored a "loose-type" organization fell back fighting an obstructionist, rear-guard action at New Orleans. Raising points of order and floor challenges of every conceivable kind, this group fought bitterly to prevent the adoption of the revised constitution. L.W. Weil, president of the Southern Association of Bell Employees, a group later found to be "company dominated" by the NLRB, who headed the opposition to the forming of a national organization, denied being "an obstructionist" but reiterated that his group "did not favor a national organization but rather 'favored national conferences.' " His organization, he said, "did not feel the necessity for the establishment of a national organization existed, and if a conference of the officers of the various organizations throughout the country met for the purpose of exchanging ideas, that would be sufficient for their needs." Failing to secure the conference approach, the opposition then sought passage of the weaker Chicago constitution with its limited powers and scope. Stevens of Northwestern declared that he failed to see why the Chicago document needed revision, the cost of the New Orleans meeting was exceedingly high ($3,500 a day) and money could be saved by the speedy adoption of the Chicago document, and the "attempt to sell a national organization to his people was based too strongly on expectations and visions and not on accomplishments." He also objected to a provision in the new constitution requiring organizations applying for membership must "prove to the satisfaction of the National Assembly by approved questionnaire that they are bona fide labor organizations." Some organizations, he said, "whose members were not as labor-minded and as financially well-off, might feel the cost to be prohibitive."

Bert Horth of Wisconsin presented the constitution as revised by a committee consisting of himself, Pansy M. Harris (Traffic Employees League of Southern California), Leo George (president, Hoosier Telephone Association), Kenneth Blount (Ohio Federation), Joseph Beirne (W.E. Sales), D.E. Bishop (chairman, United Brotherhood of Telephone Workers, Southern California), L.W. Kirk (president, Associated Commercial Employees, Pacific Tel. & Tel.), and R. McNair, (Chairman, Illinois Plant) chairman. "You will note," Horth told the delegates, "that in the preamble 'We, the telephone people' was changed to 'We, the telephone workers,' having in mind that we are workers; *that,* the majority of telephone people believe, and to use any other term is to describe ourselves other than that we are supposed to [be] . . . It was felt that the majority of people had come to the conclusion that we are telephone workers, at least that we work . . ." After Horth's overview, the delegates took up the constitution paragraph by paragraph, debating nearly all its provisions at length. When Beirne offered a motion setting the per capita dues to the national organization at twenty-five cents a year per member, Miss Anna J. Ryan, president, New England Telephone Operators, wanted to know if there would be a differential between men and women. After some discussion, it was decided that for the first year, women were to pay twelve cents per capita, men twenty-four cents. At first, the women, at least some, were inclined to accept the differential. Then, in part as a consequence of a behind-the-scenes struggle to reduce national dues, the women caucused, reconsidered and favored equal dues, which were set at ten cents a year per member.

During the debate, the fear surfaced, which was felt by many of the men present, that the traffic groups, numerically the largest bloc of telephone workers and staffed predominantly by women, would come to dominate the new organization. One delegate stated that he believed women ought to have a separate department. According to Griffith, women had very little to say at the first two conferences but were more active in New Orleans. "They appeared quite satisfied," Griffith recalled, "to leave the oratory to the men, except from time to time in the committees the women reminded the committee members that in any dues structure or any expenses the majority of most of the payments would come from the women—and they shouldn't forget that little item. Other than that, they were quite retiring." Beirne recalls that the men did not trust the women. This distrust turned up in the bloc-voting procedures laid down for the national assemblies, which provided that an assembly was to be "composed of accredited delegates from each member organization, one of whom shall be entitled to vote."

Finally, the debate drew to a close, after extending the planned three-day meeting into a fourth day, and the weary delegates approved the constitution, appointed a ratification committee, named Griffith chairman *pro tem,* and Horth secretary *pro tem,* for a constitutional convention to be held in New York City the following June. The constitution was to be "in full force and effect" if and when ratified in convention by ten or more qualified applicants for membership. There were ten nominees for the ratification committee, and, interestingly, the five chosen were all from Bell associated companies. Even though Ernest Weaver, president of the Western Electric installers group, the Association of Equipment Workers, played a prominent role at the convention as a spokesman for a strong national organization, he was not elected, nor was R.L. Spauling, Long Lines chairman (AT&T) and a leading spokesman for the weaker, Chicago document.* Elected were: Horth (Wisconsin), a "transmission man doing work neces-

*Others nominated were: R.F. Johnson, president, Telephone Employees' Association (Northwestern Bell); T.M. Riall, vice president, United Telephone Organization (New York), and Walter McPherson, chairman, Pacific Tel. & Tel. Commercial (Plant) Employees.

sary and dealing with transmission;" Bishop (Southern California), "one half time test board and one half time maintenance of ship-to-shore radio;" Stevens (Northwestern), "switchboard installation, repair and toll tester;" Griffith (Ill), "equipment engineer's office, plant department;" and Miss Harris (Southern California traffic), a "supervising operator." On balance, the committee reflected the majority at New Orleans, moderate but leaning towards a strong national organization.

When Paul E. Griffith rapped his gavel against the podium in the College Room at the Hotel Astor, New York, on Monday, June 5, 1939, at four-fifteen in the afternoon, the National Federation of Telephone Workers was launched, a jerrybuilt but, nonetheless, seaworthy vessel. A press statement claimed "ninety-five delegates of forty-two independent labor organizations representing 165,000 telephone workers" present at the federation's first constitutional convention. Of that number, however, only sixty-one men and sixteen women were authorized to speak for NFTW affiliates, representing 92,130 workers. (Kenneth M. Blount, president of the Ohio Federation, was on hand to speak for his organization, which had not as yet applied for membership but would soon do so.) Jacob J. Schacht, up from St. Louis, Mrs. Nancy E. Franks and Miss Hazel White represented the largest affiliate, the Southwestern Telephone Workers Union with 16,000 members in all departments; New York's United Telephone Organizations sent a large delegation, headed by president J.F. Broderick and vice president Thomas M. Riall, representing the second largest NFTW affiliate, with 9,363 plant workers; Long Lines, the third largest affiliate with 9,084 members in all departments, sent in a new leadership, including Stanley H. Burke, chairman, and Dorothy F. Handy. The Illinois Plant group, with 4,496 members, sent an impressive delegation, headed by Rexford McNair, president, and included two new voices destined to play vital roles in the history of the union, Alfred B. Herrington and Carlton W. (Slim) Werkau. Mrs. Emma I. Jascot and Miss Martha Wolkman represented the largest traffic affiliate, the 6,844-member Chicago Area-Illinois Traffic Federation, and Mrs. Anne C. Benscoter and Miss Margaret C. Fitzpatrick, the second largest traffic group, with 3,640 members in Illinois (State). Miss Janice Hagy, president of the 4,017-member Northwestern Bell Telephone Operators' Association, represented the third largest traffic group at the convention. Miss Pansy M. Harris came from southern California on behalf of the fourth largest traffic affiliate, the 3,528-member Telephone Traffic Employees League. Charles H. Flax, chairman of the Western Electric Independent Labor Association, spoke for 7,200 manufacturing employees at the Hawthorne plant; George C. DuVal, for 3,000 at the Kearny plant in New Jersey; Ernest Weaver headed the four-man delegation from Western Electric Installation, the 3,600-member Association of Communication Equipment Workers, and Joseph Beirne, the 3,129 Western Electric salesforce.

The interminable wrangling over a constitution was now at an end: Not that the document remained inviolate, for it was amended even at the first convention, but that the delegates could also get on with other business. They proceeded cautiously, however, in part out of inexperience and in part because of the uncertainties inherent in their situation as an independent labor organization. The NLRB, the courts and other governmental institutions were well geared to cope with the recognized bodies of organized labor, the AFL and the CIO and their respective affiliates. Policy vis-a-vis independent unions, in 1939, was as yet not clear. Legally and in theory, workers were as free to choose independent unions as they were to choose either an AFL or a CIO union. Still, there was little precedent to build upon and as for the political arena and in the legislative halls, even less. For example, would the new telephone workers' federation be recognized on federally-formed industry committees? The delegates authorized the NFTW president to appoint a committee whose "sole duty" would be to watch activities concerning the application of the Fair Labor Standards Act to the telephone industry but they could not be assured—as an AFL or CIO union would—that there would be proper representation for telephone workers on any committee appointed by the government for the industry.

At New Orleans, during the last hour of discussion on problems faced by telephone workers, Joseph Beirne stated his belief that there were two matters of serious concern: the establishment of an office "to keep abreast of legislative action, which might be detrimental to their interests, and which would be impossible unless an experienced and qualified representative was in charge and paid a decent salary" and the establishment of "ways and means for exercising influence on members of the legislature." As debate at New York would show, the NFTW was not prepared to undertake political action, as well as a "recognition program" to secure "proper recognition as a labor organization" by other labor organizations, management, the government and the general public," the majority agreeing that such a development was "premature." The question of a Washington lobby waited on the necessary finances, and the federation was not in a position to implement Beirne's suggestion until 1941. Still, a seed had been planted.

A part of the democratic process, in unions as in society, involves exploring various avenues in seeking solutions to problems of all kinds and of varying gravity. The delegates at the 1939 convention, as an instance of one of several ultimately dead ends, authorized a committee to explore the possibility of "taking advantage of the combined AT&T stock held or controlled by employees." It was thought that "representation on the Board of Directors . . . would be the most efficient way of obtaining the influence desired by the federation and that through exercise of stock ownership the viewpoint and requests of the workers would be conveyed directly to the owners of the business." The possibilities for a Telephone Labor Act and for a Telephone Retirement Act based on similar legislation enacted by

Congress for railroad workers were also to be explored, as well as a "recognition program" to secure "proper recognition as a labor organization . . . by other labor organizations, management, the government and the general public."

The delegates, however, did not ignore collective bargaining as an alternative way of obtaining their goals. They authorized a "survey of employment conditions throughout the Bell System," a necessary first step in the bargaining process and the first move towards setting up a research department. Among the first "demands" to be raised were a greatly strengthened pension system, including the raising of the minimum "to an adequate amount," especially a higher pension rate for workers in the lower brackets; a reduction of hours to seven per day and thirty-five a week, "with no decrease in pay;" retraining and the retention of older men in connection with dialization, one of the first attempts by American workers to cope with automation, and, finally, the implementation of the slogan, "Telephone Work for Telephone People," a drive to counterattack the Bell System's contracting out of installation and other work to outside firms.

Even now, as the new national organization began to take shape, telephone workers were chary of the strike, the ultimate sanction in collective bargaining. Operating employees, in particular, were conscious of the "public-relations angle," although Western Electric employees had taken strike votes on occasion as a last resort. As Griffith phrased it, "We wanted to have a strong, independent union of our own, but we did not want it to be affiliated with any of these other unions because we agreed, with our employer, that the maintenance of continuous service was absolutely paramount and that we should do nothing to interfere with that." Nonetheless, the delegates declared that NFTW affiliates would "not become strike breakers," and went on record "as opposed, both in principle and practice, to assuming the work of any organization which belongs to the National Federation of Telephone Workers, while said organization is participating in economic disputes." As Jack Barbash noted in his pioneering study, "This was an interesting viewpoint for a group new to unionism. The affiliated groups were in the position of expressing a willingness to undertake a sympathetic strike to support the objectives of another affiliate without being too sure as to whether they would strike to support their own demands." It was, in truth, an extraordinary expression of maturity and of independence.

The constitution was amended to provide for voting at conventions based on numerical strength—each affiliate being entitled to one vote for 2,000 members or less and an additional vote for each additional 2,000—and for representation on the executive board by regions. Paul E. Griffith was elected president, Stanley H. Burke, vice-president, and Bert Horth, secretary-treasurer of the new organization. S.M. Adams, New Jersey Bell;

Pansy M. Harris, Southern California Traffic; W.J. McPherson, Washington-Idaho area; and Kenneth T. Stevens, Central Region, were elected members of the executive board. The president was allowed a salary of $200 a year, the secretary-treasurer, $180 a year. The total budget was set at $10,000; however, it was never fully collected. Griffith would operate from a desk in the offices of the Illinois Union of Telephone Workers and Horth, from a cubbyhole in the headquarters of the Telephone Guild of Wisconsin. It was not an entirely satisfactory arrangement, but it seemed practical and fitted the limited budget of the fledgling NFTW.

Institutions have a way of throwing up the leadership they need at a given time. This, of course, is no more than a sociological rule of thumb; men and times are sometimes out of joint. But the new officers elected by the delegates meeting in New York were both suited to and representative of the new institution just coming into being. As George DuVal later described him, Griffith was "a very compassionate man [who tried] to weld all these groups together knowing that there were some weak sisters and some very strong radical members in the group . . . and I think he did a good job at that time." Joseph Beirne was more critical, seeing Griffith as "one who went with the group after the group voted. Yes, there was nothing aggressive about him. But that was necessary in '39; it was necessary in '40 . . . Paul was built just *laissez faire*. He was built to sit there and maintain order." Though "bland," Beirne added, Griffith "was a necessary personality."

As such, Griffith was able to assuage the suspicions of those who looked upon national organization unionism, with jaundiced eyes while retaining the confidence of the militant wing of the new organization of telephone workers. A handsome, sturdily-built man in his early forties with that openness of character so typical of the American midwest, he was the perfect chairman. Born on August 7, 1899, in a rural community east of Greeley, Colorado, where his parents had moved from Nebraska (and before that, Indiana), Griffith considered himself "a rugged individualist." His father worked, for a time, as a ranch hand and was active in Colorado politics, serving as a school board member in Milliken. His mother was "a kind of suffragette of the time." She organized the womens' club, founded the town library and inspired in her son a determination to go on to college after graduation from Milliken High School. We take such a step so much for granted nowadays that we forget how unusual such a decision was for a young man from an agricultural community. Griffith studied engineering at the University of Colorado at Boulder, graduating in 1922 with a degree in mechanical engineering.

After graduation, Griffith went to work for Western Electric at the Hawthorne Plant near Chicago, Illinois. It was, as he later recalled, "quite an experience" for Hawthorne was "a very lively place" and "quite a bit different from northern Colorado." He worked on the first dial system ever installed within the Illinois area and afterwards was transferred to Atlanta, Georgia. The early dial equipment was "full of bugs," imperfections in the circuitry, which the young engineers were expected to straighten out. After stints in Pittsburgh, Kansas City, Missouri and Chicago, Griffith was laid off for a stretch in 1924. He drove a cab, marking time until his recall and then transferred to the equipment engineering department of the Illinois Bell Company working in the central division on the Chicago Loop. During the early 1930s Griffith became active in the Illinois Bell Telephone Employees' Association, serving as an officer of the engineers' local and later on the central division and joint plant councils. He was among those who, as he phrased it, were actively "purifying" the organization of company influence. As chairman of the Illinois Federation of Telephone Unions, he was drawn into the founding of the NFTW.

During those early, formative years, Griffith's temperament admirably suited the needs of the federation. He toured the country, arguing the case for a moderate national organization. "In each of these places," he recalled decades later, "I told [the audience] about the autonomy clause, our desire that the member organizations remain 'forever free and autonomous,' that I was determined that that would be; that their own president had signed the ratification document on that basis; that I was very certain that it was very safe for them to have done so, and that the organization that they had approved would remain basically as it was from then on, at least in the foreseeable future; that any changes made would be changes that everybody agreed upon, but in no event would there be any change of this particular clause."

Soon, however, a storm would blow up over the immutable clause that would change forever the organization Griffith gave so much to create.

V

Coming Together

Of 1939, Winston Churchill would later write, "Summer advanced, preparations for war continued throughout Europe, and the attitudes of diplomatists, the speeches of politicians, and the wishes of mankind counted each day for less." Closeted with aides in his eyrie at Berchtesgaden, Adolf Hitler plotted his first moves of the coming war. Details of the pact with Stalin were worked out; "incidents" were devised to provoke the Poles. And all through a beautiful clear night, tanks, guns, lorries and division after division of armed men moved along the roads of Germany towards the Polish frontier. At dawn on September 1, 1939, the guns opened fire and Hitler's war had begun.

Americans were apprehensive as Stukas divebombed Warsaw into near rubble and as Hitler and Stalin divided a prostrate Poland between Germany and Russia. "Here in Washington the White House is very quiet," President Franklin D. Roosevelt wrote the country's Ambassador to Great Britain, Joseph Kennedy. "There is a general feeling of sitting quiet and waiting to see what the morrow will bring." Few envied the President's task to somehow keep the United States neutral, yet also to aid the beleagured victims of Hitler's blitzkrieg as well as prepare our own defenses. "Passionately though we may desire detachment," the President cautioned his countrymen at the outbreak of war in Europe, "we are forced to realize that every word that comes through the air, every ship that sails the sea, every battle that is fought, does affect the American future."

So the war would. During the "phony war," the winter of 1939–1940, while armies waited and the Allies sought desperately to re-arm in time, America, in historian James Burn's phrase, "was stuck on dead center, somewhere between neutrality and effective aid to the Allies." After the broad shattering sweep of Nazi Panzer divisions across Europe to the Channel's edge, America began to rally behind the President and his call for "equipment and training equal to the task of any emergency and every defense." Communication is at the heart of modern warfare, so telephone workers were drawn early into the defense effort. Paul E. Griffith began his second term as president of the National Federation of Telephone Workers with this pledge: "We are willing to do everything possible in America's preparedness program. The Executive Board of the National Federation of Telephone Workers has so offered the national defense board in Washington. Our offer has been accepted by the White House on behalf of Sidney Hillman, labor representative on the national defense board. We are ready to go ahead."

Griffith, however, cautioned the delegates to the NFTW June 17 to 21, 1940 convention at Salt Lake City, that "steps are being taken right now to guard against industrialists who would take advantage of the defense situation to exploit our labor. We are willing to do our part, but we expect industry to do its part as well." After passage in March 1941, of the Lend-Lease Act, which authorized the President to sell, transfer, exchange or lease arms and other equipment to any country whose defense was deemed vital to that of the United States, the NFTW pressed the telephone company to convert various facilities to defense work. AT&T, for example, had planned to funnel all defense contracts to Western Electric manufacturing plants and to phase out, or reduce to skeleton strength, the facilities and personnel of the twenty-odd sales distributing houses throughout the country. Skilled distribution house workers were to be "rehired" in the Western Electric manufacturing plants over a period of a year to work on defense contracts. As a scathing editorial in the publication of the Association of Telephone Equipment Workers, *The Cable,* then edited by Frank Novotny, pointed out, this practice would delay the war effort by six months to a year. "Is the Western Electric Company Sabotaging the War Effort?" *The Cable* asked. The question was more than rhetorical; it demanded action. Under pressure from the NFTW affiliate, Western Electric management changed its short-sighted plans. The number of distributing house employees rose from about 7,000 to roughly 13,000 within a year. As Frank Novotny proudly recalls, "We received many commendations from the government."

Delegates to the 1940 and 1941 NFTW conventions worried about the fifth column, urging that "a voluntary aid plan be formulated" to combat such activities and sabotage by Nazi, Fascist or Communist sympathizers. (Hitler, as yet, had not turned on his partner in the division of Polish spoils, Joseph Stalin.) Reflecting the disquiet of the time, the NFTW's executive board expressed "disapproval of any use of alien labor" within the vulnerable telephone industry and recommended that affiliates seek information on the number of aliens employed by the telephone companies. Though the latter recommendation was adopted by the delegates at the Fifth National Assembly, nothing ever much came of it. The 1940 convention also acted to protect the interests of NFTW members called into active service. Officers were instructed to negotiate job protection upon demobilization and "security" for [draftee] families. Telephone workers subscribed enthusiastically to the purchase of defense bonds, a step heartily recommended by the delegates to the Sixth National Assembly in Omaha, Nebraska, June 16 to 21, 1941.

These were characteristic of the responses of most workers to the war soon to envelop the world. Patriotism, however, does not wash away in waves of good feeling crucial economic social problems. Indeed, for the infant organization of telephone workers, the NFTW, the coming of the war posed the problems of collective bargaining and recognition in a new and acute form. For it soon became apparent that wages and working conditions would be subjected to regulation, if not outright determination, by the federal government. In the late 1930s collective bargaining became a right as a matter of public policy; during the war, it would, in a sense, become an instrument of public policy. In calling forth the immense effort necessary to make America "the great arsenal for democracy," the President acted at once to involve organized labor. He appointed the indefatigable Sidney Hillman, a founder of the Congress of Industrial Organizations and president of the Amalgmated Clothing Workers, as an associate director of the Office of Production Management. Hillman was to be responsible for manpower supply, strike prevention and mediation, and the safeguarding of labor standards. His co-director, the General Motors production genius, William S. Knudsen, would concentrate on production and priorities. Hillman's presence in Washington guaranteed a role for organized labor in the defense effort but whether or not this would include the independents as well as the American Federation of Labor and the CIO remained uncertain. For example, would the NFTW be recognized in Washington as a national labor organization? Sam Houston, then counsel to the Washington, D.C., Federation of Telephone Employees, had been assured by Hillman's "office" that the NFTW "would be accepted as the dominant but not sole labor organization in the telephone industry." However, in view of the growing telephone company practice of farming out to contractors work formerly performed by company employees, Hillman's negotiation of an exclusive agreement with the AFL building and construction trades on behalf of government agencies concerned with defense construction was far from reassuring.* From the start, NFTW's founders were anxious to secure "proper recognition," as a 1939 resolution put it, from other labor organizations, management, the government and the general public. The war and

---

*NFTW affiliates interpreted the agreement as a "decision" to award telephone installation to members of the AFL building trades although the work had been performed by telephone company employees since 1900. John J. Moran, president of the Long Lines Federation, telegraphed the President: "Any attempt to deprive [telephone workers] of this work [telephone wiring on defense construction] by the circuitous method of compelling the American Telephone and Telegraph Company to subcontract such work will be bitterly resented and resisted." Telephone workers threatened to strike if the government carried out this "decision," and the Long Lines group instructed its members to refuse to connect equipment to telephone wires installed by AFL electricians. Other NFTW affiliates soon followed suit.

the proliferation of wartime agencies gave the question a new urgency. And as it turned out, the struggle for recognition, in the broadest sense as well as before wartime agencies, would transform the NFTW from a loose-knit confederation of associations into an industrial union.

Recognition by the associated companies and by Ma Bell herself naturally was of prime importance to the fledgling NFTW. At first, they were encouraged by AT&T. As the vice president then in charge of personnel, Karl W. Waterson, once remarked to NFTW leaders in the course of talks concerning pension matters, "We're not unfriendly to your organization." Recognition by the associated companies of NFTW affiliates, initially, came rather easily. Or, perhaps one ought to say, easily when compared to the turbulent sit-down strikes in auto, steel and rubber a few years earlier. Actually, telephone workers had to exert considerable pressure on the associated companies to get them to come around. In New York, for example, the telephone company signed its first collective bargaining agreement ever on July 18, 1940. But did so *only* after some 10,000 installers, maintenance and repairmen threatened to walk out and tie up telephone work in the metropolitan area. The signing of the agreement marked the culmination of two years of struggle. NFTW President Griffith and Vice President Stanley H. Burke made a special trip to New York to extend NFTW support to its embattled affiliate. Charges that the company refused to bargain collectively were filed in February, 1939 and were withdrawn, of course, when the company agreed to recognize the NFTW's New York affiliate, the United Telephone Organizations (UTO). The contract, which was to run one year, froze basic pay scales and wage progression during its term (remember pay cuts were more likely in 1940 than raises), and, interestingly provided $2 a week pay boosts for lower paid workers in surrounding counties bringing their wage scales into conformity with those of New York City. Other provisions included seniority rights, thirty days' notice of layoffs with termination allowances ranging from one to three weeks' pay based on length of service, and vacations with pay. The company also agreed to the arbitration of grievances, authorizing the State Mediation Board to pick an arbitrator when disputes could not be resolved through negotiations. The company also accepted the idea of "telephone work for telephone people," and agreed that it would not let out work belonging by custom to members of the UTO.

NFTW leaders skillfully exploited their labor and the law—and the New Deal agencies—to secure recognition. John J. Moran, the new chief of the reorganized Federation of Long Lines Telephone Workers, ably seconded by Dorothy F. Handy, Mrs. Norma F. Naughton, Ray T. Beveridge and Mrs. Franklin Folk, negotiated the first labor contract with Ma Bell. The Long Lines group, embracing 10,000 Ma Bell employees in eleven cities, called on the United States Conciliation Service to mediate a year-long negotiations effort. Labor attorney Henry Mayer guided the union officers through the legal maze as he did other NFTW affiliates in the New York region. As a result of the agreement signed on October 21, 1940, grievances were to be arbitrated through the services of the American Arbitration Association. Seniority rights and paid vacations were guaranteed in the contract. The union also won the unique right to decide whether adjustments in the labor force were to be effected through part-time work or layoffs. This had been a treasured management prerogative and this victory, in its way, set an invaluable precedent for protection secured by the union in the post-World War II years against the consequences of automation. A $2-a-week wage increase was granted towards the adjustment of regional differentials, a first step towards "equal pay for equal work." A highly novel feature of the agreement provided for a comparative wage study by the United States Labor Department as a basis for an adjustment of Long Lines wage scales.

However willing to negotiate under pressure from NFTW affiliates—not from the government—Ma Bell balked at extending formal recognition to the NFTW. In part, she did so because AT&T management did not want to acknowledge the extent of its control over the associated companies. NFTW president Griffith paraphrased AT&T President Walter Gifford as saying, "In so many words, he did not want to reduce the presidents of the operating companies to the role of Charlie McCarthys [Edgar Bergen's ventriloquist dummy of the popular radio program]." NFTW leaders met with AT&T officials in February 1940, where the company's position was spelled out by vice president Waterson and his assistant, Jacob B. Taylor.

Reviewing a NFTW proposal that "a basis be established for dealing and consultation" between the federation and the parent company "on questions not settled satisfactorily between the associated companies and the member organization," Waterson answered by taking the "associated autonomy" stand. Taylor stated AT&T's willingness, NFTW officers reported to the 1940 convention, "to discuss with us informally any question we raised," but added, "they could not see their way clear at this time to do any actual collective bargaining." As Ma Bell viewed the question, Taylor continued, that "to take jurisdiction in a collective-bargaining matter away from an associated company was to accept responsibility for the results that followed, and that the organization was too big to do this." Taylor, according to the executive board report, "acknowledged in this connection the right of the AT&T Company to replace an associated company management and to influence and control an individual associated company policy, in respect to matters affecting service, etc., but that this was done by voting the stock rather than by direct intervention in the management affairs. He acknowledged that they did make 'suggestions' to the companies and that the 'suggestions' were often followed."

After a subsequent meeting on May 6, 1941, with Cleo Craig, the succeeding AT&T vice president in charge of personnel on which AT&T President Walter Gifford also sat, the NFTW sought some clarification of the company's position. AT&T President Gifford replied, "I have an open mind as to what, if any, formal relationships can be established between the National Federation of Telephone Workers and the American Telephone & Telegraph Company . . . Up to the present time, I have been unable to see any practical basis for such an agreement." This was to remain AT&T's posture until telephone workers mustered the necessary muscle to change it.

NFTW's affiliates, for their part, were reluctant to give the Federation real power to bargain collectively with AT&T, holding the autonomy clause inviolate. This reluctance was evident even in providing labor relations information. At the 1941 convention, W.J. McPherson, chairman of the Labor Relations Committee, reported that only ten of the affiliates had replied to a questionnaire seeking detailed information about wage scales, job classifications and the like. And there were other internal divisions. Operating company people still looked upon Western Electric people as "second cousins" in Joseph Beirne's recollections of that time. A move to elect Beirne as an executive board member in 1939 was defeated by this unwillingness to accept the Western Electric affiliates of the NFTW as full partners with operating company affiliates. Beirne was elected vice president in 1941, the Western Electric groups presenting a united front at the time.*

Despite conscientious efforts, there were unresolved tensions between the predominantly male plant work force and the predominantly female traffic labor force. Delegates to the 1940 convention, recognizing that "the nature of the problems and interests of . . . women workers differ in so many ways from the problems and interests of the male workers represented in the federation," resolved that "in order to most equitably represent the will of the women workers and to best serve their interest, the elected feminine member of the executive board [Pansy M. Harris of Southern California Traffic Employees League] shall be in attendance at all conferences where the opportunity may present itself to plead their cause." In the 1940 election of officers, Miss Harris was elected unanimously, along with Griffith and Horth, to the three members-at-large positions on the executive board. (At

---

*The six Western Electric unions, representing 26,000 hourly-rated employees, formed the National Committee of Communication Equipment Workers. Beirne, head of the sales group, was elected chairman; Ernest Weaver, president of the Association of Communication Equipment Workers, vice chairman, and George DuVal of the Kearny Employees Association, secretary-treasurer. Their success at securing bargaining on a company-wide basis, including a wage progression plan, provided a model for the NFTW. But this National Committee did not survive the jealousies of the installers and plant men.

the time, the president, vice president and secretary-treasurer were elected from among the executive board members by the delegates.) But Mrs. Theresa Donahey, from Ohio, was defeated by Leo George, head of the Hoosier Federation, and Miss Dorothy F. Handy, from the Long Lines Federation, was defeated by J.J. Schacht, head of the Southwestern Telephone Workers Union, for the central and southern region positions on the executive board respectively.

The following year the traffic member organizations met before the Omaha Assembly and threatened to withdraw from the federation unless traffic gained greater representation on the executive board. The failure to select a woman to fill one of the two additional posts created by the enlargement of the executive board in 1940 exacerbated feelings already running high over a failure to gain equal pay for equal work in negotiations and to secure the reclassification of telephone operators as skilled workers. Operators were then classified as unskilled workers, touching on a worker's pride as well as her pocketbook. A motion to recommend the election of three traffic members to the executive board was defeated. Delegates opposed to the traffic resolution objected to the "ultimatum," argued that women were not confined to the traffic department and claimed that many of the problems involving or affecting women workers were being successfully handled by the plant and other organizations. Others objected to fixing the number of representatives from any one group and urged that candidates ought to be advanced on the basis of their "qualifications." Proponents countered that considering the proportion of traffic members it was only "reasonable" to have at least three instead of only one on the executive board. (Approximately sixty-two percent of Class A telephone company employees in 1941 were women; the percentage of the NFTW's 106,964 membership may have been even higher since most, if not all, of the executive and supervisory employees excluded from bargaining units were male.) Adequate feminine membership on the executive board, other delegates argued, was a prerequisite "to a proper understanding and effective negotiation and action . . . on the problems of women workers." The presence of women on the board, too, in a predominantly womens' organization, would "aid in dispelling any suspicion of domination by the male members of the executive board." The revised resolution, which dropped the threat of withdrawal, adopted on a roll call of fifty to twenty-two, recognized the demand for more traffic representation. (Of the 110 delegates to the convention, thirty-nine were women.) Miss Pansy M. Harris was re-elected to the executive board, and Mrs. Theresa Donahey added as the fourth member-at-large. (Mrs. Donahey again contested Leo George for the Central Regional post, but lost.)

In an effort aimed at giving the NFTW more clout, delegates to the 1940 convention urged on affiliates the "termination of all labor contracts on a certain uniform date." But little was accomplished in this area, at least over the next few years. Delegates to the Sixth National Assembly, over June 16 to 21, 1941, in Omaha, debated the NFTW's approach to collective bargaining. Should the Federation continue to work solely on the objective of obtaining recognition by AT&T as a collective bargaining agency, or should the NFTW attempt to bargain for the member organizations at the associated company level, continuing meanwhile the effort to obtain a general bargaining arrangement with AT&T? Delegates wrangled over the need for detailed procedure to delegate collective bargaining authority to the federation. There was resistance to the idea, a fear that bargaining by the NFTW would erode affiliate autonomy. Finally, the delegates approved the continuation of the efforts being made to achieve recognition by AT&T. But the character and extent of the actual powers to be exercised by the federation were limited in scope. As the 1941 convention resolution spelled the approach out, "The officers or agents of the NFTW *shall stand ready* as in the past *to assist or conduct* bargaining on behalf of/or with the officers of any member organization so *requesting this assistance* or transferring jurisdiction of specific matters to the National Federation of Telephone Workers with the provision that the expense of such bargaining be borne by the particular member organization unless the bargaining subject is national in scope and approved by the Executive Board or authorized by a majority of the member organizations in assembly or by mail." (My italics.) In short, there was little room for Federation initiative. This weakness was fully acknowledged the following year when the executive board recommended to the Seventh National Assembly meeting in Baltimore, Maryland, over June 8–14, 1942, that "efforts to obtain bargaining recognition from the Bell System, as such, should be indefinitely deferred. It is felt that the federation will not only have to obtain more members, but that it may have to revise the autonomy provisions of the constitution before it will be in a position to request, through governmental agencies or otherwise, the establishment of the Bell System as an appropriate Unit for collective bargaining purposes."

By then, the United States was at war. On December 7, 1941, the Japanese attacked Pearl Harbor and a declaration of war against Japan, Germany and Italy, the chief Axis powers, followed immediately thereafter. During the ominous closing months of 1941, it became apparent that labor relations were to be a federal matter and the country's interests were to be set above those of the contending, labor-management parties to any dispute of any magnitude. Unfortunately, the NFTW's status as a bona-fide spokesman for telephone workers remained uncertain. Strike threats bubbled up all during 1941, indicating a growing dissatisfaction with wages and working conditions throughout the Bell System. A walkout of 8,000 Western Electric installers was forstalled when the Association of Communications and Equipment Workers, headed by Ernest Weaver, reached an agreement on a six cent an hour wage boost, union recognition and other gains. But it had been a near thing, with NFTW President Griffith and Vice President Beirne warning AT&T chieftain Walter S. Gifford that Bell System employees throughout the country would refuse to cross any picket lines thrown up by the equipment workers.

When AT&T brushed aside an eight month Department of Labor study demonstrating, as Attorney Henry Mayer put it, that its wage policy was "unsound," the 15,000 Long Lines workers voted in October, 1941, ten to one for a strike. The company insisted on maintaining a wage differential as high as $21 a week for identical work in differing locations around the country. On the eve of the strike, set for November 14, 1941, Long Lines president Moran and attorney Mayer stated, "The onus for the disastrous consequences of the strike will belong to the company because of its stubborn attitude and to the government agencies for their refusal to give this organization [the federation] the privilege of using the government's machinery, in accordance with President Roosevelt's expressed wishes." The strike was postponed at the request of United States Conciliation Service Director, Dr. John R. Steelman, and in order to give the union time to work out arrangements to meet requests from the Army and Navy and the news services that critical communication services be maintained. What the union wanted, John J. Moran asserted, was to have the dispute referred to the National Defense Mediation Board. The dispute was settled a week later when the company acceded to union demands reducing differentials and agreed to a $3 million wage settlement. Yet, a company statement issued at the time boded ill for future relations, even under the aegis of a wartime government. "We cannot believe," the statement declared, "that employees of the caliber which the public has been accustomed to depend on for vital service—and who enjoy wages, working conditions, and degrees of security which are truly enviable—would hastily disrupt long distance telephone service . . ."

Telephone workers, however, did not find wages nor working conditions "enviable" at all times, nor in all places. As D.L. McCowen, the popular chairman of the Southwestern Telephone Workers Union, liked to remind his NFTW colleagues, "A repairman in Weatherford, Texas, is entitled to the same pay as a repairman in New York City." The wartime wage freeze created, in the words of a 1945, War Labor Board report, "gross inequities", and instead of bargaining over wages the NFTW—and its affiliates—had to prove "claims" before the War Labor Board for necessary adjustments in pay scales, a somewhat different process. This called for a degree of recognition for the NFTW but not an entirely satisfactory one, for the independent NFTW was not consulted in the framing of wartime economic policies as were (to a larger degree) the AFL and the CIO. As Joseph Beirne remarked about the no-strike pledge given by William Green and Philip Murray, "I couldn't understand how a couple of guys could stand up there and give such pledges for *all* labor . . . Absolutely no one had asked anyone in [the] NFTW how *they* felt about it." Largely because of its uncertain status before federal agencies, the NFTW did not give its pledge not to strike. "We did have a pretty long agenda of things we *had* to do within certain time frames, if they were to be done at all, in the building of the union," Beirne once explained. "We didn't want to give away any options, and one option would be a strike . . ."

Few believed, however, that the strike option would prove to be necessary within the quasi-legal wartime system of adjusting wage claims. When the War Labor Board worked out the so-called Little Steel formula, allowing raises based on a fifteen percent rise in living costs (first granted within the steel industry, hence the name), the Bell companies balked at applying the formula to telephone wages. To force the Ohio Bell Telephone Company to grant increases in accordance with the Little Steel formula, some 2,100 maintenance, installation and repair workers walked out on August 5, 1942, engaging in the NFTW's first strike. Operators refused to cross picket lines maintained by members of the Ohio Federation of Telephone Workers, and though the strike lasted but two days it was effective, forcing Secretary of Labor, Madam Perkins, to certify the dispute to the War Labor Board.

Although the Ohio strike was rooted in a wage dispute, it reflected the NFTW difficulties before federal agencies and its relations with the telephone companies. Recognition frustrations exacerbated a growing dissatisfaction within the NFTW over the course of the federation and its leadership. The two top officers became full-time staffers in 1941 and the Milwaukee and Chicago offices were consolidated, first in Chicago and then moved to Baltimore after a search for Washington space proved futile. A Washington Contact and Information Service was established with an appropriation of $1,200, and in April, 1941, Charles V. Koons, later NFTW and CWA attorney, was appointed to keep an eye on federal developments. As necessary as these moves were, they did not avert the crisis that developed in 1942.

NFTW activity had outpaced its income, a gap that unfortunately measured the uncertainty of support from among its affiliates. The federation was approximately $25,000 in the red, even though membership continued to rise, reaching 145,000 in 1942. In February of that year, the executive board recommended a dues increase of two cents monthly, bringing the monthly per capita to five cents, but by the June Baltimore convention only eighteen out of thirty-eight affiliates had approved the increase. Three voted against it. Monthly expenses were running at $12,000 a month. In an economy move, the executive board voted to revert the president's job to part-time, to cut per diem allowances for executive board members on NFTW business, and to restrict the activity of regional staff serving as organizers. The crisis cut deeper, however, than the financial picture reveals. The situation was, as NFTW President Paul Griffith later put it, "intolerable." As he later recalled, "I talked to several officers of member organizations concerning this total situation . . . They, too, said that they would propose changes at the next assembly [agreeing with an observation of Secretary-Treasurer Horth], but if the majority did not go along with the changes, that they would withdraw from the National Federation of Telephone Workers. Quite a sizable percentage of the national membership was within this group. I can't recall offhand just what the percentage was, but I think it would possibly be more than fifty percent who were fully determined to split off and form another organization, or else allow the minority to split off and go their own way. What they were determined to do was to preserve our federation-type of organization and to maintain our independence." As a consequence of this feeling of pressure to *dissolve* the federation, the executive board called a special assembly to be held at Cincinnati, Ohio, over February 1–6, 1943. As Chairman Beirne told the delegates, "We would also like to clearly establish the fact that the Executive Board of the Federation considers itself as being somewhat 'on the spot.' "

This, in truth, was something of an understatement. NFTW president Griffith had decided to resign, accepting a commission as captain in the Signal Corps: "I did not relish the idea of a family squabble that would most certainly wreck the organization and cause two organizations to be formed, neither one of them having the prestige that the present federation had already achieved." Vice president Beirne became acting president, and began to draw together the reins of responsibility. Secretary-Treasurer Horth believed that there was a majority among NFTW members favoring a federation with each affiliate remaining "forever autonomous." And he had some grounds for believing so. Floyd C. Maize, the executive board member from the Mountain States Federation, held this view as did former board member, Miss Pansy M. Harris, leader of the Southern California traffic group. The Illinois Union of Telephone Workers was among several large blocs within the federation favoring continued "autonomy" or "dissolution." Beirne, however, prevailed upon the executive board to recommend the establishment of a union unhampered by the restraints of "autonomy." It proposed such a course in Resolution Number One, by a vote of six to one.

As Beirne would say many years later, the Cincinnati meeting was "a gut-buster." The delegates came, as one Westerner later put it, "loaded for bear," and the questions of autonomy and re-organization were all entangled in the general dismay over the state of finances and the disarray of the NFTW books. Secretary-Treasurer Bert Horth became ill, and so the convention opened without him. Ever astute, Beirne seized the advantage this gave him and the proponents of a strong union. As he explained it years later, "With the meeting opening and there being no secretary present, I appointed Slim Werkau of Illinois, who was the leader of the Illinois delegation, as acting secretary-treasurer. And that took the leading proponent of the dissolution movement off the floor.* And when appointing him, when he came up to the platform, the thing I told him was, 'Now, Slim, you've just changed sides.' And he knew he [had]. He knew he was mouse-trapped, and he was, for now he had to act like an acting secretary-treasurer. Now, to the mores of the telephone worker, that's very important. He made his choice. He had to change sides, and I made it clear to him what was happening. There was no hanky-panky. It was out in the open. And his acceptance meant that he would do that, and the telephone worker is built that way. He's overly, sensitively honest in his position and in the exposition of his principle. And Werkau did not decline. He accepted—which also meant something to me. It meant that their inclination for the dissolution was not so hard as we all thought it would be when we opened up."

Beirne acted promptly in opening the Cincinnati assembly to defuse highly charged emotions and to disarm deeply buried suspicions. Despite the straightforward agressive thrust of Resolution Number One, Beirne was conciliatory. "Let each of us remember that none of us may be the wisest men in the NFTW," he told the eighty-four delegates, "and let us respect the opinions and judgement of those who may differ with us and let's make our final decisions and judgement this week based on whatever facts are available. We have, I believe, an enormous job to do. The success or failure of unionism in the telephone industry may be in the balance and I think it is something to which the voting delegates in particular, and everyone of us, should give serious consideration." The first item on the agenda, an unusual reversal of position, was "good-and-welfare." It was thought, Beirne said, that "the best way to get us all on common ground would be to have free and unchecked discussion . . . without the assembly being burdened by any motions."

"Good-and-Welfare" did help clear the air, as did an extensive and critical discussion of the NFTW financial report. Many criticized the executive board for putting President Griffith on part-time, and that criticism as well as those of the financial report appear to have cut across autonomy/strong union lines. The discussion, however, revealed various crosscurrents at work within the various affiliates, a movement that ultimately created a majority behind Resolution Number One. Frances Smith, executive board member and head of Michigan Traffic, stressed the need for authority, but also reported that "back home we have not grown as fast as we should. Our members are not as union-minded as they should be and there is always the problem of the unwillingness of the members to pay the freight." William M. Dunn, then president of the Cincinnati Federation and later assistant to CWA president Beirne, first raised the question of newly felt pressures, saying, "It has been very impressive to us that some organizations have been

---

*According to Griffith, "They split Bert's [Horth] constituency right down the middle by nominating Werkau of Illinois to be secretary-treasurer."

dealing with other national organizations." Ernest Weaver acknowledged that his group, the Association of Communication Equipment Workers, had participated in the founding of the Confederated Unions of America, a group of independent and unaffiliated unions. Weaver was, for a time, a CVA president. While the ACEW had no intention of withdrawing from the NFTW, Weaver told the Cincinnati meeting, it did feel the need for greater protection. "We have for a long time thought of the NFTW as a third labor party, but recently came to the conclusion that the NFTW set up as it is could never become a third labor party. Our political influence in Washington will depend upon the number of people in our organization, and we as yet don't even include all of the Bell System. I sincerely doubt the chances of an NFTW man on the War Labor Board. The best I think the NFTW can do, and I doubt this, is to get someone on the FCC. We are going to have to get some political pressure somewhere. Let's guide our actions along that line. The CVA may flop . . . this may not be the time for such an organization, but there are several organizations that need help and if they don't get it from groups like us they are going to get it somewhere else. There are numerous groups going into the CIO and AFL, and you can foresee the time when we will be the only non-members left. The worst thing in the world would be to bust up the NFTW, but if you can tie in with some other organization with the same ideals and principles in order to increase your political influence, well and good."

J. J. "Jack" Moran, president of the Long Lines group, then reported on inquiries his organization had made about possible affiliation with either the AFL or CIO. Since the AFL promptly replied that any affiliation would have to be with the NFTW archrival, the IBEW, that line was quickly dropped. The CIO was less adamant about affiliation through its American Communications Association (ACA), particularly strong on the West Coast. (The ACA was expelled from the CIO in 1948 as a Communist-dominated organization.) Moran and his associates met with Allan Haywood, CIO director of organization and who later would be instrumental in securing the affiliation of the CWA, and found him, contrary to his expectations, "a high type of labor man." Haywood expressed interest, but advised "that we join as a unit and under no circumstances let ourselves be split up, whether we join the AFL, CIO, or whether we stay independent." After some discussion, the Long Lines group voted to stay with the NFTW. As Moran shrewdly foresaw, "We have lots of ideas but what comes out of this will probably be a combination between going the whole way and what we now have. We are at the point where we must realize that even if one large member organization withdraws, it would be difficult to continue. I believe the NFTW should try to organize the Bell System into one organization."

While the difficulties the NFTW faced in organizing the Bell System, before wartime agencies and within itself, seemed to make the prospect of affiliation tempting, those very same factors worked to draw the affiliates together. No one wanted to go into the AFL as a branch of the IBEW, a craft union by tradition, and the encroachments of the ACA on the West Coast and incursions by the CIO's United Electrical Workers, also under Communist influence, discouraged those who otherwise looked favorably upon the CIO. At the same time, these outside threats—and the need for a united front in Washington and in dealing with AT&T—tended to push those anxious about autonomy towards acceptance of the fundamental proposition of Resolution Number One: ". . . changes are necessary to effectuate the objectives which dictated the formation of the NFTW." So, after a lengthy debate, the delegates voted 114,947 for the resolution and 27,372 against, with 3,941 abstentions.*

Acknowledging that "there exists a difference of opinion among the member organizations . . . with respect to the proper type of union organization," and arguing for the need of change and that the present structure "makes it difficult to control duplication of effort" and that there presently exists "no proper difference or designation of authority to accomplish the several purposes set forth in the constitution," the delegates resolved: "That the telephone workers establish a national telephone workers' union in which the following principles shall be observed:

1) That member organizations be chartered locals.
2) That the national union shall be empowered to bargain collectively on all matters pertaining to said telephone workers.
3) Jurisdiction claimed by this organization shall be the entire telephone industry of the United States and its possessions, and all work performed in connection therewith or incident thereto.
4) That supreme authority shall be contained in the said national union, its constitution and bylaws.
5) That individual members be members of the national organization.
6) That proper machinery be established in said constitution for the determination of the proper jurisdiction between locals and national."

And the delegates instructed their officers:

"That a constitutional committee be appointed with the purpose of writing the constitution and bylaws in accordance with the above principles."

Sensitive to the divisions that still existed within the NFTW, chairman Beirne cautioned the assembly. The action taken, he said, did not permit the delegates to go home and say, "We now have one union," but rather

---

*The vote on a motion to table Resolution One, to enable a vote first on a much weaker resolution on reorganization, perhaps more accurately reflects the division within the NFTW. Those opposed were the strong advocates of Resolution One. The vote was as follows: in favor, 50,352; opposed, 68,904; not voting, 26,706. Delegates, it will be remembered, cast weighted votes based on their respective memberships.

that "we have expressed ourselves, indicating that this is our desire and it should be recognized by everyone that this is the thinking of the representatives gathered here which may or may not be confirmed by our constituents." Nonetheless, between the emergency assembly in Cincinnati and the regularly scheduled June 1943 convention in Cleveland, the NFTW leadership carried on a vigorous campaign on behalf of Resolution One. A.B. "Al" Herrington, a construction dispatcher from Illinois and the new editor of the *Telephone Worker*, carried on an extensive educational campaign and debate within the pages of the NFTW magazine. In the first issue, following the Cincinnati meeting, Herrington hailed Resolution Number One as "the answer to the representation problem of the telephone worker." For the first time, he reported that a "mutual understanding was evidenced at a national meeting, to the extent that ninety per cent of the delegates voted to become an integral part of the National Federation of Telephone Workers, leaving the 'AUTONOMY' clause to the vote of all the telephone workers of America. This is a long step forward . . . Get behind it and support it. A cause was never more worthy."

The months between the emergency and regular 1943 conventions were anxious ones indeed. Jack Moran headed a committee charged with drafting a new constitution. Appointed by the executive board to work with Moran were: Frances Smith, board member and head of Michigan Traffic; Emma I. Jascot, president of the Chicago Traffic group; D.L. McCowen, out of the Southwest; George DuVal, president of the Western Electric group in Kearny, New Jersey; E. Baumhofer, head of the Northwestern organization, and Donald Buckley, president of the California United Brotherhood of Telephone Workers. The *Telephone Worker* continued the debate, with the May issue cover proclaiming:

NATIONAL	UNION
Pro	Con
It will organize an entire industry in one Union.	It will take Union dollars to the top level.
It will give Telephone Workers Social and Political Significance.	It will sacrifice autonomy for strength.
It will provide greater opportunity for job improvement.	It will require strong hearts, true faith and ready hands.

As Beirne later said, "We had from February until June to clean up everything that might be wrong. Of course, we didn't clean up everything, but between February and June we made giant strides . . ."

But there were ominous signs that all was not well. Acting president

Beirne, in an April 1943 effort to shake loose some twenty-four cases before federal agencies, threatened a general telephone tie-up. Fearful that a presidential executive order freezing all wages and wage levels would prevent "correcting inequities" in cases under consideration by various wage boards, Beirne protested to President Roosevelt that his latest order was discriminatory. Pointing out that many telephone workers' cases had been before government agencies for as long as a year, Beirne said that the new order "will unquestionably lead to serious dislocation of communication services within the telephone industry." He reminded the President that neither the AFL nor the CIO spoke for telephone workers, and declared that "175,000 aroused telephone workers must be heard if our country's economic structure is to remain unaffected and telephone communications are to be continued with our outstanding efficiency."

NFTW's militancy, however, was immediately undercut by leaders of the NFTW affiliates in Illinois representing maintenance men and office workers. Instead of backing Beirne, the Illinois group asked that his statement be corrected so as not to convey an impression that telephone workers would openly defy the government. The Illinois traffic group, however, promptly declared that it would not give up the right to strike. The Illinois action bode ill for NFTW's newly developed solidarity. On May 3, 1943, the United States Supreme Court added another complication to the NFTW's future by upholding a National Labor Relations Board order disestablishing the Southern Association of Bell Telephone Employees as a company-dominated group. J.J. Schacht, director of the NFTW Organizing Committee and the southern regional member of the executive board, had already begun the work of forming a new organization. But the high court decision, as the *Telephone Worker* pointed out, "opens wide the gates to other unions."

All in all, perhaps February to June were not propitious months for the NFTW. As the May 1943 issue of the *Telephone Worker,* rather nervously put it, "The ninth national assembly may be the Magna Carta of workers in the industry, or it may be the Inquisition." The editor then accurately summed up the state of the NFTW: "A tremendous storm has been brewed from the wording of Resolution Number One of the eighth national assembly in Cincinnati. Its legality has been questioned. Its purposes have been translated and mistranslated in a dozen ways. Its very potency and power has frightened officers in various organizations affiliated with the national [assembly]. Some are perturbed about the effect on their members if autonomy is relinquished. Some are worried about the effect to themselves and their position in the newer more centralized organization. Still others believe that the loose-knit organization we now have can be made to serve all the needs of telephone unionism."

The eighth assembly, as it turned out was neither a Magna Carta nor quite an Inquisition, but it sure was tumultuous. By a weighted vote of 86,382 to 35,621, the delegates moved to reconsider Cincinnati Resolution Number One. At that point, the delegate from the Illinois union, C.H. Formby rose to inform the delegates, "If it is the wish of the assembly to again adopt the resolution of the Cincinnati meeting, it will be necessary for the Illinois Union of Telephone Workers to withdraw its members."* The delegates waffled, bending here and circumnavigating there. A motion to rescind the Cincinnati action failed to secure the necessary two-thirds majority for passage, but it did get a majority of the weighted vote. The Illinois union, with 4,791 votes, did not vote on either motion. (The motion to reconsider was passed 86,382 to 35,621; the motion to rescind failed with 65,558 for, 57,304 against and 4,751 not voting.) In a revealing moment, a delegate asked the chairman to poll the voting delegates—one for each of the NFTW's thirty-four affiliates present—to determine how many believed in industry-wide or regional bargaining. According to the proceedings, about fourteen delegates favored industry-wide bargaining while about ten opposed system-wide or national bargaining. Called upon to make some observations about the legalities of Resolution One, acting counsel Al Kane bluntly told the delegates, "I think that there is a great deal of mutual mistrust among you people . . . I think some of you very definitely wanted to retain your character as company unions . . . Some of you were anxious to cut all ties with the company [and] make a lot of noise and kick up a lot of fuss. And I think that—I know very definitely that your constitution was the result of a compromise . . ." He urged the delegates "to forget a good deal of your sectionalism. You have got to forget the jealousies that might exist between groups or between geographical regions."

After a week of debates, the delegates called for the appointment of a new committee, "to draft proposed amendments to the constitution embodying the said principles [those of Resolution One] so far as may be practicable, consistently with the existing constitution of this federation, and report the constitutional amendments so drafted back to the member organizations within two months." And there the constitutional question would rest for two years.

While the delegates to the ninth Assembly at Cleveland, in a sense, put off resolution of the troublesome autonomy question, they acted with a commendable decisiveness in picking a new leadership. Joseph A. Beirne was elected president, J.J. Moran, vice president, and C.W. Werkau, secretary-treasurer. George DuVal, John Crull, Ernest Weaver and Donald Buckley were elected the eastern, southern, central and western representa-

*The threat was serious. The Illinois Union withdrew almost immediately following the June 7–12, 1943 NFTW Cleveland Assembly. The Federation of Women Telephone Workers of Southern California followed suit soon after. Later, the Connecticut Union of Telephone Workers also broke away to become an independent group.

tives on the executive board; Frances V. Smith and Ione Trice as members-at-large for traffic. One can analyze the make-up of that board in several ways, but it certainly was weighted for an aggressive, strong union. Interestingly, three members of the nine-man executive board—Beirne, DuVal and Weaver from Western Electric—were traditionally militant and were originally considered "outsiders" by those from the associated companies. Two others, Crull and Trice, were from the aggressively pro-union Southwestern Telephone Workers Union, the largest single group affiliated with the NFTW. Moran, Smith and Buckley had been among the leaders in the fight for Resolution Number One at Cincinnati. Of the nine, five represented affiliates that had voted no against rescinding Resolution One, and four of them had voted against reconsideration. Four had voted yes on both motions.*

Clearly, a new leadership had emerged out of the uncertainties of the Cleveland meeting. Ahead lay a cruel, testing time.

*For the record:

Reconsider	Rescind	
Yes	Yes	National Association of Telephone Equipment Workers—Delegate Beirne
No	No	Federation of Long Lines Telephone Workers—Delegate Moran
Not voting	Yes	Indiana Union of Telephone Workers, casting a proxy vote—Delegate Werkau
Yes	No	Western Electric Employees Association, Kearny—Delegate DuVal
No	No	Southwestern Telephone Workers—Delegate D.L. McCowen
Yes	Yes	Association of Communication Equipment Workers—Delegate Weaver
Yes	Yes	United Brotherhood of Telephone Workers—California Delegate Buckley
No	No	Michigan Traffic—Delegate Smith

VI
Towards One Union

Joseph Anthony Beirne, at 32, had been elected to an uncertain command. The Cincinnati mandate for one union was certainly unsettled by the actions of the Cleveland assembly and undermined by the departure of two major affiliates. Ma Bell showed an increasing aversion towards her company-spawned unions, rather like that shown by a high-flown society matron towards the illegitimate offspring of her wayward youth. The recognition the NFTW—and its affiliates—so desperately needed was to secure rank-and-file rights before government agencies, which in wartime remained tenuous and unsatisfactory given the unique telephone wage structure. And as an independent, without ties to either house or labor, the NFTW was forced to stand alone, a Promethean organization with rivals pecking away at its very guts.

Leadership embodies many qualities, political and social, and, ultimately, those of character. "When you're head of a union," Beirne once said, "you've got to be a sociologist, marriage counselor, father confessor, psychiatrist, economist and legal expert all wrapped into one." Sitting in the cramped NFTW quarters in Baltimore, or later, in a Washington storefront, or, out in the field talking up one union for all telephone workers, Beirne was surely all of these. The sum, however, was something more. Whether scratching aid out of an inadequate budget for Bill Smallwood and the southern telephone workers beleaguered by the IBEW, or urging on the educational efforts of Ruth Wiencek, or counseling Bill Dunn about his work on various government boards, or backing Mary Gannon whenever her Washingtonian telephone operators staged a quickie walkout to right some wrong, Beirne exhibited those qualities the historian Edward Gibbon attributed to the Emperor Diocletian—a "steadiness to pursue his aims, flexibility to vary his means," and a remarkable tenacity. President Harry Truman once said, "If you can't stand the heat, get out of the kitchen." Joe Beirne could withstand the heat and he remained in the kitchen during those difficult times when it often appeared that the NFTW itself might not last out the long day. He coaxed, cajoled and convinced telephone workers into building a union, and in that sense one can paraphrase Emerson to say that the organization that emerged

75

in the mid 1940s was "the lengthened shadow of one man."

Joseph Anthony Beirne was born in Jersey City on February 16, 1911, the son of Michael Joseph and Anne T. Giblin Beirne, both from County Roscommon, Ireland. The acute listener could discern in his speech the accents of Jersey City and Ireland. He was raised in a devout Catholic home, and Beirne always felt that his mother sacrificed a good deal to send him to St. Aloysius parochial school with the "high-tone kids." His father worked for thirty-three years and three months for the Pennsylvania Rail Road as a locomotive engineer. He refused to cross a 1921 picket line, and when that strike was declared an outlaw strike by his union, the Brother-hood of Locomotive Engineers, he was offered a job as an oiler in the roundhouse. That was too much for his pride, and he never returned to the Pennsy. The elder Beirne was not embittered, as many people might have been, by his experience. As his son recalled it many years later, "He never indoctrinated us with any thoughts that the union had sold out or anything of that kind." Joe's brother and sister were union members in the 1920s. "There was a union family, a union background, but not union talk. [My father] was not of the socialist stripe that was very prevalent in the late teens, the early '20s. He was not a rabble-rouser who went to meetings and raised hell against the establishment and the institutions. He was a dues-paying member, and when the real test came he met it." As many young-sters then did from working families, Joe went to work at an early age (he was sixteen), to help out, starting as a stock boy in a local "five-and-dime" and, later, as a utility boy, earning 32 cents an hour for Western Electric at the Kearny, New Jersey, plant's inspection department. Later, he trans-ferred to the company's New York Distribution Sales House.

Slender, dark-haired with beetling brows and thin-lipped beneath pierc-ing dark brown eyes, Joseph Beirne was an ambitious young man; where others gave up, he persevered. He married Anne Mary Abahaze in 1933 and while working to support a growing family found time to go to school nights to get his high school diploma and to go on to Hudson City College, the night division of St. Peter's College in Jersey City. He also managed to be active in the debating and elocution societies. By 1937 he had accumulated enough college credits, roughly two years of work, to consider a career in law. He was taking courses at night at New York University when, as it sometimes happens to young people, Joe Beirne found his calling quite by accident. As he later told the story, "I was quitting work at five-fifteen. I had a seven-thirty class at New York University. So I had two hours to kill [and] only a fifteen-minute walk to school." As it happened, in Beirne's phrase, "the leaders selected by the company" called a meeting to adopt a constitution for a new organization. "So I went to the meeting. Now, if I had had an earlier class, I wouldn't have gotten to that meeting. If I had no class at all, I doubt if I would have gone to that meeting. I would have gone home." Beirne spoke up, and people listened. By late 1938, he was chairman of his own local union and president of the national sales group. "I knew I had to make up my mind whether I was going to continue my night school and get my degree or quit to give attention to the undertaking I had accepted. And, of course, in a year's period, as you get immersed, and as you meet the company management, and as you get involved . . . Hell, my interest—and I guess it came from my home environment; it was dormant—suddenly came out, and I was interested then in what I was doing." So, Joe Beirne said to himself, "Okay, go full-time. Whatever the hell the boatride may be, whatever the rapids will produce, go with the organization. Go with the union."

Even with hindsight it was difficult to choose priorities among the host of problems confronting the newly elected leaders of the NFTW. The problem of AT&T recognition was, of necessity, deferred; and the goal of one union, as a practical matter of internal politics, lay ahead. Rival unions were nibbling at the foundation, wooing the rank-and-file, as affiliates pursued their independent ways. "If the hard-core hadn't stuck together," William Dunn has said of the time, "these in-and-outers would have ruined us." Someone has said that unions are a cross between an army and a town-meeting; the NFTW lacked the discipline of the former and possessed the quarrelsomeness of the latter to an almost destructive degree. It was also exceedingly naive; even the leadership knew little about the ways of trade unionism. At the Denver assembly, in June 1944, a day was given over to the discussion of the very rudiments of trade unionism. Fran Smith delivered a paper entitled "Union Security—Benefit or Detriment?;" strike director I. R. Hudson, lead a discussion on the "Strike Weapon;" Jack Moran read a paper, "The Menace of the Non-Member;" and education director Ruth Wiencek gave a talk on "Union Education as a Means of Promoting Economic Democracy," and showed a film, *Labor's Challenge,* borrowed from the Detroit American Federation of Teachers AFL, local. While NFTW counsel Al Kane and Bill Dunn led technical discussions on legislation and the workings of wartime agencies, this was hardly the normal stuff of national union conventions of the day. This is not to decry its importance or usefulness, but merely to illustrate the structural weakness of a new organization as yet unable to carry on a national program of education among its affiliates.

Despite defections, the NFTW managed to hold its own through 1943, dropping slightly from 126,784 members to 122,427 in 1944. The wartime expansion of the Bell System labor force, and the successful organization of the Southern Federation of Telephone Workers, among others, brought the total membership to 165,178 at the war's end in 1945. All things considered, it was a respectable showing but the union still had a ways to go. The number of Bell System employees alone increased from 321,422 in

1941 to 396,198 in 1945 and would jump to 508,564 a year later. Per capita dues rose steadily, from ten cents a year in 1939 to thirty-six cents in 1940 and 1941, sixty cents in 1943 to $1.20 in 1944 and 1945. The budget also grew from $10,000 in 1939 to $204,043 in 1945. Growth brought confidence, even in the face of adversity, and Beirne would be able to remind the delegates to the 1944 Tenth Assembly at Denver that the NFTW had survived the skeptics' prediction that it would not last six months. "Let us keep our place in the labor movement," he declared after his first year in office. "Let us do those things which will represent to the public at large and impressively to our organizational rivals, that the telephone workers know that they are workers, not a part of the aristocracy of labor, but rather people who work hard at their trade, and calling, and that their leaders know and have experienced and can adequately take care of those problems which are pertinent to labor and which demand protection or which may demand defense."

Increasingly, as the war wore on, what was demanded by more and more workers was protection against the rising costs of living, the steady erosion of their standard of living. By the end of 1943, the Bureau of Labor Statistics reported a rise of 23.4 percent in the cost-of-living index since January 1941, the base-period for the Little Steel Formula, which allowed wage hikes of up to fifteen percent. (Application of the formula resulted in a "pattern" of $2 a week increases for telephone workers.) The AFL and the CIO, in a unusual demonstration of unity, immediately challenged the BLS finding. Working together, labor economists demonstrated a cost-of-living increase of 43.5 percent. Later, a Presidential commission's findings, in November 1944, announced a twenty-nine to thirty percent increase. CIO president Philip Murray angrily retorted that he was not relying solely on the reports of experts, but on "the best economist in the country—the American housewife." The NFTW possessed its own built-in economist, the telephone operator. During hearings before the War Labor Board in Chicago, the Illinois traffic union reported on the living expenses for an operator in October 1943. She paid $13.14 a week for room and board, $3.76 for clothes, $2.05 for entertainment, $2.50 for war bonds and $4 in income taxes —a *minimum* of $25.74 a week. The starting rate, at the time, was $17 a week, increased at regular intervals *over a thirteen year period* to a maximum of $29 a week. An average weekly rate of $21, however, meant that an overwhelming number of the Chicago operators were unable to meet the minimum necessary expenses of living.

The Ohio Federation of Telephone Workers drew up a chart of the top and starting rates for telephone operators working for seventeen Associated Bell System companies. It revealed starting rates, as of November 1944, that varied from a low of $16 a week to a high of $23. Top rates ranged from $26 a week to $34. But a Wisconsin operator, for example, starting at $16 a week, could not reach the maximum of $27 short of *sixteen years*. This worked out to an annual increase of 69 cents a week. A New Jersey operator possibly started at a higher salary, at $20 a week, rising to $33, doing this in the munificently short time of eleven years. This amounted to a gigantic annual increase of $1.11. Only four associated companies granted significantly shorter progression rates—New York, Michigan and Illinois, nine years each; Southern New England, eight years. Annual increases for those lucky girls ranged from $1.11 a week to a $1.55 a week. A *Telephone Worker* editorial wryly put it, "The Bell System really has a system."

The editorial went on to describe how the system worked. "Operators come into the business and, generally, before they have received their first raise are doing a satisfactory job at the switchboard. Within a maximum period of two years they are doing a thoroughly competent job." And then what happens? "Discouraged by the low wages, the long road ahead and the inadequate top rates even when attained, the operator quits and seeks more remunerative employment. In many cases she goes to work operating a private switchboard at wages $10 to $20 a week higher than the 'system' paid her." She also left for war plant work, learning new skills and earning a good deal more than what was attainable in telephone work.

Did this bother Ma Bell? Not particularly, for the Associated Companies deployed an elaborate recruiting mechanism that seemingly brought in a never-ending stream of new, young recruits. In 1943, for example, the system hired 128,000 new operators, mostly to replace those who could no longer take the strain at working at peak performance for subsistence wages. "As a result of this policy," a NFTW spokesman concluded, "the average level of service remains low, but more important from the company's standpoint, *wages* are kept down." This process also kept other costs down since operators were not employed long enough to be eligible for sick benefits or vacations, never mind being around long enough to collect a pension.

Progression schedules were truly stretched to a maximum by the Bell System. The predominantly male work force in the plant earned more than switchboard operators, but they, too, had to wait for their "reward." Starting salaries in the plant were not much higher, roughly $20, say, for a central office repairman. A New Jersey repairman, however, had to wait eleven years before hitting the top of the scale at $69 a week. This worked out at an annual increase of $4.36 a week, larger than that granted to operators to be sure but not exactly munificent. A Wisconsin repairman worked ten years before reaching the top-of-the-pole $55 a week from a start at $18 a week. A New Yorker did better, rising from $20 a week to $70 over nine years.

Wartime wage policies were milked to Mother Bell's advantage. As bold as brass, the companies sought to have the War Labor Board rule that all wage *progression* increases must be regarded as an application of the Little

Steel formula. As the NFTW quickly pointed out, this would mean no wage progression increases for the duration of the war. In trying to correct wage inequities, the War Labor Board sought to apply certain economic rules-of-thumb, comparing wage rates within a community, say, and establishing a "bracket," a range of comparable job rates, and allowing increases *if* workers' wages fell ten percent below the bracket minimum. As it worked out, what labor came to call "the bracket racket," worked against working people, since, for example, highly skilled workers found their wage rates being compared to workers with perhaps the same skills but employed in small, non-union plants at much lower hourly rates. So the telephone companies went one better than other employers by claiming that the only applicable "bracket" for telephone operators was the Bell System wage rate. This, too, meant no increase whatsoever.

Still, even economic giants cannot abort economic laws entirely. The loss of experienced operators to war plants and other more attractive jobs accentuated a growing labor shortage. It became increasingly difficult for telephone exchanges located in large defense centers or in major cities to recruit new employees, particularly at the industry's depressed wages. So, the companies began hiring operators from out of town, so-called transferees, and paid them an expense allowance to make the job more attractive. During wage negotiations in 1943, the Ohio Federation discovered that Ohio Bell had "transferred" 100 operators into Dayton. They were short-service employees, hired and trained in other towns, then paid an $18.25 a week "expense allowance" above the going base rate on transfer to Dayton. Operators with thirty or more years of service, permanently located in Dayton, were making $8.25 a week less than the newly-employed transferees.

The union demanded that either the transferees be returned to their home territories and/or that the company grant an equitable starting rate so that local Dayton workers might be hired. The company refused to consider the matter, fearing a revision of pay structures. The dispute went to the Regional War Labor Board where it met the fate of most telephone-wage cases at the time. The NFTW complained to the National War Labor Board Chairman William H. Davis that the regional boards had been "notably slow" in deciding telephone cases, largely through their inability to understand the complexities of the Bell System wage structure. "One of our biggest jobs," NFTW President Beirne said, "has been educating the members of the regional panels." Beirne also charged, in a November 1944 *Telephone Worker* editorial, that "the Bell System has the War Labor Board under its thumb." Walter T. Margetts, an industry member of the Board, a law partner of Walter Gordon Merritt, was in Beirne's words, "the chief labor union buster in the United States," and labor attorney for the telephone companies. "Snooping around the other industry members,"

Beirne asserted, "as well as the public members, on behalf of the Bell System is the biggest job Margetts has." Beirne urged the immediate formation of an industry commission to handle the specialized telephone cases.

Dispute cases began piling up in an alarming manner. Twenty-eight unresolved cases involving NFTW affiliates were before the National War Labor Board by mid 1944 and another fifty-seven were stalled in the regional boards. As Pearce Davis and Henry J. Meyer pointed out in their classic study of labor disputes in the telephone industry, the regional board system was "eminently suited" to local labor markets "where there were many separate business units . . . competing for workers to perform comparable jobs." But such a policy, Davis and Meyer concluded, "could not be applied to an integrated national industry, a public utility occupying a non-competitive, monopolistic position in each operating area, an industry whose wage structure was the result of these factors and its own peculiar history." Clearly there was a need for a specialized agency for the telephone industry if justice were to be done for telephone workers. Above all, the issue went to the heart of the problem of recognition. As the delegates to the 1944 Denver Assembly noted in a resolution, the labor members of the regional War Labor Boards "are universally appointed from among the membership of the CIO and the AFL and the experience of the NFTW and its affiliated unions has been that many of the members so appointed are hostile to the purpose of the telephone workers . . ." Rival unions—the American Communications Association, the IBEW and the United Electrical Workers—boasted of their "pull" within wartime agencies as a means of tempting telephone workers away from the NFTW and its affiliates. As NFTW president Beirne pointed out in the first of a series of radio broadcasts sponsored by the NFTW, "When Donald Nelson recently met with labor representatives to get the workers' slant on production, etc., only delegates of the two larger unions were invited. Telephone communications, including the manufacture thereof, is certainly vital to our economy, yet *no* representative in this field attended the meeting . . . *We want equal justice and fair representation in the governmental agencies* during this period when the agencies have replaced collective bargaining. With almost an *equal* number of workers in independent unions, as in either the AFL or CIO, we are *not* unrealistic in requesting *equal* representation."

Appeals to the public, however, did not suffice. The powers that be were unmoved until the NFTW resorted to the classic strike weapon. A wave of strike threats during the summer of 1944 produced some softening on the part of the National War Labor Board (NWLB). By August, John J. Moran of Long Lines, George DuVal of Western Electric (Kearny) and William Dunn of the Cincinnati Federation were serving on NWLB committees reviewing telephone cases on appeal from the regions. Delays, however, persisted; Beirne branded the current procedure as "grossly inefficient and inadequate." The crisis peaked in November when the Dayton telephone operators took matters into their own capable hands.

On the morning of November 17, 1944, the Dayton operators decided that they had had enough shilly-shallying over the then two-year-old starting-rate dispute and simply walked off the job. Earlier in the month, the Ohio Federation had served a thirty-day strike notice on the company, the NLRB and other governmental agencies. The strike action was held in abeyance while the union leaders sought to meet with an NLRB request that the issue be "clarified." Then the Dayton operators learned that women were available for work but that the War Manpower Commission would not release them for employment with the telephone company because it felt that the existing starting rate of 52.5 cents an hour was too low but would do so at sixty cents an hour. Furious, the Dayton operators walked out. As Robert C. Pollock, president of the Ohio Federation of Telephone Workers, told the press, "No union leader could conscientiously order a girl making $21 a week to work beside a girl making $39.25 for exactly the same work." The Ohio Federation voted its full support, and the strike spread overnight to Columbus, Toledo, Xenia, Tiffin, Findlay and Wellsville. Soon major Ohio communities were totally without service, long-distance calls were handled by scabbing supervisors only on an "emergency or priority" basis. Akron, Canton and Youngstown operators joined the spreading walkout, and before the first three days were over some twenty-five cities were "down" and roughly 10,000 telephone workers were out on strike. Four thousand were out in Ohio alone with others preparing picket lines in Washington, D.C. and Detroit as well as in other parts of the country. Plant workers refused to cross operator-maintained picket lines. A supervisor was promptly jailed in Dayton for punching a picketer in the stomach, causing her to be hospitalized. Ernest Weaver, NFTW regional director, warned the NWLB that "indications tonight [the third day] are that the nation is facing probably the worst communications strike in its history."

As the nation teetered on the verge of a communications crisis, the Regional War Labor Board in Cleveland issued a show cause order and NWLB Chairman Davis sent a telegram to the union stating that under labor's no-strike pledge the members should return to work "at once." Nathan P. Feinsinger, a prominent arbitrator and a public member of the War Labor Board, told NFTW leaders, "You are taking on the Government of the United States. That's the effect of your action. No union has done that yet and succeeded. We will take every step necessary to see that this strike doesn't succeed in the face of a violation of our order." The NWLB insisted that the company could not make the union an offer, nor even negotiate while the workers were on strike. NFTW officers reminded government officials that the telephone workers were not bound by a no-strike pledge given by leaders of the AFL or the CIO. But, speaking for the

Ohio strikers, Pollock pointed out, "We are anxious for a settlement. At the same time we are unable to understand why the doors between the company and the union are completely locked." Worried lest the strike spread, and concerned that the Dayton walkout would disrupt services to the Army-Airforce bases nearby, the Wright and Patterson fields, NWLB board chairman Davis warned that he would recommend to President Roosevelt's government seizure of the Ohio Bell Telephone Company.

Closeted with government officials for two days in Washington, NFTW officers, including unit leaders J.J. Moran and Ernest Weaver, remained steadfast, refusing to call off the strike until the government showed some concern for the workers' plight. "If the government takes over," a NFTW spokesman declared, "it will mean at least a moral victory for the workers." Reluctantly, the NWLB backed away from an ultimate confrontation. It agreed to take the matter out of the hands of the regional board and promised a special national panel to consider the question "immediately." Confident that the NWLB, in the words of Ohio Federation president Pollock, would "proceed expeditiously" and that its decision would be "fair and equitable," the union called off the strike the evening of November 23. Telephone service shortly returned to normal.

The Dayton walkout was a milestone, marking a new period of telephone worker militancy. The willingness to strike secured a major goal of the NFTW, the creation of a specialized agency to handle telephone cases. It was a major step towards recognition. In a resolution passed on December 15, 1944, the War Labor Board established a national telephone panel, a tripartite body comprised of people with some knowledge of the particular problems of the communications industry. John J. Moran and William Dunn were named as permanent labor members of the panel. Industry members were Frank N. Stephans, vice president of Ohio Bell, and B.A. Phillips, vice president and general manager of the Central Telephone Company, Sioux Falls, South Dakota. Pearce Davis, who had been assistant director of the NWLB wage stabilization division, and Henry J. Meyer, chief of the compliance section of the Board's disputes division, were named chairman and vice-chairman of the panel respectively and served as public members. The panel started its business with a workload of 110 cases.

Later, the authority of the panel was extended to "finally" approve voluntary wage increases. Six months after the panel was formed on January 1, 1945, it became a full-fledged commission empowered to decide all disputes or voluntary cases (where both company and union agreed to submission) within its jurisdiction, subject only to appeal to the full War Labor Board. Cases were considered on an industry-wide basis, a perspective, as Jack Barbash phrased it, "not available to a regional board." The operations of the panel and the commission would ultimately affect approximately 350,000 telephone workers. The National Telephone Commission introduced an element of orderlines into the telephone wage structure, providing, as it were, a platform for post-war union achievements. As Davis and Meyer summed it up: "The upward reevaluation of the traffic operator classification within the hierarchy of telephone jobs, the re-alignment of intra-Bell System wage rate differentials, to accord more realistically with the present-day pattern of inter-regional wage levels, the shortening of automatic wage progression schedules were notable and valuable contributions." The commission, in effect, forced Bell System management to deal with telephone union leaders on a basis of approximate equality. The Dayton strike, the consequent operations of the telephone panel and the commission demonstrated, for the first time, what the NFTW, as a national organization, could do for telephone workers in improving wages, hours and working conditions.

Collective bargaining, however, was limited by the exigencies of the war. The NFTW existed, as it were, in a limbo, neither fully recognized by the government or by Ma Bell. Whatever strength the federation had was derived from its autonomous affiliates. It was an umbrella organization, but one of paper with flimsy ribs and badly in need of strengthening. The affiliates, too, had their share of weaknesses, vulnerability. When attacked by AFL or CIO unions, they could not save themselves by acting alone. Increasingly, the affiliates began to turn to the national center for assistance of all kinds. When Peoria traffic threatened a walkout in November 1944, protesting the demotion of a fellow worker, an operator with twenty-two years of service, NFTW president Beirne was promptly notified. He participated with the local leadership in presenting the union case before a conciliator from the U.S. Conciliation Service. When the company refused arbitration, the union pressed for an emergency hearing. And after four hours of argument, Beirne and the local leaders forced the company to agree to reinstatement. It was a small victory, but significant as it pointed up the interdependence of all telephone workers.

NFTW affiliates emerging so recently from the era of company unionism were open to challenges from AFL and CIO unions. While affiliation with a national organization was considered evidence of good-faith unionism, the NLRB and the courts waffled when it came to assessing affiliation with the NFTW. Frequently, the IBEW, the UE or the ACA charged that NFTW affiliates were "successor" organizations to the old company-dominated associations and, therefore, still tainted and not truly independent. So, it was with considerable relief that the NFTW leadership accepted NLRB assurances that it would not entertain charges of "successor" relationships against any NFTW affiliate. But the assurances were less than firm. As the *Telephone Worker* subsequently editorialized: "Telephone unions might as well realize that they have been given the double cross and are being made the victims for a campaign to use the National Labor Relations Board to further the organizational objectives of the AFL and the CIO. Telephone unions might as well face this situation together now as face it, one at a time, later. Even if it requires a nationwide telephone strike to show that telephone unions aren't fooling, that step, if necessary, must be taken."

As it turned out, that step was not taken, but the NFTW soon faced a major challenge in the South, a confrontation that organizationally helped make it a true union. It all began when two telephone operators in Shreveport, Louisiana, acting on behalf of the IBEW, sued and won the disestablishment of the Southern Association of Bell Telephone Employees (SABTE) an NFTW affiliate in the fall of 1941. At the time, the SABTE was in transition, caught somewhere between the old associationism and trade unionism. As Lonnie Daniel, a toll test man in Baton Rouge and later an area director with CWA district 3, recalls, "We had what was called an association . . . which really was a company union. Supervisors all came to the meetings, and the district management usually encouraged the selection or election of its officers." Bill Webb, a line and station repairman in Memphis and later an assistant to the executive vice president of CWA (Glenn Watts), reminds us what it was like to belong to what he calls, "the squawk association." A young repairman developed some trouble with the veins in his legs and his doctor ordered him not to climb poles for a couple months. His fellow workers agreed that he could do the ladder work and the wiring inside the houses; they would climb the poles. But the foreman fired the ailing worker. "We hired you to climb, and if you can't climb, you're fired." As it happened, according to Webb's recollections, there was a meeting of the "squawk association" that night. When the chairman, a foreman named Shorty Harris, got to new business, the young worker rose to complain. He was called "out-of-order," and told that he had no grievance. "So several of us young guys," Bill Webb's recollections run, "raised points of order on different things and see, my foreman is over whispering in my ear right quick, 'Boy, are you tired of working here?' "

Nonetheless, SABTE was changing as other NFTW affiliates were. "I thought we were on the way to converting the thing [SABTE] peacefully into a real union," CWA executive vice president George E. Gill, then a cable-helper's splicer in Montgomery, Alabama, remembers. "We did all of the things that were recommended to us to separate ourselves from this stigma, one was to kick all of the supervisory employees out, which we did with pleasure." SABTE, Gill acknowledged, "was company-dominated in the sense that they met in company meeting rooms, and they were somewhat subsidized with respect to office equipment and clerical work . . . Many locals, however, of that group were not company-dominated. The leadership operated on a voluntary basis and were not dominated." Gill himself was the president of the Montgomery SABTE local, moving it in an increasingly independent direction. In the interim period between disestablishment of the SABTE and the final victory of the NFTW, Gill voluntarily quit his leadership post and dropped out "to protect us from challenges" and because "there might be some legal challenge then on the basis of continuity." Lonnie Daniel adds, "But some of the leaders in the SFTW locals, as it was formed then, were the same that were active and pressing for a union when SABTE was disestablished. However, they were not supervisors."

In truth, the NLRB order disestablishing the SABTE as a company-dominated union created a certain confusion. The IBEW, the major challenger, appeared interested only in picking up local unions here and there. By the time the case reached the Supreme Court, which upheld the NLRB order on May 3, 1943, the IBEW had filed for certification in only one place, Paducah, Kentucky, where it claimed a majority of the traffic employees. When NLRB hearings were held December 1943, the IBEW argued for local bargaining units—the CIO, for state-wide units while the Southern Federation of Telephone Workers, ably represented by its counsel, Robert T. Speer with assistance from Henry Mayer, attorney for the Long Lines and other NFTW affiliates, successfully pressed the case for a company-wide regional unit. Each labor group, of course, argued from its position of greatest strength.

As Gill is quick to point out, "When the Supreme Court disestablished the old ERP plan, it left a backbone of organization there. Officers of one sort or another in every town, local unions of some kind in every town and the people had been encouraged to join this organization by the company." It was an organizing edge, the organizers of the newly-formed Southern Federation of Telephone Workers would exploit successfully in the campaign ahead.

"A few of us," Bill Smallwood recalls, "felt that the decision [of the Supreme Court] was bound to come." A soft-spoken, mild-mannered Atlantan wearing rimless glasses, Smallwood—"I was just a young pup without too much responsibility"—then worked in the central toll office in Atlanta. He began cautiously to draw together a small group, "people we felt we could trust." They shared one view; in Smallwood's words, "We needed a good union." Discreet inquiries were made—to the AFL, the CIO, "even to the Mine Workers," then independent and a potent group in the South, especially in Alabama where the United Mine Workers, historically was the backbone of trade unionism. "Because of our past history," Smallwood has explained, "the mother-knows-best attitude, which was worse here because it was compounded by the fact that unionism was a dirty word, an anathema, we realized we could not win a majority for any one of these groups. We reached a consensus that we have got to set up an independent organization that is *bona fide,* that's clean, that's honest, that wants to give real representation." Some eight groups in nine states began to work together, forming the Southern Federation of Telephone Workers. Sam Sims was named head of the Atlanta group, and Smallwood became the first SFTW president.

The NFTW was eager to reorganize the South, but the southerners, worried about wooing a majority in a drive for certification by the NLRB, urged postponement of the question of affiliation. "Of all the known organizations," Smallwood told NFTW president Beirne, "none have a chance to organize this group, but the NFTW has the greatest chance to win acceptance." While acknowledging that they could "use some guidance," Smallwood argued against direct NFTW intervention. "This is not the time," he told Beirne. "But Joe being Joe, he wasn't willing to let anything slip away," he said. Nonetheless, Beirne had to give way before certain realities. The NFTW simply did not have the resources for a major organizing drive. The Southern Federation adopted a $1 for men, seventy-five cents for women, dues which was collected by hand. "We were unable to get time off the job for anyone to organize full-time," Smallwood says, "while the IBEW had organizers out in the field. We assured Joe we could pay the overhead, but not the salary for an organizer." The Southern Federation, on July 17, 1943, petitioned the NLRB for recognition as bargaining agent of all non-supervisory employees of the Southern Bell Telephone Company. The question of full time staff became imperative.

As it turned out, Beirne had to beg and borrow from NFTW affiliates to get the job done. But organization of the South was done *through* the NFTW. J.J. "Jake" Schacht, an executive board member, assigned the task of coordinating the southern effort. He arrived at the old Piedmont Hotel in Atlanta in June 1943, with a few names jotted down on a card—Sims, Smallwood, Hugh L. Wallace, first vice president of the Southern Federation, and Paul Meiere, its first secretary-treasurer. "My main objective was to hold meetings, talk to people. So we started that sort of routine." Smallwood remembers their first meeting, "Jake showed up, a short, heavy-set, dark-complectioned individual, who talks with a Brooklyn accent though he was born in Harlingen, Texas, in the Rio Grande citrus region." Smallwood finally worked himself up to broach a touchy subject, "I don't know how to be diplomatic about it, Jake, but you've got a couple of strikes against you. You could come off Third Avenue in New York, look Jewish and talk Brooklynese." Schacht taught himself the southern drawl, "and my folks at that time lived in Texas, so I became a Texan real fast. Well, as *that* got around a little bit, why, it kind of opened up. I could start talking to people, start telling them what *we* had done, and the things we had gained through our organization or being organized." At that, Schacht recalls a few times when he was offered two choices—"one to be *run* out, or I could get out by myself." Schacht could not hope to cover the entire south, so he concentrated on the big locations, setting up committees "that could get out and start talking to the majority of the people." As he recalls that hectic period, southern telephone workers "weren't union-minded by any extent. They were *anti*-union as a majority, and they didn't want to be taken in by some carpetbagger that came down there to organize 'em in something that they didn't know anything about. But I was a telephone man, and I was talking their language, and I knew what problems they had, and obstacles that they were running into or had run into, so they had something that had to be done and done fast. So that was to our advantage."

Compared to a latter-day CWA organizing campaign, the southern drive was crude indeed. As Smallwood points out, it was "a bootstrap operation." One full-time man couldn't possibly hit every telephone location in nine states, nor could the volunteers, even "deadheading" company circuits, call everyone. Farrell Beaver, working the toll board in Charleston, South Carolina, heard of the drive by word of mouth, "mostly from Western Electric installers who were at that time working amongst us, and they were NFTW members." Beaver called Joe Beirne, then headquartered in Baltimore, and asked him what the NFTW could do to organize a real union. "He told me to call the Piedmont Hotel in Atlanta and get in touch with either Mr. Jake Schacht or W.A. Smallwood, which I did . . . They sent me cards, and I traveled over the State of South Carolina as other men did in other states." Beaver, who later served as a CWA special representative, hit the four or five major cities in South Carolina, "in the two days I was on the road back in 1943." The Telephone Company, at that time, "had two locations in practically all the towns they operated in . . . the main exchange building and the storeroom [where the outside and plant men worked] . . . I'd hit that place at seven o'clock in the morning and get everybody I could and talk to them on the street and tell them what I was doing . . . I was handing out cards right and left . . . Now, usually at noontime, there's a going in and out of people into the exchange . . . And I would usually get that place. And then I would move on to some other city and get the garage of the storeroom after five o'clock at the end of the tour." Beaver remembers "deadheading" plenty of calls, just by talking to night operators and night plant men in a town 200 miles away . . ." The road was more or less already paved for me when I got there because in most cases I had someone earmarked to contact."

The NFTW stepped up its assistance over the 1943–1944 winter months. "Our largest project was the Southern Bell," NFTW secretary-treasurer Werkau later reported, "where we spent two years at a cost of $1,200 a month. We had an organizer permanently located there. Other people were shifted down there as needed." Sam Sims credits the Long Lines, Western Electric installers and distributing house groups scattered throughout the South with providing "invaluable" aid, especially "contacts" in places outside Georgia. Joe Beirne, Ernie Weaver, and J.J. Moran were NFTW executive board members who made excursions into the South from time to time during the organizing drive. Bill Dunn made trips into Kentucky and

Tennessee from Cincinnati, talking up "Federation." Nancy Franks, a toll service assistant from St. Louis, Missouri, came to Atlanta on loan from the Southwestern Telephone Workers. Anne Benscoter, an executive board member, came down on leave from the Illinois Telephone Traffic Union. An ex-chief operator from Peoria, busted by the company, put in ten-twelve weeks, working with the traffic group in Atlanta, some three to four thousand strong. "She could be as smooth and diplomatic as the best in the business," Smallwood recalls, "or as rough as any lineman." Mrs. Franks remembers, "When I went down, they put a trailer over a rented lot, and I signed people up and talked to them over there . . . I was there a month, and then we got a majority in Atlanta . . . We had a contract, see, before they did, and [I'd] tell them what we had in the contract, and their wages was low down there. Of course, the South has always paid less because the company said you didn't have to buy as many heavy clothes and as much fuel oil, and I don't know what all, in the South. So then we talked to them about their wages and their working conditions, the differential, the holidays, the Sundays, and the vacations, and the termination pay, because they knew they were going to be concerned with dial conversion as well as anybody else."

By mid winter, the SFTW had signed up 11,000 out of the 26,000 eligible in Kentucky, Tennessee, North and South Carolina, Georgia, Alabama, Florida, Mississippi and Louisiana. After more delays, occasioned by challenges leveled by the IBEW, the NLRB scheduled the election with balloting in twenty-one locations over May 10, 11 and 12, 1944. Employees outside those locations voted by mail ballot. Since the IBEW was unable to muster sufficient strength in petitions, the choice on the ballot was between SFTW and "No union." The SFTW won 14,714 "yes" votes to 1,515 "no" votes. Sixteen months after the long campaign began, the SFTW was certified by the NLRB on September 12, 1944, as the bargaining agent for all of Southern Bell's non-supervisory employees. At a special convention of the Southern Federation, Smallwood and his fellow officers reported "the assistance we got from the NFTW, and we recommended that the Federation cast its lot with the NFTW." And, so the convention voted, John Crull was sent to the South to help negotiate the Southern group's first contract. Summing up those organizing years, Smallwood said, "The real success of unionism in the Southeast was that a lot of people had one common objective, to get a union that had the strength to speak for them. A lot of people poured a lot of love, a lot of sacrifice into building the union."

"There are signs," a *Telephone Worker* editorial declared in October 1944, "which indicate that the member unions in the federation are much closer to a 'National Union' philosophy than at any time in the history of the NFTW." Among the signs, of course, was the success scored by the union in the South. This encouraged further efforts with affiliates securing more and more aid from the national organization. When the NLRB disestablished a company union at the Point Breeze, Maryland, plant of Western Electric in the summer of 1944, Slim Werkau, NFTW secretary-treasurer, supervised an organizing drive undertaken by the Maryland Plant union. Later, the drive became the responsibility of Walter Petry, organizer of the Western Electric sales house in Boston. The Machinists, the IBEW and the UE intervened, but the Machinists soon dropped out in favor of the IBEW.

The Point Breeze company-dominated union had not been affiliated with the NFTW, and the plant was the focus of a war-time conflict over the hiring of black workers.* Western Electric had been forced by the Fair

---

*Until 1943, hardly a single black operator was to be found in the entire Bell System. Gloria Shepperson, now an assistant to CWA Secretary-Treasurer Knecht, remembers being one of the first black women, if not actually the first, hired in New Jersey; and to secure that, encouraged by her mother, she had to fight an anti-discrimination case to win her job as an operator. Black installers were hired in Chicago for the first time in 1942. What happened is revealing of the times. Harry Fleischman and James Rorty tell the story in *We Open the Gates,* a pamphlet published by the IUE, AFL-CIO, in 1958.

Al Herrington, one-time secretary-treasurer of the independent union at the Illinois Bell Telephone Company (now a national staffer for the Communications Workers of America, AFL-CIO), tells how a combination of education and prodding worked in Chicago during World War II.

It all began when management called the union executive board (which also served as a bargaining committee) into the plant manager's office to report that the Urban League was pressing the company to hire Negro installers. "We told them we couldn't do it," the plant manager firmly declared. "We know your union members would refuse to work with Negroes. And besides we're not going to put up separate facilities for Negro workers."

The company was in for a shock.

"Who said you could speak for us?" asked the union committee. "We don't object to working with Negroes. The Negro janitors are in our union, and if you hire Negro installers, we'll work with them too. What's more, you don't have to have to put up separate facilities. We can all use the same."

Arrangements were made to hire a limited number of Negroes as phone installers, giving first crack to Negroes already employed as janitors and porters. But despite this sensible agreement between the union executive board and management, a rank and file revolt started. At the next membership meeting, one member after another condemned the board's action. A committee was picked to see the plant manager and protest the hiring of Negroes.

"I'm sorry," replied the manager, "but this agreement was worked out with your board. It stands."

The rank and file committee reported back to the membership. "The board sold us down the river. Maybe we can't keep these Negroes out of the plant, but we *can* keep them out of the union."

The next month, after a number of Negro installers came on the job, the opposition members had a new idea:

"Look," they said, "we have to pay out good money to support our union. Why should these Negroes be free-riders and get the benefit of all our gains without paying a cent? They've *got* to join the union and pay dues. But we won't let them come to union meetings."

Another month and another membership meeting later, the rebels changed their tune again:

"*We* have to come to meetings to build up the union. Why should the Negroes go to

Employment Practices Executive Order 8802, issued by President Franklin D. Roosevelt on June 25, 1941, to hire black workers. Fred D. Waldeck, an assistant to CWA executive vice president George Gill then working as a set-up man in the punch press and tool press department at Point Breeze, tells what happened when the presidential ban on discriminatory hiring took effect. "Well, Western had a policy of not hiring Negroes except maybe for janitorial work, that type of thing. So, when they started hiring Negroes —and at that time that plant was up around 6,000, 650—700 Negroes, well, what developed was we had a Jim Crow strike where people walked off the job when the Negroes got there . . . Well, it was the company union that pulled it. But I was convinced in my mind then, and I haven't changed my mind, that this thing was instigated by the company. I think they used the company-dominated union to trigger it. Well, most of the Negroes worked and all the whites stayed out. Well, that strike lasted about two weeks. And then the United States Government moved the Army in and they took over. And they ordered everybody back to work or be subjected to being inducted into the armed forces. Then they went in, and people went back to work, and the Army stayed there about six months running the place."

The federal seizure was the immediate background for the disestablishment of the company union. Waldeck, Elmer House, a tradesman at Western, and Ted Brown, another skilled worker at the plant, met with Werkau. The NFTW national office was then in Baltimore, not far from where the Point Breeze men lived and worked. Walter Petry was brought down from Boston to organize the plant for the NFTW. "Well," Waldek's recollections continue, "by the summer of 1944 we had a real campaign going. It was a campaign between the IBEW, the UE, the CEW, and the NFTW. And on the first ballot, we topped it, with the UE coming in second, and IBEW a poor third. 'No Union' was last. They only got about twenty-five votes as I recall . . . 'No Union.' And IBEW got a little over 600. And then we had a runoff between the UE and the NFTW, and the NFTW won by about a two-to-one margin in the runoff."

It was a famous victory for the Point Breeze campaign [and it] was the first truly NFTW effort. The Southern drive operated through the NFTW but was largely financed by affiliates and, technically, was mounted by an independent, the Southern Federation. J.J. Schacht was sent to the West Coast to organize there. Anne C. Benscoter, a member of the executive

---

the movies while we're attending union meetings? *They've* got to come to meetings too —but they will have to sit in a separate section."

You guessed it.

Before long, Negro phone workers were coming to union meetings, sitting with the other unionists, taking full part in all activities. But it didn't just happen.

In the long weeks between meetings, countless talks among union leaders, shop stewards and rank-and-filers paved the way for the change.

board, and Nancy Franks, of Southwestern Telephone Workers, were assigned to the Mountain States territory to assist the federation in organizing operators in Colorado and Utah. It was another first for the NFTW, with the federation filing charges of company domination against two traffic groups. Traffic was organized first in the Mountain States area through the help of D.L. McCowen. As LaRoy Purdy, an assistant to CWA president Beirne and then a traffic manager in Colorado, put it, "Nancy Franks and Anne Benscoter, who came to Colorado, and did a hell of a job in organizing Traffic and got the group recognized . . . We did the plant job later . . . The women were much more interested. They were the pioneers in the business." Mrs. Franks started in Denver then, with the help of Mrs. Benscoter, went on to Pueblo, Colorado Springs, Boulder, Fort Collins, Loveland, and on into Utah. "They were unhappy," Mrs. Franks later recalled, "most unhappy about the seniority in the traffic department. From moving from one board to another and taking their seniority away from them. And after you worked for a company that long, you feel that your seniority belongs to you as an individual and should be recognized. Therefore, they weren't hard to sell that they should be organized, and they were very helpful, and they were very thankful. They did have a lot of problems, and these were solved in the first contract. Anytime you make a first contract, I tell you, you make mistakes, and nothing is perfect, but it was certainly a big help to start it on the right road. And they all got their seniority back. It took them six months to figure up their cards and get them back in operation on their overall seniority." The Mountain States Federation scored substantial victories in Colorado against the Colorado Operators' Association, by 286 to fifty. By the Eleventh National Assembly in Chicago, June 11–16, 1945, the NFTW executive board was able to report a membership gain of 40,000 secured through its organizing efforts. At the war's end, the NFTW encompassed forty-seven affiliates with 170,036 members.

VII
An Oath in Blood

Mary Gannon's girls jumped the gun, leaving their posts at noon, Friday, October 5, 1945, two hours before the scheduled nationwide telephone-worker "meeting" called earlier in the week by the NFTW. Mrs. Gannon was that kind of leader. Mrs. Eleanor Jane Palmer, Washington Traffic's secretary-treasurer, described her as "a very dynamic woman, who commanded both respect and a following. She had the people working right with her, and we had so much regard for her that you might call it blind faith. I think if she said, 'jump,' we'd jump and then ask later," The Washington operators were practiced militants. Mrs. Madge Giles, a steward and later president of Washington Local 2300, has given us the full measure of their discipline. "On getting the word from Mrs. Gannon, the stewards would go and ask a friendly service assistant, 'May I get in position?' " Obtaining a quick nod of approval, Mrs. Giles continues, "I would pick up the SA stand. A ring on every one at the same time with the keys open. 'We have a work stoppage. We'll explain later.' And they knew that when I said, 'We'll explain later,' it would be explained later." Some 200 work stoppages occurred in the year following the end of World War II in that manner, and not all of them were over *local* D.C. issues. Washington traffic occupied a sensitive position, routing calls to the White House and other government offices and the operators were willing to use the strength that gave them for other telephone workers as well as on their own behalf.*

That fall, at the War's end, Charles W. Whittemore, a National Labor Relations Board trial examiner, had recommended the disestablishment of the NFTW affiliate, the Western Electric Employees Association (WEEA) at Kearny, New Jersey, as a company-dominated union. He acted at the instigation of the then CIO union, the United Electric Radio and Machine

---

*Mrs. Palmer gives an example: "Whenever anybody in the country was out—I remember at one time in St. Louis the traffic girls were trying to get some air conditioning put in, and the only thing the company would offer were the tubs of ice. You've heard about them. In order to get some satisfaction on their grievance, they could have had a work stoppage, but they weren't in the prime position where they were really disturbing the country or upsetting the country. So what they did was call to Washington and ask our president if she could give them some help."

Workers of America, and his decision was a blow to the very existence of the NFTW as a *bona fide* labor organization. Henry Mayer, counsel for the WEEA and for several other NFTW affiliates, had based his defense not only on the proven seven-year record of struggle with the company but also on the WEEA's affiliation with the NFTW. As he pointed out, it had been the NLRB's practice to dismiss charges of company domination whenever leveled at AFL or CIO affiliates and that justice called for the same parity of treatment to be extended to the NFTW and its affiliates.

In reviewing the case in a letter to the *New York Times,* Mayer pointed out that the WEEA had been in existence for eight years. "It became an affiliate of the National Federation six years ago. When the charges of company domination were filed by the CIO in 1942, the association, denying the charge, also called the board's attention to its administrative policy and insisted that it be applied in this case even though its parent body was not an affiliate of the AFL or the CIO.

"The Board was then consistent and refused to issue a complaint. Two and a half years passed and during this time much pressure was exerted on the board to reverse its decision. In September 1944, it finally succumbed and thus placed itself in the anomalous position of having one administrative rule for AFL and CIO unions and another for unaffiliated unions." In the course of the Western Electric hearing before Charles W. Whittemore, the board's trial examiner, the company and the board entered into an agreement to settle the case. The settlement contemplated disestablishment of the Western Electric Employees Association and release of the company from any liability to pay back to its employees about $1,250,000 checked off their payroll for dues. "On behalf of the association, which was a party to the proceedings, I vigorously opposed the settlement and suggested instead that an election be held at a time to be fixed by the board with the Western Electric Employees Association, the CIO and any other union that demonstrated an interest going on the ballot. The board rejected my proposal, insisting that nothing would satisfy it short of complete extinction of the Western Electric Employees Association. It denied to that union the right to appear on any ballot.

"In effect, the board said that 30,000 workers at Western Electric did not have sufficient intelligence to determine for themselves, despite the recent dynamic and educational years, that their union was company dominated by voting against it at a secret election conducted by the board itself. . . . The board obviously arrogated to itself the right to deny freedom of choice to any group of workers who do not want the AFL or CIO by making it exceedingly difficult, if not impossible, for them to select an independent union."

NFTW president Beirne charged that NLRB examiner Whittemore had been guilty of "gross discrimination" against independent telephone workers unionism. As Beirne told a mass meeting of New York and New Jersey

NFTW members at Manhattan Center, "We want someone to get it through their thick heads that we are as intelligent as the CIO and the AFL and that if we choose to remain independent then agencies and managements better respect our choice." Operating on the principle, phrased by Beirne as, "Hurt one of us and you hurt all of us," the NFTW executive board called for "simultaneous" and "continuous" mass meetings of Bell System employees from coast to coast on Friday, October 5, 1945, from two in the afternoon until six in the evening. The meetings were to serve both as a protest against the trial examiner's report in the Kearny case and as a means of asking the NFTW rank-and-file to authorize a nation-wide strike vote should that prove to be necessary. "We are not against the National Labor Relations Board," J.J. Moran, head of the NFTW Long Lines affiliate, declared, "but we are against the policy of kowtowing to AFL and CIO unions." And as Beirne explained, "While we feel certain that the three members of the NLRB, who are legally constituted to administer the act, will reverse the hearing officer, we nevertheless believe that our members have enough at stake to carefully review the entire history of the Kearny case. The telephone workers are prepared and will resist any encroachment by the UE-CIO or any other Communist-dominated CIO union."

It was a truly remakable demonstration of solidarity. "We were all asked to leave our jobs for a period of four hours," Miss Nelle Wooding, then a leader of the Dallas traffic group, recalls, "And believe me, some of the people had to be almost carried out. They wanted to go with the union, but the idea of walking off their switchboard was just appalling to them. But they went . . ." In Detroit, Michigan, Mrs. Helen W. Berthalot and another young lady passed out their first handbills in front of the main telephone building. "It had never happened before," according to Mrs. Berthalot. "We passed out handbills telling the kids to walk off the job and come to a meeting that afternoon—a four hour meeting. And the president of the company came along, and he said, 'May I have one?' and I said, 'Sure.' And he said, 'Well, so you are going to take the people out. Do you think that you can do it?' and I said, 'Yes, sir,' and he said, 'How are you going to get back?' Then he stood in the door that afternoon and watched all of his people walk out—there were very few that stayed in the building. And in some places I know—I went out to the office that I used to work in and walked into the operating room and told the girls to come on, and only one girl stayed back, and she walked out to the rest room and then walked back in again. All the rest of them came."

And so they did, over 200,000 telephone workers in all parts of the country.* Members left their jobs at switchboards, desks, in exchanges and

*A firm figure on the number of workers involved is hard to arrive at. ATT declared that it was impossible to say what total percentage of operations was affected, but acknowledged that 100,000 workers had left their jobs. Henry Mayer, WEEA attorney, estimated on the day of the mass meetings that 200,000 had participated. The *Telephone Worker*, in November,

manholes, in manufacturing plants, and on subscribers' premises to attend meetings where they heard details about the trial examiner's report on Kearny and discussed appropriate counteraction. The meetings passed resolutions authorizing the NFTW officers to call for a nationwide strike vote under the War Labor Disputes Act, still in effect, if such action proved to be necessary to win fair treatment from the National Labor Relations Board. Other resolutions instructed members to ask their congressmen to prevail upon the NLRB to reverse the Whittemore findings. In some cities, resolutions authorizing the strike vote were coupled with a demand that such a strike, should it develop, should not be terminated until a satisfactory agreement was reached with respect to the nationwide demands of the telephone workers for a twenty-five-to-thirty percent wage increase. Mrs. Norma F. Naughton, chairwoman of the Long Lines New York City Branch 101, led a festive walkout, en masse, of operators, from 32 Sixth Avenue to St. Alphonsus Church, a block away at 308 Broadway, saying "I defy anyone to call us company dominated now."

It was the first nationwide tie-up in telephone history. While dial telephone service was not affected appreciably, according to company figures Long Lines was down to eleven percent of its normal operation in Cincinnati, thirteen percent in Buffalo and Pittsburgh, fifteen percent in Detroit, sixteen percent in Louisville and Kansas City, seventeen percent in Boston, nineteen percent in Chicago, twenty-eight percent in Philadelphia, thirty-six percent in Cleveland, and twenty-four percent in St. Louis. In Newark, New Jersey, Gilbert Hunsinger found he could not rely on the telephone service; he sent word home to his wife in Bloomfield that he would be late to dinner—by homing pigeon. Reports to the national office of the NFTW showed meeting attendance "varying" from ninety-five percent to one hundred percent in the Southwest, in towns, large and small, all the way from St. Louis to the farthest corner of Southwestern Texas. Meetings varied in size from 4,000 in St. Louis to three in Norton, Kansas, where there was a 100 percent turnout. Indiana reported "99 and 44/100 percent participation." In Southern California, Bell Company management read statements to their employees, urging them to stay on the job as a "patriotic and public duty." Despite this attempt at intimidation, plant, commercial, installer and sales NFTW members walked out, as did the employees of the independent Associated Telephone Company. Michigan Bell ran quarter page advertisements in the daily papers urging workers to remain on the job, but Fran Smith mobilized her forces to gain ninety-nine percent participation

counted 250,000. Forty-three of the forty-seven affiliates participated; the combined membership of the four nonparticipants was about 5,000. The NFTW membership at the time was in excess of 200,000. The June 1945 convention credentials committee reported a delegate strength of 153,485; the June 1946 convention, 191,919.

throughout the state. One line foreman who refused to allow any of his crew to take his car to the job on the morning of the meeting was loaded into the company truck at 2:00 P.M., driven to town where the hopeless foreman was left in the truck while the workers attended the rally. Mountain States reported a ninety-eight percent turnout in Plant, but the turnout varied— from 100 percent to fifty-one percent in Traffic—depending on the state of success in the then ongoing organizing campaign. The Denver meeting was so crowded that many members were forced to stand in the hall of the Shirley Savoy Lincoln Room. Despite the great geographic spread of the union district, ninety-nine percent participated, and in one case, the members of one local, residing 170 miles away from the union headquarters, drove all the way to join the demonstration. Over ninety percent of the workers represented by the Southern Federation in 947 towns throughout the nine southern states attended the four-hour meetings. Ohio reported the demonstration as "very effective" with at least ninety-five percent participation throughout the state." While the Commercial Telephone Workers and the Federation of Telephone Workers, Illinois NFTW affiliates, refused to join the action, Illinois Traffic, the Hawthorne plant workers and local units of Western Electric installation and sales participated fully. Lexington, Kentucky, plant and traffic walked out with the exception of one operator and a toll girl. Members had to be restrained from dragging one of the offenders out of the office. Ninety-nine and one half percent of Connecticut members left their jobs, and 99 and 99/100 percent did so in Maryland. Twenty-three separate meetings were held in Virginia, and members were standing in the hall rented by the Seattle telephone workers for the four hours. Wisconsin met in forty-three different locations and service was at a standstill except in Milwaukee where the traffic and commercial groups were not fully organized. And in Washington, D.C., the normally unflappable Bill Dunn was so carried away that he began explaining to the members that the mass meeting was a forerunner of a strike and if one occurred what might happen. "Such things as operators taking their cords home with 'em, plant men being loose with solder fittings dropping down in the equipment before we went out." And the prestigious *Washington Post* carried an editorial the next day, saying "Telephone leader . . . advocates sabotage."

The four-hour meetings were a smashing success, and if the public read into them rather more than the NFTW leaders wanted, or would allow, the public, in a sense, was right. Henry Mayer, attorney for some seventeen independent telephone unions, some affiliated with the NFTW and some not, had interjected the wage issue, as had several of the "meetings" in their resolutions on the proposed protest strike over the Kearny case. NFTW president Beirne and vice president J.J. Moran, the Long Lines chief, took considerable pains to issue a disclaimer shortly after the demonstration. "The NFTW has denied any of the affiliates or non-affiliates who took part in the unity demonstration meetings yesterday, or who may take part in any future action in connection with these meetings, the right to introduce wages as an element of this particular demonstration. The demonstration meetings were designed solely to foster a principle and were in no way associated with wage demands." Nonetheless, the four-hour meetings were weather vanes veering around in sharply increasing winds of militancy, and wages were assuredly an element in the approaching storm.

Wartime controls were still in effect but were operating rather like a badly latched lid on a pressure cooker. The American Federation of Labor cogently argued that workers needed an immediate eleven percent pay increase to match increases in the cost of living. While telephone workers scored wartime gains through the efforts of the NFTW, they lagged in comparison with others. In 1945, the industry's average weekly earnings were $40 as compared with $32.74 in 1941, roughly a $2 a year gain. But Bureau of Labor Statistics figures showed durable goods industries averaging $49.50 a week; non-durable goods industries, $38.29; electric light and power, $50.05; telegraph, $37.98, and wholesale trade, $44.07.

Four days after Japan surrendered on August 18, 1945, President Harry S. Truman authorized voluntary wage increases that did not affect prices to become effective without War Labor Board approval. He also pleaded for a continuance of the wartime no-strike pledge, at least until his labor-management conference could fashion machinery for the peaceful transition from the war to the new economic situation ahead. (The NFTW, incidentally, was not invited to participate in that conference.) But the President's hopes for keeping the lid on inflation were soon shattered. Labor quickly chucked the no-strike pledge as members chafed at spiraling living costs. In the last four and a half months of 1945, man-days lost due to strikes shot up to 28,400,000 more than double the wartime peak of 1943, when the great coal strikes wracked the nation. And this was but a prelude to the great strike wave of 1946.

Telephone workers were quick to press their just demands. In November, some 8,700 local and long-distance operators and clerks represented by the Illinois Telephone Traffic Union walked off their job, forcing the company to finally talk turkey over long delayed wage increases. Despite a drizzling rain on the first morning of the walkout, determined pickets marched in front of exchanges, carrying signs declaring, "The Voice/With A Smile/ Will Be/Gone/For/A While," and other rhymed protestations. As the operators marched, Mrs. Anne C. Benscoter, ITTU president, Mrs. Decima Kelsall, vice president, Mrs. Hazel Richards, executive board member, and attorney Edwin R. Hackett met with the company. Other NFTW members refused to cross the traffic picket lines, and, in other cities, refused to handle Illinois calls. Mid-strike, on November 22, NFTW president Beirne flew into Chicago (plane flights were by no means as common then as now) to join in the negotiations. Beirne also alerted all NFTW affiliates for a possible nationwide strike. After seven days, the company capitulated, granting the operators a $6-a-week raise, $4 of it retroactive to May 9, 1945, and an additional $2-a-week beginning not later than February 1, 1946."

The Illinois traffic strike demonstrated what might be accomplished on the picket line, and the four-hour meetings encouraged telephone-worker belief in the efficacy of united action. Yet, there were many hurdles to overcome, and not least among these was a lack of agreement as to how to best conduct the struggle ahead. The issue of autonomy clouded the available choices, and the affiliates were rife with rumours of NFTW favoritism towards Western Electric groups. "Personally," F.J. Meskill, a leader of the Connecticut Union of Telephone Workers, told NFTW secretary-treasurer Werkau, "I think Messrs. Beirne, Weaver and DuVal should not be heading up the NFTW. I do not think operating and manufacturing groups fit together. Most of the trouble we have had is because of actions taken by the Western Electric Unions within the NFTW." Maryland traffic also made similar charges—and threatened withdrawal—over the Kearny case. There were other differences. As Werkau explained to a Connecticut group, "Some groups feel you should start with a high figure and work down to what you really want. Ohio works that way. Others feel you should go in and ask for what you want and stick to it. Southwestern works that way." And in a November letter to John Crull, NFTW president Beirne worried, "We could quite possibly be on sympathy strikes or direct strikes fifty-two weeks out of the year, if the opinions of some of the heads of our members organizations were to prevail."

To work out a common strategy, the NFTW called a Presidents' Conference, the week of December 2, 1945, in Milwaukee. At the end of October, NFTW President Beirne sent a letter to all affiliates urging them "to coast" on their wage negotiations until after the Milwaukee meeting. In a subsequent explanatory letter to the head of the Virginia Federation, Stuart A. Napier, Beirne outlined the executive board's strategy: "Our plan calls for negotiations sometime in the early part of 1946. We have been limiting the participating organizations to those which have contracts which expire between the months of January and April of 1946 so that there can be some reasonableness to the demands we will make upon each of the companies, and the AT&T, for negotiating with us in the early part of 1946." For those whose contracts expired earlier, as apparently was the case with the Virginia group, Beirne suggested, "If your contract termination is in September [1945] and you are on a month-to-month extension then it would be possible for you, in the event you wish to participate, to carry on your present contract until the time the NFTW actually sits down to negotiate for the participating unions." Beirne's conciliatory tone accurately reflected uncertainties inherent in NFTW's national bargaining stance. The affiliates had to be cajoled into taking a united stand.

At Milwaukee, the assembled presidents—thirty-eight out of forty-seven

NFTW member unions participating—did hammer out a uniform program. It set four basic goals: a $2-a-day wage increase or its equivalent; a 65 cent an hour minimum wage; retroactivity to August 18, 1945, and a return to the normal 40-hour work week. The latter, of course, reflected the necessity of adjustment from the wartime economy to that of peacetime. But there were practical reasons, spelled out in the next issue of the *Telephone Worker:* "Agreement on a uniform demand for immediate return to the normal work week is based on the firm belief that if the companies would eliminate the practice of 'selective hiring' and increase starting rates it would no longer be necessary to work extended tours. Further, that the extra wages earned as a result of working longer hours actually conceals the full effect of the need for higher base wages."

The Milwaukee deliberations also secured a commitment to a common strategy. It was, as events would soon show, a bit shaky and very tentative. The delegates were cautious, noting that no two strike situations were alike, and that each strike situation required a separate analysis. It was resolved that no NFTW affiliate should be required to go on strike in support of another "unless the striking union has prior approval from the NFTW executive board." To implement the wage policy, each organization was directed to send weekly progress reports on negotiations to the NFTW president, and summaries of these reports were to be sent to each affiliate. The NFTW statistical director was directed to provide essential data— company financial reports, interpretation of tax laws, governmental orders, reconversion information and the like—to all affiliates engaged in bargaining. And most crucially, "no affiliated union is to make a settlement below the established policy without consulting the NFTW president." The executive board was instructed to appraise the progress of negotiations by mid-February and, "if in the opinion of the Executive Board, sufficient progress has not been made," it was to call another Presidents' Conference "to consider a general strike." Voting delegates to that conference were to "come prepared to take positive action."

Behind the rather bland, even evasive language lay some rather explosive emotions. As Beirne later recalled, "So here we met, and we had all been in our separate negotiations. In the NFTW we were supposed to do some sort of a coordinating job. Well, that was a joke, and I termed it such. I couldn't sit in my office, as the president of the NFTW, and through the process of writing letters and telephone calls, all of which was exhortation: 'We must stick together. We must stick together.' That was the basic theme. . . . we just went no place with that one, and so first we called a meeting for the purpose of looking at where we all stood in collective bargaining. We were able to call that meeting on the basis that we had certain responsibilities in the NFTW for coordination, and the letters and telephone calls were not coordinating very well. 'So let's all get together and find out what we want to do,' because the bargaining was getting up to the point where agreements were going to be reached real soon.

"So we met. We spent a week, and out of that one we'd taken an oath in *blood* that we were going to stick together . . ."

The symbolic comingling of the blood of brotherhood, however, could not compensate for the fundamental weaknesses of the NFTW. Leaving aside the question of Ma Bell's willingness to bargain nationally with the NFTW, which was by no means certain, NFTW affiliates voluntarily had to "transfer" their respective bargaining "rights" to the NFTW bargaining committee before national bargaining could begin. It was a cumbersome procedure at best, and few affiliates had done so by the end of the year when NFTW leaders were rather desperately trying to hold to a common strategy. At Milwaukee, only two affiliates had reached agreements on post-war terms, but neither were of sufficient standing to serve as an industry "pattern." But on leaving Milwaukee, Chicago Traffic "signed off." Others soon followed suit, eagerly grabbing settlement offers of $3-a-week increases for starting wages and $4 and $5-a-week increases for the top. As Beirne graphically put it, "They fell over like duckpins." Seventeen affiliates, however, held firm to the Milwaukee Commitment.

Desertion, however, was only one of the difficulties faced by the NFTW leadership. Other affiliates were all too eager to hit the bricks, to demonstrate their militancy. Smarting under charges of company domination leveled by the CIO's UE, the Western Electric Employees' Association called for a strike on January 3, 1946, and 17,400 workers walked off their jobs in twenty-one plants in the New York City metropolitan area. Post V-J Day downgrading jeopardized an average hourly wage of 80 cents earned in producing telephone switchboards, carrier telephone equipment, cable, vacuum tubes and other communications equipment; Western Electric rejected out of hand the WEEA's request for a thirty percent wage increase, and a 65-day strike ensued. On the first night, four pickets were fished out of New York Bay after their 26-foot skiff, the union "Navy," sank and they had to be treated for shock, immersion and frostbite. Five supervisory employees, who had parked their automobiles in a lot adjoining a Western Electric plant in Manhattan, reported that tires had been slashed. On the second day, management massed 1,000 "executives, supervisors and maintenance employees" at the Kearny, New Jersey, plant gates in an effort to break through the picket lines. "With all the perseverance of the Spartans at Thermopylae," A.H. Raskin reported in the *New York Times,* forty-two WEEA pickets fought off the assault. Flailing about with fists, feet and picket staves, the strikers upset the determined dash of the strikebreakers. "Fifteen policemen," by Raskin's count, "who had been standing around looking disinterested earlier in the morning while hundreds of individual non-strikers were being turned away from the gate by the pickets, charged into the struggling group at the main entrance when hand-to-hand fighting broke out." By then, "the pressure of the crowd had driven the pickets, still battling with those in the front ranks, several feet inside the gate. The police, as they separated the contestants, ordered every one to fall back. When the clouds of battle cleared, all the non-strikers found themselves back on the street, except forty who had managed to slip inside in the confusion."

As the WEEA strike settled down, erupting only occasionally in minor scuffles, the Washington Traffic group took on its management in a contest over "excessive and dictatorial" supervision. Under a new "service program," supervisors were ordered to "observe" experienced operators as well as trainees. Systematic spying reinforced these orders: "Keep a plug in your hands at all times, be alert, use a courteous tone of voice at all times, keep your eyes on the board at all times, don't talk to the adjacent operator, keep your headset adjusted ⅛ of an inch from your mouth.

"Do not change headset from one ear to the other without calling your supervisor, sit up straight with both feet on the rail, keep hands on the edge of key shelf, if the customer says 'good morning,' don't answer him, hold the plug at a forty-five degree angle, don't take an aspirin without being relieved from your position."

Provoked by unwarranted strain, the Washington operators sat down at their boards for an hour on January 4, and six days later, 3,000 held a "continuous meeting" that lasted eight days. Finally, the company capitulated, agreeing for the first time in Bell System history that workers were entitled to "good working conditions." A joint committee—three from the union and three from the company—instituted "a study of the work assignments" with a view to making "recommendations for any changes that may appear desireable." An invaluable precedent had been set.

Meanwhile, the 7,704 Western Electric installers belonging to the Association of Communication Equipment Workers were chafing at the bit. They had a grievance rooted in a four-year-old wartime dispute, a failure of the War Labor Board in 1942 to grant Western Electric installers "a wage structure with wage levels comparable to the wage structure and wage levels of telephone plant employees." The installers wanted this disparity resolved before negotiating post-war wage standards. On Wednesday, January 9, 1946, at about one in the afternoon, NFTW officers received a letter from ACEW president Ernest Weaver seeking approval of a strike already underway. Since the installers, a nationwide group, planned to picket exchanges wherever they worked, the NFTW was confronted with the possibility of a cross-country shutdown over old scores, while the affiliates were as yet unprepared for united action on belief of their own post-war program.

The installers' move was not entirely a surprise, though the timing of the letter to the NFTW officers was awkward. Both Frank J. Fitzsimmons, president of the Kearny group, and Ernest Weaver, head of the installers, had pressed the NFTW for a "sympathetic strike" in support of their own actions. The NFTW affiliates were being polled on the question of a sympathy walkout in support of the Kearny strike just as the installers quit their jobs. William S. Leary, president of the Pennsylvania Federation of Telephone Workers, announced that his 5,000-member union was opposed to a sympathy walkout, adding, however, that they would observe installer picket lines. The Connecticut Union of Telephone Workers was even more adamant in opposing a sympathy walkout. Telephone workers in Nevada and Northern California promptly pledged their support to the installers. Beirne called NFTW executive board members to a meeting in Washington, and while they were en route he talked with Secretary of Labor Lewis B. Schwellenbach. At the urging of the Secretary, the ACEW and the company agreed to a late afternoon conference on Friday, January 11. In return for this and NFTW sanction of the installers' strike, Weaver agreed to postpone the planned picketing of Bell System exchanges. But Weaver failed to convince the ACEW executive committee, and pickets were posted at midnight. A confused picture was further complicated by Washington Traffic's "extended meeting," which effectively interrupted long-distance service and disrupted local calls as well. As Werkau later explained, "We sat there [in the NFTW Washington office] not knowing what the score was. About four A.M., Joe Beirne and myself drove to Laurel, Maryland, and got a call through to Jack Moran." He had set up temporary strike headquarters in Philadelphia. From Moran, Beirne and Werkau learned that Weaver had arranged a conference call with his ACEW board members and that they had thumbed down his recommendation postponing picketing of the exchanges. "They had got so far," Werkau said, "they had to go ahead and it could not be stopped. Mr. Weaver was outvoted and the National Federation was left holding the bag."

Understandably, that weekend meeting of the NFTW executive board was a tumultuous affair. Fitzsimmons and Weaver were, in Werkau's words, "both advised that it was the opinion of the executive board that their action was ill-advised and not in the best interests of the telephone workers, and that the board would recommend to the affiliates that it was not necessary under the rules of the game as written and interpreted that they support either of these striking unions." Fitzsimmons and Weaver were visibly upset. Paul Williams, ACEW secretary-treasurer and strike director, told Weaver he would not honor the order postponing the picketing. "I wouldn't even listen . . . I'd quit as secretary-treasurer if the picketing program was abandoned." Bell System companies went to court to secure injunctions against even peaceful picketing on the grounds that the strike was a secondary, not primary walkout. Injunctions were obtained in several cities in Kansas and Texas and state-wide in Georgia, Oklahoma. Long Line and local operators observed installer picket lines in New York; Washington; Chicago; Philadelphia; Pittsburgh; Cincinnati; Detroit; Newark, New Jersey; Columbus, Cleveland and Dayton, Ohio; Baltimore; Albany; Reading, Pa.; San Francisco and Los Angeles. Picketing was also successful in Maryland, Ohio and in the southwest. What the *New York Times* headlined as "Telephone Tie Up/Worst in History" was well underway before the weekend was over.

The NFTW was confronted with a runaway nationwide strike over a *local* dispute. It risked exhaustion over a grievance rooted in wartime anomalies, but with no immediate bearing on the post-war program hammered out in Milwaukee. Conceivably, Western Electric could settle with the ACEW after a weary strike, leaving the rest of the NFTW affiliates to grapple with Ma Bell, emptied of emotional and economic reserves. Recognizing, in Werkau's phrase, the fact that "the fat was in the fire," the NFTW executive board gave the ACEW until 1:00 P.M. on Sunday "to bring about a meeting of the minds with the company." When negotiations collapsed, the board met for five hours, and NFTW president Beirne emerged to inform the press that a strike of the entire membership would be called but the timing of the walkout had been left indefinite. The hesitency over timing reflected a two-fold bind: few of the affiliates had, as yet, delegated bargaining rights to the NFTW and thirty-day strike notices had not been filed as required by the wartime Smith-Connally Act which was still in effect. Acting on orders from Labor Secretary Schwellenbach, government officials began preparations for a presidential takeover of the Bell System. Beirne, meantime, conferred with NFTW attorney's emerging shortly after nine o'clock, Sunday evening, to announce that the strike call would be deferred for thirty days to comply with the law and that the ACEW was being asked to call off its walkout and turn the issues involved over to the NFTW for resolution.

"In order to avert a series of piecemeal strikes which would keep telephone service in a constant state of turmoil," Beirne informed the country in a nationwide radio broadcast, "the NFTW has requested all affiliates to file notice of intent to strike as required by law. We have requested unions on strike to defer their strikes and remove picket lines pending a strike on an industry-wide basis."

The ACEW promptly complied on the assurance that strike notices would be filed by affiliates and that a presidents' conference would be called. One was set for the week of February 17 in Memphis, Tennessee. WEEA's Fitzsimmons huffed his displeasure, "We carried on alone this far and will continue to do so," but he agreed that there would be no further picketing of Metropolitan New York exchanges by his group. Member unions were notified by the NFTW that their members were not obligated to respect picket lines if striking affiliates refused to comply with the instructions. To "defer their walkouts was, all in all, a remarkable exercise in discipline on the part of the loosely federated NFTW, and a unified course of action soon developed. Before the month of January was over, seven major affiliates designated the NFTW as their bargaining agent on the basis of the Milwaukee program."* (The remaining ten of seventeen unions holding to the Milwaukee line were to "coordinate" their bargaining with the NFTW effort on behalf of the seven.) At a January 24 policy meeting, it was decided that the "Federation of Long Lines Telephone Workers shall be used as the spearhead of this coordinated bargaining." The reason for this choice is simple: it would force Ma Bell directly into national bargaining. While the ACEW installers could, as could Long Lines, precipitate a national strike, they were not in a position to set a "pattern" for other telephone workers. Long Lines was at the heart of the System, reaching out through the country, and was an AT&T replica of the member companies with comparable jobs, wages and working conditions, while the installers were a single craft working nationwide for Western Electric, an AT&T subsidiary.

As Slim Werkau explained NFTW strike strategy to the press, a Long Lines strike would be using the wires of the telephone company itself as a picket line. "Suppose," said Werkau, "we station one picket in front of the AT&T Building in New York. The wires from the building radiate throughout the United States. That, so far as our federation members are concerned, constitutes a nationwide *bona fide* picket line and each one of us will respect it."

This, of course, depended on *all* the affiliates respecting the picket lines of striking telephone unions. And this is what Memphis was all about. Over 100 delegates from forty-two of the forty-nine affiliates were present on February 18 in Memphis and, unlike Milwaukee, they were empowered to act, though this did not make for *less* debate. Seventeen unions, representing about 150,000 of the Federation's 250,000 members, had filed strike notices and were asking for support from the others. To drive home the necessity for unified action and the need for discipline, the executive board proposed the censure of two of their members, Anne C. Benscoter, member at large, and George Lawson, Western Regional Member, for having "caused to be executed agreements with their respective companies in violation of the policy adopted by the executive board of the federation, without reference to the federation or affiliated organizations which might be seriously damaged thereby . . ." In debate, the proposed removal of the two board members was softened into an "investigation into the charges," and the amended resolution was passed by a small margin, 76,668 to 76,490. Still, a point had been made. "In a nice way," Beirne later said, "we cut

---

*The seven were: Cincinnati Federation of Telephone Workers; Federation of Long Lines Telephone Workers, Inc.; Illinois Telephone Traffic Union; Indiana Telephone Workers Union; Michigan Telephone Employees Federation, Inc.; Telephone Guild of Wisconsin, and the Washington Telephone Traffic Union.

them to ribbons for having agreed in Milwaukee and then [having] ignored what they had agreed to do."

For two days, the delegates debated various courses of action, thumbing down an immediate strike call as well as a proposed "concentrated" strike —at Kearny and in Michigan—with financial assistance coming from "all affiliates." In measured tones, D.L. McCowen, seconded by Bill Smallwood, proposed that the Memphis meeting authorize the NFTW Executive Board to "be empowered to call a nationwide telephone strike at such time as the executive board considers it proper . . ." The motion was passed 121,997 to 30,761 not voting. The delegates snake-danced around the hall and sang as NFTW president Beirne announced their decission to a waiting press outside. Their morale was given an additional boost by the affiliation of the New Jersey and Indiana traffic groups, headed by Mrs. Mary Hanscom and Mrs. Mae Mann.

After some hesitance—Beirne opposed setting a strike date; Moran favored it—the executive board called for a strike at 6:00 A.M., March 7, 1946. On Friday, February 22, Beirne announced that the seventeen unions in a position to conduct a legal strike "will leave work at the time directed" and that the remaining thirty-three affiliated unions would respect picket lines established by the seventeen. For a week and a half after the Memphis Presidents' Conference, events unfolded in slow-motion with AT&T meeting with Long Lines negotiators in New York City and member companies with the seventeen NFTW affiliates around the country. Ma Bell finally balked, holding fast to an offer of 13.8 cents-an-hour. As the strike deadline approached, negotiations flickered into life, intensifying into a concentrated movie-frame speed. "Using the knowledge we had of government here in Washington, and getting Schwellenbach right into the scene," Beirne later recalled, "we were not only able to get Craig of AT&T, who was a top man, vice-president of AT&T, down into Schwellenbach's office, but we were able with Schwellenbach to keep the pressure on."

NFTW clearly had the edge; Ma Bell was nervous, perhaps fearful of a presidential seizure. Nonetheless, AT&T did not acknowledge the national character of the bargaining until late in the last day before the strike was due to begin. With Labor Secretary Schwellenbach "standing by," AT&T vice president Cleo F. Craig entered the Long Lines negotiations at the eleventh hour. After a brief conference between Craig and Director of Conciliation Edgar L. Warren, NFTW president Beirne was called to the Department of Labor and his arrival placed the negotiations on a national basis. To make that certain, Beirne sent a telegram to all NFTW affiliates, warning, "Strike is inevitable." Testifying in 1950 before a Senate subcommittee, Beirne said, "There were conferences between Secretary Schwellenbach, Mr. Craig, and myself. We reached a deadlock." Craig later denied participating in the bargaining, as he told the Senate subcommittee, "It is my impression that it was just the final buttoning-up of the thing. They really were in agreement except that they hadn't agreed that they were in agreement." He also claimed that his staff canvassed the member companies the night of March 6 as to their willingness to bargain with their respective unions on the basis of a settlement in Long Lines. And, though "no company delegated any authority to me to bargain," they "did say that I could bind them; that they would make an offer to their union."

While federal conciliators moved between the parties, the NFTW held fast to its positions, as described by Beirne to the press: "What would avert the strike would be for the companies to consider all the disputes as one, and that any pattern developed be applied in all cases, subject only to local variation and with all so-called fish-hook clauses eliminated and no fringe issues included in the money amount of settlement." As the long hours of night unfolded, Long Lines bargainers, Moran, R.T. Creasey, A.S. Douglas, Dorothy Handy, Loreta E. Emnia and O.L. Adams, thrashed out details with company officials, J.E. Dingman, S.W. Landon and G.S. Dring, agreeing on an 18.2 percent wage offer, or an average hourly increase of 17.6 cents an hour. Copies of the agreement were given to Beirne, Craig and the Secretary of Labor. "We were queried," Beirne reported later, "as to whether or not what had occurred in Long Lines could serve as a pattern for the other sixteen unions and sixteen managements." Beirne and Craig agreed, initialing a famous "document" that settled the 1946 dispute.*

The strike was called off at 5:45 A.M., March 7, just thirty-five minutes before the strike was set to begin. Terms of the settlement established the following increase formula, taken from the *Telephone Worker* of March, 1946:

"For plant workers—$5 at starting rates, $8 at top rates.

"For traffic workers—$5 at starting rates, $7 at top rates.

"For clerical workers—$5 at starting rates, $7 at top rates.

"For janitors, house service and dining room workers, etc.—$5 across-the-board.

"For administrative workers—engineers, staff technicians, etc.—$8 across-the-board.

"For manufacturing workers—17.6 cents per hour, distributed in any way the union and company can agree to."

In Long Lines, for example, operators were to start at $27–$31 a week,

---

*In its entirety, the Beirne-Craig memorandum reads:
1. Settle Long Lines.
2. Use dollar pattern in Long-Lines settlement for occupational groups for application to associated companies. Determine cents per hour in Long Lines settlement for application to Western Electric. Fringe-issue settlement which is applicable only to Long-Lines to be excluded in above computation.
3. Craig assures union of this agreement.
4. Beirne and Moran assure Craig of said agreement and call off strike immediately.
The memorandum was initialed by Craig, Beirne and Peter J. Manno of the Department of Labor Conciliation Service.

governed by area differentials, with a top wage of $39 to $45 a week. Top plant men received $62 to $80 a week. In some instances, the union sacrificed maintenance-of-membership in return for a check-off of dues. The WEEA strike was settled the next day on basically the same terms. The rival CIO-UE withdrew its charges of company-domination the following month.

Operators were already walking off the job in Washington, Philadelphia, Cleveland, Detroit, Dallas and elsewhere when the word of the settlement was flashed from the nation's capital. A policeman informed a lone picket outside the Dallas exchange that the strike had been settled. "The radio said so." But the young man had been warned, "Don't go by the newspapers; don't go by the radio." So he continued pacing until Miss Nelle Wooding, head of the Dallas traffic group, arrived to confirm the calling off of the strike. Mrs. Mae Mann, head of Indiana Traffic, recalls, "Joe [Beirne] called me at about six thirty in the morning, and he said, 'The strike is off.' But in many places in the state of Indiana, we couldn't get to all of them . . . Indianapolis was gone; they were just out. South Bend was out. Evansville was out . . ." Mrs. Mann, however, had little trouble with her management, and soon telephones were working without interruption in the Hoosier state.

But in the southwest a hitch did develop when the Southwestern Bell management tried to act as if it were an independent entity. Craig got on the telephone to talk with George Gephart, vice president of personnel for Southwestern Bell, and John Crull, who was present at the Texas end, tells the story: "We were able to hear both sides of the conversation between Craig and the Southwestern company's vice president. The phone was that good, that sensitive. And Mr. Craig said, 'George, this is Cleo.' He said, 'What seems to be the matter down there?' and George said, 'Well, these folks down here are trying to talk us out of our shirt.' And Cleo said, 'Well, what have you offered them?' " Gephart detailed his offer. "And Craig said, 'Well, George, that's not the pattern! I have agreed with Joe Beirne that the Bell System would give the pattern.' " Gephart demurred. "And Cleo said, 'Well, now listen, George, understand now, we have agreed that there's not going to be a strike. We have agreed that these folks are entitled to this pattern. Now, you give them the pattern. And call me back as soon as you've settled.' " A chastised Gephart complied, and when the accounting group pushed for a particular provision, beyond the pattern, Gephart declared, "Well, you got everything out of us including the flagpole off the building. You might as well take that."

As Beirne would say again and again, the agreement with Craig was "*the first signed national agreement.*" Although Craig would repudiate the idea later, AT&T had engaged in national collective bargaining with the NFTW. Admittedly, it was not "by-the-books," as Beirne would make plain to the

Senate Subcommittee looking into labor-management relations in the telephone industry four years later. "If collective bargaining means that two people have to be certified, or two representatives have to come from organizations which are certified by the National Labor Relations Board as being the appropriate collective bargaining agents, then I would hasten to say that Mr. Craig had no standing as a bargaining agent, and neither did Mr. Beirne, because neither of us was from an organization that the NLRB had certified . . . But, if collective bargaining is not confounded by a lot of legalistic fandangles, we were bargaining, and we reached agreements, and a strike was settled." What clinched the matter was not only Craig's demonstrated power in getting the Bell System companies to fall in line on negotiations involving the seventeen standouts, but the private verbal agreement he made with Beirne that all previously signed contracts would be reopened and their terms brought into line with the basic Long Lines settlement.

As Beirne later exclaimed, "We had stuck together and we *did* move the giant. But then to put the frosting on the cake, we had more money put into the pockets of those who had signed off . . ."

It was a remarkable accomplishment.

VIII

One Strike . . . Two Rivals

The lift in telephone worker morale from the success of the 1946 Beirne-Craig agreement lasted on into 1947. It encouraged the NFTW leadership to proceed with their plans for revamping telephone unionism. It encouraged the rank-and-file to take on Ma Bell once again in a national struggle. But it could not be sustained, and the fragile, newly-established unity of the NFTW was soon shattered, in Hegel's phrase, "amid the pressure of great events." The turbulence within telephone unionism in the closing years of the 1940s, however, illustrates another adage of the great German philosopher, "Nothing great in the world has been achieved without passion."

The extension of the gains won for the seventeen NFTW affiliates under the Beirne-Craig agreement to the others, that signed off at lower rates earlier, strengthened the hand of the advocates of one national union. "Of course," Beirne once explained, "we capitalized on it, and it became one of the strong reasons for the lack of opposition in June, a couple of months later in 1946, when the convention acted with the *terminal* date on constitutional changes. For it was in June of 1946 that the positive decision was made to destroy the federation and to set up the Communications Workers of America." Bill Dunn acknowledges that there was some bitterness, "not bitterness to the extent of wanting to expel them or anything like that from NFTW. But there was bitterness that they had not stuck with us. However, also we recognized that by getting the company to go back and pick 'em up—leadership standpoint I'm talking about now—we could prove even to them that we had to have one union, which was the objective." Emboldened by their success in the 1946 negotiations, the NFTW officers, for the first time, actually moved to discipline affiliates. The Chicago Telephone Traffic Union and the Communications Workers Union of West Virginia were asked to withdraw from the federation for actions "deemed detrimental to the welfare of telephone workers" during the 1946 struggle. The traffic group had voted not to support the strike, and the West Virginians had instructed their members to "disregard" NFTW picket lines.

Fran Smith of Michigan, chairman of the NFTW constitutional committee set up at the Milwaukee meeting, argued the case for a national union. "Organic limitations," she wrote in the *Telephone Worker*, "have grown

110

increasingly important in recent years. The difficulty of mobilizing all NFTW affiliates in striving toward a national pattern, to strike together, and to settle together—these, plus the lack of constituted authority for the NFTW to protect the wishes of the majority against the recalcitrant minority—have demonstrated the need for a next step, a step toward a still higher level of national solidarity—one which local whims cannot break or destroy.

"Any possible doubt as to the need for a new structure was resolved by the recent wage crisis in which the $5 to $8-weekly increase pattern was developed for 350,000 telephone workers by the courage and militancy of 150,000 of them. Seventeen of the fifty-two NFTW affiliates took the bit in their teeth, assigned the necessary authority to the NFTW, and resolved to strike if necessary to win their demands.

"Some other affiliates, who had negotiated smaller settlements earlier, renegotiated their contracts to get the extra money won for them, despite their violation of the wage policy established democratically by majority rule.

"We are not condemning these affiliates for what they did. We do, however, point to the weakness of the present NFTW structure which made it possible for them to do it. Under the 'local autonomy' clause of the present constitution, affiliates may depart from established policy, no matter how adverse the effect may be on their own members, or on members of other affiliates."

The move toward one union gained momentum, from Milwaukee through Memphis and on to Galveston. It proceeded along two lines—reform and, ultimately, reorganization of telephone unionism and a quest for affiliation. Acting on instructions from the Milwaukee Presidents' Conference, NFTW president Beirne appointed a committee of four to explore the question of affiliation. Richard W. Long, president of the Federation of Telephone Clerks of Illinois, William A. Smallwood, president of the Southern Federation, Ray Waldkoetter, president of the Indiana Telephone Workers Union, and Miss Ruth Wiencek, NFTW education director, met with Frank Fenton, director of organization of the AFL, Allan S. Haywood, CIO director of organization, and John L. Lewis, then majestically alone. First impressions, we are assured by the psychologists, are important, so, in the light of later events, Miss Wiencek's impressions are of interest. "Our first impression of the AFL," she recalled, "was that it was a completely quiet building. It was almost like a mausoleum, sort of a chill. Somehow we felt that they didn't get the import of what we had to offer and why we were coming there." The CIO was different, Miss Wiencek added. "They knew we were coming. They made pains to see to it that the regional directors from the areas that we were from would be present also. We found them in the main to be young people, young men in their thirties. We found them vital and interesting. We were shown around the CIO headquarters, and it was quite different from the treatment that we got when we came to the AFL. We saw there was a bustle of activity, people writing for the *CIO News*. We met the directors of education and research . . . We were able to get pretty straight answers, too, about the differences between the international unions and the CIO itself . . . We were quite impressed."

The AFL and the CIO were asked to send representatives to the 1946 Memphis Presidents' Conference. James Preston, assistant to the IBEW president, explained the craft structure of the electricians' union to the delegates. George Googe, AFL southern director, explained that the IBEW held charter rights to the telephone industry and that, if the NFTW decided to affiliate, it would have to do so through the IBEW, possibly as a "council" or department within the union. Allan Haywood, speaking for the CIO, offered the NFTW full international status within the CIO. He stated his belief that any jurisdictional squabbles between the NFTW and the UE would be resolved. He counseled the delegates against dividing up, saying, "Probably the most effective way to increase bargaining strength would be through strengthening and solidifying your national union. Whether or not you affiliate with the CIO, you should do that." At the Galveston NFTW assembly, the affiliation committee reported its belief that affiliation was "advisable" in "the long term" and urged that any organization refusing to grant "international status" be rejected. After a lengthy debate, the delegates decided that "no presently apparent benefits" were to be gained through affiliation and so to remain independent. At issue was a question of priority, and the delegates were eager to establish a truly national organization first.

"We were up to our eyeballs in constitutional committee reports," Beirne once remarked, "we had one in every damn convention." When it appeared that the Galveston Assembly would bog down in a point-by-point discussion of a rough draft of yet another constitution, the delegates referred the question to a subcommittee headed by John Crull. Crull and the members of his committee—Maurice J. Hebner of Southern California commercial, Edwin R. Hackett of Chicago commercial, Elmer F. Reinker of the Ohio Federation, and attorneys Everett E. Cotter, Henry Mayer and Al Philip Kane—met with interested delegates all day Wednesday, June 4, and reported the following day to the convention as a whole. The Crull committee concluded that "it would be futile to attempt the formation of a national union on the base of the memberships of the unions affiliated with the National Federation of Telephone Workers unless the present organizations should indicate that, as a step towards the formation of a new union, they were willing to dissolve the National Federation of Telephone Workers." The committee submitted forty principles—affecting such questions as jurisdiction ("the entire communications field"), conventions ("composed of delegates of locals") and functions and duties of officers ("set forth with reasonable particularity") to serve as the basis for a new constitution. It was instructed to proceed with the drafting of a constitution for a new organization to be considered at a special assembly, to be called not later than December 31, 1946.

The Crull committee went to work with a will, and within a month produced a draft constitution. Essentially, the Crull draft modified the autonomy enjoyed by NFTW affiliates, making them divisions of the proposed new organization, the Communications Workers of America, with their subordinate units designated as locals. The divisions were to be clearly subordinate to the highest authority in the organization, the annual conventions, and between conventions, the executive board. The national organization was empowered to grant divisional charters, to appoint administrators over locals in cases of fraud and dishonesty, and to approve strikes and contracts. The assets of divisions and locals were to be considered "trust funds . . . to be held and administered by the division or local." Still, considerable power was to remain with the divisions and through the divisions in the local unions. The divisions set dues, although the convention was allowed to "establish minimum dues," and were authorized to bargain collectively, though this right was qualified by the right of the convention to "formulate national bargaining policies." Convention delegate strength was apportioned on the basis of one delegate to each 500 members, or major fraction thereof, by divisions, with each division retaining the right to allocate the vote—one for each paid-up member—among its delegation. The chairman of a delegation "may cast the votes assigned" as a bloc, with the reservation that any one delegate might call for a poll of the delegation.

The NFTW leaders clearly hoped to dissolve the federation at the Denver Assembly, held November 4 to 16, 1946, and adopt the new constitution. In August, a draft constitution was sent to member unions for review, suggestions and comments. NFTW president Beirne toured the country, urging the imperative need for "one national union" for successful bargaining in 1947. Drawing on the Milwaukee-to-Memphis experience, he told telephone-worker audiences, "Even that one little inkling of unity last March broke the $3 and $5 pattern the companies were trying to put across on telephone workers." In the call to the Denver Assembly, Beirne requested that the organizations come to Denver prepared to operate the second week under the new constitution. While some affiliates held referenda on acceptance of the proposed constitution, others did not. Several organizations, notably Kearny's WEEA, objected to the bloc-voting provisions in the new constitution while others expressed fears that their assets would be "seized" by the new national organization. On the first day a poll of the blizzard-bound convention showed that unions representing 3,658 members were authorized to immediately adopt the "one national union" constitution while unions representing 214,782 did not possess that authority. After ten days of debate, the delegates, by a vote of 148,017 to 33,894 approved the report of the constitution committee as amended. By a vote of 163,440 in favor, they decided to dissolve the NFTW, to order a referendam on affiliation to the proposed new national union, and to establish the Communications Workers of America when charters had been issued to divisions "having an aggregate membership of 115,000." By a unanimous vote, the delegates named Joseph Beirne temporary president, John J. Moran temporary vice-president and Carlton W. Werkau temporary secretary-treasurer. A new union being born, but, in truth, telephone workers entered the 1947 negotiations in a rather anomalous position, neither fish nor fowl, a NFTW-not-quite-CWA.

In public, Beirne put up a bold front; in private and behind the scenes, he was a worried man. The telephone workers were feisty enough but far from unanimous as to priorities. Richard W. Long and his Illinois Commercial group held that only pensions should be bargained on a national basis in 1947. Others agreed with an Ohio Federation spokesman, "We feel that only certain [items] should be bargained this year," namely wages and the check off of dues. The Denver Assembly established a bargaining policy committee composed of one representative from each of the forty-nine NFTW affiliates and instructed president Beirne, with executive board approval, to name a Coordinated Bargaining Committee to head actual negotiations. He appointed John L. Crull of Southwestern, Robert Creasey of Long Lines, Richard W. Long of Illinois Commercial, Robert G. Pollock of Ohio, Frances V. Smith of Michigan, Frank J. Fitzsimmons of Kearny, and S.R. Nestle of Upstate Telephone Workers Union (an independent). While the delegates accepted the union shop and check off, improved vacations and pensions as "objectives," they referred wages, differentials, progression schedules and several other matters to the executive board "to secure comments from the member unions" and "to establish objectives regarding them."

The executive board acted promptly, and on December 19, NFTW president Beirne announced a ten-item agenda for national bargaining. "We are starting early to give the industry plenty of time to reach a settlement," he declared. An eighteen-page draft of detailed contract clauses were sent to member unions for directions in filing their demands upon Bell System companies. In summary, the 1947 bargaining agenda was:

1. $12-weekly increase across the board required to offset increases in the cost of living.
2. Union shop and check off of dues.
3. Area differentials: wage rates should be determined on the basis of job content, not on the basis of artificial classifications of cities.
4. Length of schedules: the present eight-year period is too long and should

be replaced by a five-year schedule—no comparable crafts in other industries require such a long period to reach the maximum.

5. Town classifications: the spread between towns is left to local bargaining, but there should be not more than four classifications within an operating area.
6. Establishment of job descriptions for service assistants.
7. Jurisdiction over work: a clear statement of the telephone work for telephone workers principle.
8. Leaves of absence for union officers.
9. Improved vacations: provisions for vacations up to four weeks.
10. Pensions: minimum of $100 a month—no deduction of Old Age Security Insurance benefits from Bell pension—contract control over pension matters.

The member unions were instructed to proceed with their bargaining, to file strike notices and to hold strike votes so as to be ready for unified strike action by April 7.

"We were all pepped up and enthused about all the recent increases we'd been getting," Bill Dunn remembers. "We were very much elated with our success in the threatened strike in '46. And we were going to hang together this time!" Ma Bell mounted a counterattack. The Chesapeake and Potomac company charged that the union demands would cost one-half the company's present payroll; New York Bell saw "no justification for a wage increase at this time;" and Southern Bell made the same declaration, adding that it saw no need to completely revise work practices. In bargaining with Long Lines, AT&T grandly made one concession out of a list of fifty items under discussion. Bell System companies demanded the elimination of seniority and the exclusive right to promote and transfer. D.L. McCowen reported from St. Louis that negotiations were a farce. The company made no effort to answer union arguments, or even to dispute union figures, but spent most of the time trying to get union negotiators to acknowledge that they were not free to make a final settlement without approval of the NFTW bargaining policy committee. As the ides of March passed, Ma Bell's strategy became more and more explicit: The idea was to divide and conquer the NFTW to prevent the emergence of a strong national union of telephone workers. As the *Telephone Worker* reported in mid March, "AT&T seems more stubborn than ever in maintaining the fiction that the separate companies are individual entities in themselves, free to make their own decisions and free to enter any contract they wish." But the uniformity of Bell propaganda gave lie to its claim and pointed to a common strategy emanating from 195 Broadway in New York, AT&T's corporate headquarters. The Bell System companies were uniformly adamant. As NFTW president Beirne put it, "They choose to gamble with this so vitally needed service and seem almost to want to push us into a nation-wide telephone strike, a strike our whole program set up last November was intended to avoid."

Beirne tried to argue with his fellow officers that the reasonable proposition is when the boss wants *you* to strike, *don't!* NFTW members were balloting fifteen to one in favor of a walkout when the NFTW policy committee met in Washington on March 24. D.L. McCowen catches the mood in his recollections ". . . I won't speak for anybody but myself, but I'm satisfied most of the people in the union felt the same way and that was the company couldn't stand a strike. I didn't think it would last over three days, and I thought we'd get what we wanted within reason." Beirne prepared his argument carefully. It was "the first speech I had written to anybody in the union," he remembered later. Beirne urged that "we should not strike; that we were not structured to strike; that we should hold off any notion of a strike until we got our structure that would cause us to stay together, that would not permit running off the reservation . . . We are not equipped financially, and we are not equipped organizationally, to maintain a unified strike. And if we just follow what we said in December, the other side'll clobber us, and we'll begin to fall apart."

Beirne's sharply reasoned, impassioned appeal fell on deafened ears. "I think I impressed them for about a half a day," Beirne ruefully recalled. And so when it came to a vote, just one other fellow supported me, a guy from Indiana." After a heated discussion and amid a growing enthusiasm for a walkout, Robert Pollock of the Ohio Federation made the motion to strike, failing agreement with Ma Bell on April 7. Beirne was instructed to contact officials of AT&T to "invite them to form an industrial committee for the purpose of bargaining with the National Coordinated Bargaining Committee" on the ten-point program. AT&T's Craig replied the following day, "As you know, the labor agreements with the unions affiliated with the NFTW are with the operating telephone companies and all bargaining matters are handled by each operating company with its union." In well-orchestrated unison, six operating companies offered to arbitrate wages *locally* with prominent *local* citizens deciding whether or not the company was paying "comparable wages" in each locality. And this theme, assiduously promulgated by AT&T, resonated through the media across the nation. "The place to settle the demands is locally," AT&T publicity insisted. "The contracts are between local unions and companies. Each company has bargained cooperatively and continuously. Each has offered to renew its contracts. Some have offered local arbitration. Each company pays adequate and just wages within the community—this is the right policy and a local issue, in the same way telephone rates are established to meet local conditions. There is no excuse for a telephone strike."

Some form of system-wide arbitration may have been acceptable to the union, but Ma Bell remained adamantly opposed to any national resolution of the dispute. Knowing full well the response, AT&T vice president Craig kept insisting on local negotiations, local arbitration limited to wages. "It covers only wages," Beirne explained to newsmen, "One of ten demands. Settlement of wages wouldn't stop a strike. Local arbitration would cause a crazy-quilt pattern, meaning more inequalities and inequities between areas." The company succeeded in stalling all along the line up and to the end of March. The NFTW policy committee named three of its number— Beirne, J.J. Moran and John Crull—to a special subcommittee to "explore all avenues" towards a settlement. Under government pressure, AT&T agreed to move Long Lines talks to Washington, and a few days later, Southwestern company and union negotiators were asked to conduct meetings in the nation's capital. Southwestern company officials, at first, refused the invitation but quickly reversed themselves after a call from Craig. U.S. Attorney General Tom Clark ruled that the Federal Government could seize the telephone industry in the event of a strike. Congressman Fred A. Hartley, Republican of New Jersey and chairman of the House Labor Committee, introduced a bill enabling the Attorney General to obtain a court injunction to restrain NFTW and its affiliates from calling a strike. John Gibson, assistant secretary of labor, and Edgar Warren, director of the Labor Department's Conciliation Service, worked around the clock in an effort to bring the parties together. But they could not get AT&T or any of the Bell companies, to even make an offer, any offer. As Gibson told the NFTW policy committee on the eve of the strike, "Since there are no wage offers, we had hoped we might work toward arbitration of some sort or other." But it was "no go" from Ma Bell, and at 3:45 A.M. on Monday, April 7, Labor Secretary Schwellenbach called NFTW president Joe Beirne to request a chance to talk to the NFTW policy committee. An hour before the strike was due to begin, the Secretary appeared in the Department of Labor auditorium where the policy committee assembled to plead for a postponement of twenty-four or forty-eight hours. His plea was entered without an offer from the Bell System, or any member company, and without any concrete proposals of any kind. It was heard in a stony silence.

As clocks ticked off six A.M., east to west, telephone workers began walking off the job, 325,000 strong. Joe Deardorff of Idaho and LaRoy H. Purdy were attempting to bargain, locally, for the Mountain States. "We bargained all night," Purdy has recalled, "and I frankly didn't know whether we'd have a picket line that morning or not. I went down to the door, and the damn building was completely surrounded by women. A little gal came up to me and said, 'Mr. Purdy, do we strike?' And I said, 'Yes.' She turned to the kids and said, 'Here we go.' And away they went . . . not only in front of the building but around the entire block." Richard Hackler recalls hitching into town to picket the San Francisco Chinatown telephone exchange. Ben Porch, a Birmingham lineman, quit night school, "because I could not get out of my picket line responsibilities and go to school too."

Mrs. Madge Giles remembers the round-the-clock picket lines and the District of Columbia police being fed by the company. "They'd go in the operating building, and the company was feeding them their lunch and dinners and breakfasts, what have you . . . I think the company had them right in the palm of their hand." George Gill recalls the white-capped seamen, members of the Seafarers' International Union, joining the telephone operators on the Mobile picket line. "They went because they liked to be with the girls. And it would scare the company; keep the scabs off for a day or two." Mrs. Berthalot, Michigan traffic strike director, went to Midland, Michigan, "where all the mine-workers were, and I really had to talk fast to keep them from blowing in the door of the telephone building. They wanted to help us."

As picket signs across the nation proclaimed, "The Voice With A Smile Will Be Gone For A While." Cincinnati long-distance operators walked out, leaving a call to Basle, Switzerland, plugged into the board. In New York City, operators showed up on the Monday morning picket line in their Easter finery. Mrs. Norma Naughton informed a *New Yorker* "Talk of the Town" reporter, "The girls have agreed to do two hours of picketing apiece a day. They're all being terribly goodnatured about this." And so they were —at first. With a fair number nibbling Good Humors, others chewing gum, and two singing "Let Me Call You Sweetheart," it was, according to the *New Yorker*'s man on the spot, a perky picket line. "We saw about 1,000 strikers, of whom 700 were women, and although there is no denying that there were some middle-aged and some rather plain women, they made up the fetchingest bevy of pickets that ever tripped over a subway grating . . . Skirts far outnumbered slacks, and many of the pickets were traipsing along on spiky heels. Some were wearing fur coats, others were coatless. The majority were hatless, but sprinkled among the group were just the right number of saucy Easter bonnets."

Joe Beirne joined a Washington, D.C., picket line, and the NFTW Policy Committee announced its intention to stay in session until Ma Bell knuckled under. Dial telephones continued to work, as did telephones in New England, where most of the employees were not affiliated with the striking NFTW, excepting Long Lines. Virginia, which required five weeks of conferences before striking a public utility, and Indiana, which had a compulsory arbitration law, had service as usual. But long-distance service was down eighty percent all over the country, and rural and suburban users of manual telephones were cut-off. Newspapers resorted to carrier pigeons; bookmakers used runners; businessmen relied on telegrams, and disaster control authorities lined up amateur radio "hams" for possible emergencies. For a time, however, authorized "emergency" calls were allowed on a rather generous interpretation of the word. An eight-year-old boy in Wisconsin called a local newspaper to report, "I saw four robins today;" a

Toledo farmer reported a dead cow, and a White Plains couple called to find a marrying justice of the peace. Within a fortnight, however, the biggest walkout in the history of American women—they comprised 230,000 of the 345,000 strikers—began to drag, grow bitter.

While economic issues were important, it quickly became apparent that the crux of the dispute was recognition. Ma Bell knew that a national union was in the making as well as a probable affiliation with one or the other of the Houses of Labor and she wanted no part of it. She had organized company unions to forestall unionization by the AFL, and she encouraged the company unions to go independent, after the Wagner Labor Act forced the issue, to forestall possible organization by the surgent CIO. Now that her "unions" were truly independent, Ma Bell was going to do her best to break them up. Company officials felt that NFTW was "too big for its britches," and the forceful action was in order to "prevent another John L. Lewis" in the telephone industry. At a New York City meeting in December 1946, company officials favored "holding out until Christmas" if the NFTW members went out on strike in 1947. Not once in the course of the conflict did AT&T retreat from its position that settlements would have to be made with the individual companies, a wedge-driving tactic that could set telephone union against telephone union and restore Ma Bell's primacy.

To counter AT&T's pressures, the NFTW had an economic case. The Bell System, for example, had been a pioneer in the pension field, but this was no longer so. In 1947, telephone-worker pensions averaged $50 a month, less Social Security payments. A survey of 188 industrial pension funds made by the Bankers' Trust Company of New York, a Bell Fund Trustee, incidentally, showed that eighty percent of the companies made no deduction from their pension payments for Social Security primary benefits. And seventy percent of the plans surveyed provided employees with a higher percentage of their base pay than did the Bell System. But NFTW overplayed its hand. While the Bell pension plan was clearly inadequate, the NFTW demand for a $100-a-month minimum, by the standards of the day, was much too high, too unrealistic. Ma Bell, who always knew best, simply ignored the union's plea for improvements.

The NFTW, however, had good argument for a wage increase. The BLS cost-of-living index had bounced upward from 133.3 on June 15, 1946, to 156.3 on March 15, 1947, by almost seventeen percent. Before the war, the telephone workers average weekly earnings had compared favorably with that of other workers. But by March, 1947, that comparable average had slipped—$42.51 as compared with a weekly average of $50.30 for durable goods industries, $44.89 for non-durable goods industries, $54.43 for electric light and power utilities, $50.91 for telegraph workers, and $50.80 for wholesale trade employees. A top plant craftsman earned $70 to $80 a week; operators' scales ranged from $21 to $31 at start, to $31 to $45 at the top after an eight year progression. American Newspaper Guild contracts provided for a three-year rise to the top for the same operator's skill employed in newspaper offices. NFTW's demand for a $12-a-week boost, however, bucked not only Ma Bell's obduracy but also what *Business Week,* on March 29, 1947, termed "the biggest fact on the labor front," the 11.5 cent hourly settlement negotiated in the rubber industry. Unions might argue that they could not "settle for less than rubber," and managements, that they could "not afford more," but as the magazine said of this "yardstick for 1947," "the magnitude of the second postwar round of pay boosts is becoming discernible."

AT&T possessed the good grace not to claim "inability to pay." It could scarcely do so in the light of after tax net profits of $215 million in 1946. But it could hew to the corporate line, refusing to make any money offers until other major industry settlements were in. An offer of sorts was proferred to Long Lines workers, including arbitration of wages, but the NFTW rejected the possible settlement because "this proposal . . . contained *local* arbitration [which] was not acceptable." (My italics.) The weakness of the NFTW position surfaced before the steel settlement when the policy committee, on April 17, slashed its $12-a-week wage demand to $6, with national arbitration to determine further wage increases and/or to resolve the other issues.

The public remained remarkably sympathetic to the strikers. A Gallup poll in early May showed that of those who had an opinion, twice as many sympathized with the strikers as with the company. "They need more money! The telephone company makes good profits and can pay better wages." Nonetheless, the strikers were running up against some formidable obstacles. Within hours after determined operators snapped shut their handbags and walked out, New Jersey Governor Alfred H. Driscoll seized Bell properties. When the strikers refused to return to work for the state, Governor Driscoll pushed through the state legislature an anti-strike bill inflicting $10,000 daily fines against the striking unions and $250 to $500 penalties against individual strikers. The law also provided for compulsory arbitration. The governor's special counsel, Russell E. Watson, was a director of Jersey Bell, and the law was passed without public hearings. The New Jersey strikers changed their high heels for sturdier oxfords and settled down for a long siege. Hefty policemen charged in, and when the dust settled, the state emerged with Mrs. Mary Hanscom, five-feet three in her stockinged feet, as head of the New Jersey traffic NFTW affiliate, Mrs. Virginia Wigglesworth, a tall ethereal blond, and Miss Elizabeth Ryan, a nervous bride-to-be, in its awesome clutches. The Garden State's 12,000 operators dared the state to throw them all in jail; 20,000 Western Electric strikers chimed in, and a million members of the state AFL and CIO threatened a one-day sympathy strike. NFTW attorneys managed to secure a restraining order against the jailing of the three leaders of the traffic union. Later, the law was amended to eliminate jail sentences for strikers and to reduce the fines. Bell management managed to secure a state-wide injunction against all picketing in Florida. Another injunction was issued in Kentucky and strikers were cited for contempt in Louisville. George M. Miller, Kentucky strike director, was jailed for leading a mass picket line in defiance of the injunction. Other injunctions were issued in Belleville and East St. Louis in neighboring Illinois.

"The company was always starting back-to-work movements, or at least trying to." Bill Webb, then a NFTW steward and PBX man in Memphis, recalls. "The girls were very, very militant; it was their first time you might say to really feel free." One morning the union mounted a picket line with forty operators. "The company manager there was an old fellow named Frank Flournoy, and he's the old cigar-smoking company type that looked down his nose at anybody that worked for the company that wasn't on the management level, you know. And he called some people on the Crump machine, which was running the city, and the police showed up and ordered our pickets down, and so we had quite an argument about it. The [first] two cops . . . reached back to get their clubs and were going to get out and break up the picket line when we refused to take it down, so we didn't let them out of their car." There were forty to fifty lineman also present who, according to Webb, "did not want to see these girls molested in any way, and there was going to be trouble if they got out." Finally, the police called up three paddy wagons . . . arrested forty operators and Webb, John Ross and Clay Jones. "I told him [the police inspector] that if he would just count heads, we would all walk down and meet him down there [at the police station]." He insisted on hauling off people in paddy wagons; the women refused, and so the police inspector called ten squad cars and marched the lot to the station. "All the young cops came down to 'yak' with the girls," Webb says. Meanwhile, forty more women had taken over the picketing. Finally, Webb persuaded the police to let him and the others go by threatening to file false arrest charges. The company, Webb adds, "went wild with injunctions" after that.

On April 20, the United Steel Workers settled its dispute with the steel companies for a 15-cent an hour increase. (Four days later, the United Auto Workers and General Motors negotiated an agreement with an 11.5 cent-an-hour in a direct wage increase and 3.5 cents in six paid holidays.) As NFTW president Beirne reminded reporters, AT&T had said that they would pony up when a pattern emerged. "The pattern has now taken shape," said Beirne. "The steel settlement has removed the last argument the company might have in denying us an increase." AT&T still refused to make an offer, despite pleas from the U.S. Conciliation Service. Western Electric refused to come to Washington for negotiations unless assured that its demand for union action without Policy Committee consent would be considered. New Jersey and Northwestern Bell tantalized union negotiators, indicating that they might make an offer if guaranteed that whatever was agreed to would not need approval of the NFTW Policy Committee. As a member of the Southwestern union bargaining team later said, "We spent lots of hours in the Labor building [in Washington, D.C.], but all we did was talk and play cards, with an occasional interruption whenever the Conciliator would drop in." And Beirne acidly commented, "AT&T hasn't any argument left, unless it has set out to break the union."

Rancor soured the unfolding spring. Two strikers were injured and twenty-two arrested after a picket line brouhaha with the police in Detroit. Police dispersed a mass demonstration in San Francisco. Someone cut a telephone cable in lower Manhattan, and 250 telephone circuits were slashed near Fort Worth, Texas. Telephone officials charged that lines had been cut in Tennessee, Mississippi, Kentucky, California, South Carolina, Michigan, Ohio and in Wisconsin. In Utah, a fire department turned high pressure hoses on strikers; a scab escorting his wife through a Louisiana picket line shot a striker, though not fatally. A message wrapped around a rock and hurled through the second-story window of the Weirton, West Virginia, exchange, narrowly missing an on-duty scab, read, "If you work tomorrow, you'll regret it." And Alabama strike director, George Gill tells a story ("I don't know whether it's true") that illustrates the mood of the lengthening strike. A deputy sheriff, who had been a miner, approached the lone NFTW picket marching to-and-fro in front of the local exchange in a small Alabama town, and asked, "Is there somebody in there working?" The picket gloomily acknowledged that there was. "Well," says the deputy, "I'll tell you what you do now. You go around back, and you take that sign off that stick, and you stand at the window. I'm going in and run that bitch out. And you beat her in the damn head when she comes out the back door."

NFTW strikers felt the strain. "In the City of Chicago in '47 we had 1,001 picket line arrests," June McDonald recalls. "One was a man; the rest were women. You get a bunch of women mad, baby, and you've got a problem. Women are emotional. They hit first and think later. And those girls were mad . . . at that time there were nine police stations in the city of Chicago. And they would pick our kids up. They wouldn't book them, you know. We were smart enough to find out where they were to spring them, you know. They wouldn't book them. They would take them to one police station and out the back door to another one and run us all over the city of Chicago . . . the plant was working. Accounting was out a few days. Commercial was working. It was the gals that carried the strike, at least where I was. They're good strikers and they hung on to the last."

Miss Muriel Edwards, later a District 5 CWA representative, remembers the strike as "traumatic." She was the steward of an office of about 630 people. "Things went generally well for two or three weeks. After that it began to fall apart; people returning to work, and they had a real back-to-work movement in this particular office. And we really had some problems. We picketed scabs' houses. In every town we picked one scab and picketed their homes to try to bring pressure upon the individual to see what was right, to stay out with the group to make the gains we needed to make at the bargaining table." And Madge Giles, president of the Washington, D.C., traffic local, says, "The traffic group was the last to return to work in Washington . . . No, we didn't shut the phone company down completely, no, because they had a lot of their management people that were working switchboards, and then, at that time, we had some fellow workers from the plant department that finished their tour and went into the traffic operators' switchboard and worked. This was one of the things that caused the trouble between the traffic group and the plant group. We thought this was wrong. We saw no reason why, if they had to be strike-breakers, why they couldn't go home at the end of their tour and leave the traffic operating board alone . . . We were quite a few years overcoming that feeling, but we have . . ."

Money was running low; the NFTW had no strike fund. "When the people were really hurting," Ben Blankenship, who directed the strike in Mobile, Alabama, recalls, "I would pick the prettiest little girls, you know, that we had and they had little coffee cans and had signs painted on 'em that said, 'I'm the girl with the smile that's gone for a while.' And they went down and stood around the shipyards. And when these guys got paid and came out the gates, why they dropped money into those cans. And this kept us going." The labor movement demonstrated its solidarity generously. Contributions ranged from the $25 given by the United Waste Paper Workers and the United Cigar Workers, both CIO, to $20,000 from the International Ladies' Garment Workers' Union, AFL; with inbetween contributions of $10,000 each from the United Steel Workers of America, CIO; the Teamsters, AFL, and the CIO itself; $5,000 from the Amalgamated Clothing Workers, CIO, the musicians, AFL, machinists (then independent), the United Automobile Workers, CIO, and the United Mine Workers of America, then back in the AFL, loaned the NFTW $100,000. Altogether, strike contributions to the NFTW came to more than $128,000, not a small sum in those distant days.

Heartened, NFTW president Beirne appealed to President Truman for government pressure to make the companies grant increases in line with those secured in other major industries without strikes. Edgar Warren, head of the U.S. Conciliation Service, had to acknowledge that the telephone companies were not about to budge. "They tell us that the wage increases recently given do not affect them right now. They say these other increases have not yet affected the market price for labor and they cannot raise wages for the time being." Initially, the strike had crippled telephone service, especially over long distances and where manual telephones were still in use. Slowly, however, the companies gained ground, by the fourth week AT&T claimed that the companies were handling four-fifths of the normal number of local calls and that Long Lines service was up to fifty percent. Strikers were reminded that the New England Telephone Company had broken a strike in 1921 by threatening to wipe out pension benefits. The Bell pension plan canceled accumulated seniority whenever an employee was absent from work for more than thirty days for any reason other than "illness, leave of absence or temporary layoffs." And as the thirty-day deadline approached, Ma Bell began to dangle cash money offers before strike-weary telephone workers.

In the belief that unity of purpose outweighed even an outright defeat, and sensing an imminent collapse of the tenuous unity of the telephone unions, Beirne proposed to the Policy Committee that they call off the strike and continue negotiations on a national basis. He hoped that such a move, backed by wide-spread publicity, would bring public pressure to bear on AT&T. The Policy Committee, however, turned the proposal down. Strikers straggled back to work; only a handful—a dozen in Kosciusko, Mississippi, twenty in Oak Park, Illinois, 256 in Chicago, and 500 in Atlanta—but the company made much of their number. Northwestern Bell offered an increase of $2.50 a week to strikers in five Midwestern states. It was rejected, but an offer of $3 and $4 to Philadelphian telephone workers was accepted on May 1, 1947. Representatives of four non-NFTW New York telephone unions accepted a $4-a-week deal. Members of two of the unions, however, overruled their officers, voting to remain on strike. On May 4, two NFTW affiliates, the Illinois clerks and commercial groups, the first to do so, defied the NFTW Policy Committee and accepted the $4 offer from Illinois Bell. The Illinois operators, however, remained firm. But by Tuesday, May 6, 1947, the NFTW Policy Committee had to recognize the inevitable. The Conciliation Service drew up a statement exempting the individual NFTW unions from control of the Policy Committee, and, after a vigorous debate, the committee decided that it would make no objections to member-unions signing such a document. In a ten-hour session, the committee reviewed all the bargaining information to hand as well as the overall strike situation. It was decided that committee members, "fresh from Washington, where they have been in close contact with the entire national picture," could best help break the log-jam of negotiations by going home. The committee disbanded at 9 P.M., and, later that night, conciliators announced in Long Lines negotiations that "the parties are less than two cents an hour apart." On May 8, Long Lines settled at $4.40 more a week —$3.72 for basic wages, plus sixty-eight cents for fringe issues. This proved to be the national average, with actual amounts varying from $2 to $5 a week.

The 1947 strike, as the *Telephone Worker* remarked in June, had certain unique features. "The AT&T is the largest corporation ever to have been struck. The strike extended over more territory and into more communities than any previous strike in the history of the nation. Thousands of the smaller communities had their first experience with a strike through the telephone walkout. Very few strikes have involved so many workers." And, the editor might have added, very few unions have struck with the structural handicaps of the NFTW. As Beirne said immediately after the strike, "we were trying to make a federation of unions do the kind of job which can be done only by one union in the telephone industry. The later states of the strike demonstrated that the separate organizations composing the national federation would act separately and individually—based on their own autonomy—when the going got rough."

Though the strikers held together remarkably well, structural autonomy did undercut the final settlement. As an acute analyst of the 1947 strike, Alvin Loren Park pointed out, "it was the feeling of the Conciliation Service that AT&T would accept as the final cash settlement approximately the pattern that had developed in manufacturing industries. This amounted to 11.5 to 12.5 cents per hour ($4.60 to $5 per week) with 2.5 to 3.5 cents per hour extra for fringe issues. *AT&T would not accept these figures, however. It chose instead to exploit the situation to its fullest extent,* and through the subsidiary companies, it proceeded to work out, with relatively weak local unions, settlements that were lower than the manufacturing pattern." (My italics.) As contracts were negotiated company by company, the other national issues also fared ill. Regional and local differentials were not considered, nor were pensions, while the demand for a union shop was rejected out of hand. After analyzing the wage settlements, which ranged from a low of $2 a week to a high of $5 a week, Park concluded that "these settlements were somewhat below the established national pattern of approximately fifteen cents per hour, including 'fringe issues,' or $6 per week, leaving the telephone workers in a worse comparative position than they were before the strike."

Still, there was no indication that the Bell System, in all its variety, intended to grant even the smallest of wage increases in 1947, certainly not without a strike. So NFTW president Beirne was undoubtedly correct when he remarked in a post-strike statement to telephone workers; "It was a very good thing that the Policy Committee was in session shortly before the strike began and during the major part of the strike because it prevented the company from succeeding in destroying the union during the early days of the strike . . . The united front and singleness of purpose of the Policy Committee during the time of its existence served as an influence in breaking what would have been a $2 pattern." Telephone workers, too, learned something from their strike. As Beirne pointed out, "We have demonstrated to each other that we can and will act as unionists. The agreements finally reached demonstrated conclusively that the Bell System runs the telephone industry as a single employer and not on an individual company basis." This being so, Beirne concluded, "being in one union will permit us to go forward with greater knowledge, greater experience and a willingness to make our ranks stronger."

Others, however, drew a different set of lessons from the strike. Jack Moran, in declaring his intention to lead the Long Lines group into the CIO, declared, "We believe our recent experience proves that telephone operators cannot exist and be isolated from organized labor." The Connecticut Union of Telephone Workers had already pulled the other way, departing from the NFTW in March, 1946, for fear of losing its autonomy. And while the organization of the new "one national union," the Communications Workers of America, in effect, had been deferred during the strike; members of the Pennsylvania Federation of Telephone Workers and the Maryland Telephone Traffic Union had voted, pre-strike in referenda, for withdrawal from the NFTW and against affiliation with the CWA. Though serious enough, these disaffections posed no real threat to the founding of a truly national union within the communications industry. The specter of a CIO drive, however, did.

Many believed that the fragile unity of the telephone workers had been shattered irrevocably by the 1947 strike, and both the AFL and the CIO expected to pick up the pieces. But the AFL was bound by its grant to jurisdiction over telephone work to the International Brotherhood of Electrical Workers and could not, in good conscience, charter a new international union in the field. The IBEW was willing to take in the telephone unions as a major branch, roughly the equivalent of a division or department. In a letter to Beirne, IBEW president D.W. Tracy argued the Brotherhood's case. "We have both craft and industrial [forms of organization] and get the benefit of both . . . Each branch has representatives and organizers who know the problems of their particular branch. They devote their full time to the problems of their branch. In this way we get the same result as if each branch were a separate national union—and each branch has the added strength of the whole—the support and the resources of the whole. And all this grew from long and bitter experience. We suggest that you and your associates consider what this form, this arrangement, would have meant to the telephone employees throughout the country in their recent strike. Our experience has proved that this form and arrangement would bring more support and strength to telephone employees than a new national union operating separately—without our full resources to draw upon." Though the argument was appealing, it was rejected. The future of telephone unionism lay along another path.

But *which* path to take was not entirely clear in the spring of 1947. While a majority of NFTW affiliates were preparing to take the road to Miami and to inject reorganization into the emergent Communications Workers of America, a significant minority heeded the call of CIO president Philip Murray to join the CIO's Telephone Workers' Organizing Committee (TWOC). "The CIO," Moran told the press on June 1, "has offered us an opportunity to establish an international union of, by and for telephone workers which will establish its own policy, elect its own officers, conforming, of course, to the broad general policy of the CIO in which we shall share a voice." Forty three officials and/or members of nineteen telephone unions with a combined membership of 200,000 met in Atlantic City over the May 31-June 2 weekend to form the CIO-TWOC. But not all of the delegates were committed to the new venture in telephone unionism. Bill Smallwood came up from Atlanta, for example, but he had been instructed by his executive board *not* to make a committment to the CIO. Glenn Watts was on hand from Washington, D.C., as an observer. TWOC chairman Allan Haywood estimated that about 80,000 would be solidly in the CIO camp. Moran of Long Lines was named vice chairman and a member of the CIO executive board. Ernest Weaver, whose ACEW was still smarting from its 1946 strike recall, won his group over to TWOC, becoming a vice chairman. Ted Silvey of the CIO served as secretary-treasurer and was later replaced by Richard Long of the Illinois Federation of Telephone Clerks. Long joined the TWOC largely because he felt that the new CWA was *too strong* a national organization.

TWOC was a temporary organization patterned after similar committees successful in steel, textiles, paper and packing houses, among other industries. Margaret Weiss of Maryland Traffic, Norma F. Naughton of Long Lines, James Massey and Norman Wolfe of ACEW, and Marie DeMartini, whose Northern California Traffic group had moved from the NFTW to the American Communications Association, CIO and into TWOC, all served at one time or another on the TWOC executive board. Fitzsimmons and the WEEA were present at TWOC's first meeting but never became a part of the organization. At first the WEEA executive board recommended affiliation, then rescinded its action, ultimately joining the IBEW. Some of the waffling that took place as TWOC took shape reflected uncertainties in overall CIO strategies. Haywood had been cultivating NFTW leaders for years now and actively encouraged the development of one national union within the communications field. Moran and Weaver, however, forced his hand by leaving the NFTW on the eve of its transformation into the CWA. And, too, Haywood may have been disappointed by the outcome of the 1947 telephone strike. When it began, there was the possibility that it might have set a pattern for other industries as well. But it did not, thankfully so in the view of CIO spokesmen. As a CIO statement phrased it, "Telephone workers can be justly proud of their militancy and vigor in their April-May 1947 strike. But if the settlement of that strike had become the 1947 wage pattern, applicable to all other industries, members of unions in other industries would have suffered. Happily, the CIO unions set 1947 wage patterns subsequent to the conclusion of the telephone strike. The unhappy part is that telephone workers were not included." Therefore, the statement concluded, "The CIO seeks affiliation of telephone workers in order to strengthen the telephone workers, and to strengthen the existing CIO unions."

En route to Miami and the birth of the CWA, Joseph Beirne had this to say: "The CIO issues press statements. We have the members. We have issued charters to thirty-one groups of phone workers representing 177,399 workers. It is our firm belief that even those officers of phone unions who have been dickering with the CIO will eventually go along with CWA and will come back to the union representing most phone workers."

But two years were to pass before Beirne's hopes materialized. Meanwhile, one strike had created two rivals for the affections of the country's communications workers.

IX

CWA All the Way

For the 200 delegates assembled in the ballroom of the Macfadden Deau-ville Hotel at Miami Beach, Florida, the week June 9-June 12, 1947, was a trying time. The summer soldiers had decamped and the sunshine patriots were skittery. Even those remaining steadfast were hesitant and lacked drive. The momentum created by referenda majorities of twelve to one favoring the creation of the Communications Workers of America had been dissipated by post-strike blues and uncertainties. As the June issue of the *Telephone Worker* woefully reported, "Because of the recent strike, it is not expected that CWA divisions will be in a financial position to bring to the convention the maximum number of delegates to which they are entitled." While the thirty-two CWA divisions represented at the convention claimed an aggregate membership of 161,699 with a total of 212,000 workers under contract, actual membership may have been somewhat less. The strike "left a lot of marks inside the union," Glenn Watts once observed, "I recall that in my own group [Washington, D.C., plant and commercial], which had been virtually 100 percent organized, or at least everybody belonged to the old NFTW, after the strike in '47, it literally fell apart. We didn't have fifty percent of the people . . ." There was little of that joy that usually attends a new venture; the founding convention of the CWA was a strained affair. As Joseph Beirne acknowledged many years later, that week in Miami "was one of the three of four weeks that I wouldn't want to live over."

In Beirne's words, the Miami meeting "could have been a *wake* if we had permitted it." Characteristically, Beirne plunged into the job at hand, fash-ioning one union out of a federation of unions, with an iron determination and a wry humor. "If we called the roll of those who are not here at this initial convention but who worked in the past for unity," he told the delegates in his opening address, "we would have an assortment of names and personalities that would be quite startling. Some are of happy memory while others are now engaged in other work." He was caustic about rumors then circulating that he had made "a deal" with the AFL or the CIO or John L. Lewis, who had cut himself and his Mine Workers adrift for the last time from the AFL. After analyzing the groups contending for the loyalties of the country's telephone workers, Beirne acknowledged that "the

CWA has a good sized job cut out for it. It—of all the unions presently existing or to be born—must carry on its destiny—to unite all the telephone workers first and then move on in other branches of the communication field.

"All of us," he warned, "must take a new view of our role in the CWA. No longer can we hope to act as 'autonomous' groups in scattered parts of the country. No longer should we think in terms of preference or precedence being given to a local situation if a bigger problem exists nationally. No longer should a division president permit his actions, aims or ideals be bound by a first-last-and-always view of his local problems.

"We must embrace the 'all for one and one for all' philosophy of the single CWA union.

"Our members as well as ourselves must think, talk and act in only one name, the CWA."

With a certain temerity, given the number of rivals about to take the field against the new-born CWA, Beirne proposed a 100 percent dues increase, from twenty-five cents a month per capita to fifty cents a month. With prescience, Beirne predicted the ultimate merger of the AFL and the CIO, citing the anti-labor Taft-Hartley Act recently passed by Congress over President Truman's veto as a major cause of labor unity, and requested a mandate to work for "a united labor organization" with eventual CWA affiliation firmly kept in mind. Finally, Beirne grappled directly with the problem of morale occasioned by the 1947 strike. "Everyone," Beirne admonished the assembled delegates, "can put it in his and her book for the future that strikes are never lost. You can also put it in your book that every organization coming out of a strike received certain scars which are not hard to diagnose. For example, the United Auto Workers [UAW] lost thousands of members and has been split asunder with factionalism ever since its 113-day strike last year. Yet not one intelligent union officer present today would state or claim that the UAW today is not a strong functioning union capable of adequately representing auto workers. Parenthetically, while the auto workers did not go on strike this year, they did not retain all of the benefits appearing in previous contracts.

"The aftermath of the telephone workers' strike is and will be something that all properly disposed officers will take in [their] stride. We should know and expect a period of disillusionment on the part of some rank-and-file members. We should expect some officers to be disillusioned and frustrated. We should expect defections in the movement. We should expect the companies to try and ride roughshod for a time. In short, we should have expected and should even now expect trouble from many angles." Noting that it was "organizationally and logically impossible" for a federation to act as one union. Beirne argued that a major benefit of the 1947 strike was the delegates presence in Miami. "We are today united in a single union, providing a single vehicle for telephone workers to use in protecting and advancing their economic and cultural standard." Telephone workers, Beirne concluded, "will go forward by looking to the future, relying on the past only for experience to give guidance . . . Steadiness, faith, the will to work together, will, I am sure, bring crowning success."

Success, however, lay ahead down a hard road, as yet untraveled. Jack Moran, in particular, had been an ardent advocate of a strong national union for telephone workers and his leaving for the CIO was a shock both for ideological and practical reasons. As Bill Dunn later explained, "We lost Long Lines and the Installers, and there we lost the tool we had been using for only one unit striking, but making the strike effective against the entire Bell System. Losing the two *national* units which gave us the most effective striking power was quite a blow." Those favoring one big union for telephone workers feared the formation of TWOC as an irreparable blunder. "It simply makes harder the struggle about the gravitation of telephone workers toward full membership in the labor movement," an unnamed CWA official told reporter Willard Shelton. At the same time TWOC's presence—and the rumor of a $2-million organizing fund from the CIO— thrust the reluctant into the CWA. Joe Beirne found one of his more effective arguments against TWOC to be that the CIO group, for all the talk about a "tightly knit union," was "nothing but a loose federation of unions." Still, the immediate impact of TWOC could not help but be divisive. Ohio was deeply divided, and remained outside both CWA and TWOC. Walter Schaar, head of the Michigan plant group, came to Miami with a per capita check in his pocket, "but I never gave it to them. Some folks moved in and sent us in two different directions." Michigan, according to Schaar, was "sort of split down the middle as to what we should do. We had a couple that favored the AFL and they were good talkers and did a good selling job."

Emissaries from the AFL and the CIO cajoled CWA delegates in hotel lobbies, bars and restaurants. For the first and only time in the history of CWA, delegates voted to screen visitors individually and voted on their admission as guests one by one. Bill Smallwood and Mary Hanscom had to plead with the delegates to gain admittance for attorney Henry Mayer who advocated affiliation with the CIO and represented the defecting Long Lines group as well as the Southern and New Jersey groups among others. The vote to admit him was close, but when taken it was emphasized that it gave him no privileges beyond admission as a guest. Sergeants-at-Arms Crull and Schacht were instructed to bar a Mr. Robinson from the AFL, two representatives from the IBEW, and Oscar Jager, out of Long Lines and in Miami buttonholing delegates for TWOC.

Delegates were pulled this way and that as Ray Hackney guided them through the intricacies of adopting a new constitution and Glenn Watts reported out resolutions framing policies for the forthcoming period. Joe Beirne, John Crull and Slim Werkau were elected unanimously to the three top offices, president, vice president and secretary-treasurer. The regions elected Mary H. Hanscom (Eastern), James E. Sigafoose (Central), A.T. Jones (Southern) and Joseph M. Deardorff (Western) as directors. A.C. Dietrich was elected accounting group director; Maurice Hebner, commercial, James E. Smith, independent; Louis Junker, manufacturing-research; Al Di Prospere, plant, and Frances V. Smith, traffic group director. Delegates thumbed down the dues increase proposal, sticking to a twenty-five-cent per capita, and balked at making group directors full-time jobs but compromised by instructing the executive board to establish full time jobs for the four regional directors within ninety days, moving that group directors should be full-time "at the discretion of the executive board when, in their opinion, the need justifies such action."

The question of affiliation niggled the delegates as the pea beneath the mattress bothered the legendary princess. The issue surfaced when Bill Smallwood proposed amending the constitution to provide that *"a majority of votes cast"* should determine the outcome of a referendum on affiliation "with any other labor organization." The constitution provided for a *majority of the total membership* to decide affiliation, a much more difficult attainment. Smallwood's amendment failed with 96,900 votes against to 63,900 in favor.* Smallwood then took up the cudgels for affiliation, propos-

---

*The vote on the constitutional amendment follows:

On the original motion, the secretary will call the roll, and the original motion is to amend Article XXVI of the constitution entitled "Affiliation," by changing, as the debate and discussion emphasized, the fifty-one per cent now required for favorable vote on any affiliation to a simple majority of the votes cast in the referendum called for. We will call the roll.
. . . Secretary-treasurer Werkau called the roll as follows:

DIVISION NAME AND NUMBER	DELEGATE	VOTES	YES	NO	NO VOTE
Indiana Division #1	R. O. Waldkoetter	1700		x	
Florida Division #4	C. V. Wingo	235	x		
California Div. #7	C.J. Woodsford	1097		x	
Research Division #8	H. Schroder	900		x	
West Virginia Div. #9	T. R. Null	2220	x		
Illinois Traffic Div #14	A. C. Benscoter	3784	x		
Illinois Traffic Div #14	Jessie Dillas	3784	x		
Maryland Clerical Div #15	Helen M. Smith	600		x	
Mountain States Div. #17	T. A. Lambert	1280		x	
Mountain States Div. #17	May Jameson	1280		x	
Mountain States Div. #17	John McLearen	1280		x	
Mountain States Div. #17	LaRoy Purdy	1280	x		
Mountain States Div. #17	Ben Staley	1280	x		
Sales Division #18	Louis H. Junker	6000		x	
Southwestern Div. #20	D.L. McCowen	35871		x	
Wisconsin Division #23	Ray Dryer	1067	x		
Wisconsin Division #23	Beatrice Strong	1067		x	

ing a referendum to determine "the desires of the membership on the question of affiliation with one of the major branches of the National Labor Movement, namely, AFL or CIO." Smallwood favored the CIO but out of his deep and abiding sense of fairness included both national organizations in his proposal. Mrs. Anne C. Benscoter, Illinois Traffic, joined Smallwood in the debate, saying, "I have no quarrel with either the CIO or the AFL,

Division	Name	Number			
Wisconsin Division #23	D. W. Cholvin	1067		x	
Wisconsin Division #23	Edward Peil	1067	x		
Wisconsin Division #23	Arthur LeFevre	1068		x	
Wisconsin Division #23	Harry Johnson	1067	x		
Lincoln Division #31	James E. Smith	844		x	
Virginia Div. #33	E. L. Evenson	4414		x	
Washington Div. #36	H. Robinson	2500		x	
Michigan Div. #44	Mary Horsfall	2501		x	
Michigan Div. #44	Helen McCoy	2501		x	
Michigan Div. #44	Helen Berthalot	2501	x		
Michigan Div. #44	Frances V. Smith	2504	x		
Northwestern Div. #45	R. S. Anderson	1667		x	
Northwestern Div. #45	R. W. Boustead	1666		x	
Northwestern Div. #45	J. R. Hill	1667	x		
Northwestern Div. #45	R. L. Rogers	1667		x	
Northwestern Div. #45	E. P. Kummer	1666	x		
Northwestern Div. #45	Susan M. Penwell	1667	x		
Cincinnati Div. #46	J.E. Sigafoose	2050		x	
Southern Div. #49	W.A. Smallwood	34174	x		
Washington Traffic Div. #50	Mildred Beahm	3000	x		
Indiana Clerical Div. #53	Rosemary Eller	247	x		
Equipment Workers Point Breeze Div. #54	R.T. Beveridge	1200		x	
Equipment Workers Point Breeze Div. #54	T. Hooper	1200		x	
Equipment Workers Point Breeze Div. #54	E.K. Green	1200		x	
N.J. Traffic Div. #55	Mary H. Hanscom	9515		x	
Indiana Traffic Div. #56	Mae Mann	3876		x	
Genesee Valley Div. #57	John W. Eadie	594			x
Ashland Division #58	J. D. Shepherd	190	x		
Pacific Division #61	Alberta Cleary	556		x	
Pacific Division #61	Hazel J. White	556		x	
Pacific Division #61	C. M. Good, Jr.	556		x	
Pacific Division #61	Oma M. Garay	556		x	
Pacific Division #61	Maurice Hebner	555		x	
Pacific Division #61	Wm. Lockwood	555		x	
Pacific Division #61	D. M. Chisholm	555		x	
Pacific Division #61	Donald Buckley	555		x	
Pacific Division #61	Geo. Gorman	556		x	
Equipment Workers Buffalo Div. #63	H. E. Jacobs	500	x		
N.J. Acctg. Div. #64	D. K. Plunkett	800		x	
Equip. Wkrs. No. Carolina Div. #65	C. Love	300		x	
	TOTALS	63,900	95,111	594	

but I certainly am not going to sit in a convention, and vote on a resolution that just includes the CIO." (The first resolution actually put forward did just that.) ". . . Naturally, Illinois being an AFL state, it always has been, and always will be, and we have a lot of respect back there for the AFL, and we are taking no part in anything that is just CIO." Fran Smith, Michigan Traffic, stated, "I am more kindly toward the CIO than the AFL, but I don't know for sure whether we should affiliate with them—either of them—at this time or not. But it is true that some of our members are talking in favor of affiliation with the CIO. I have reason to believe it is a minority, but I am not sure, and I believe that we should face the issue squarely and say: 'If the members want it, we as their leaders will not stand in the way of it.' And as a practical matter, we should put it before them." Louis Junker, Western Electric Sales, favored an affiliation referendum even though "we would be faced with all kinds of jurisdictional fights," and though he would "try to influence [his] members" by telling them that "this is not the time to go CIO."

D.L. McCowen headed up the fight against the proposed referendum, saying, "I do not believe we would get a majority vote in favor of affiliation with either of the two great national labor organizations in this country . . . I think the chances are that we would have a majority vote in favor of independence; but I don't know for certain. My point is that I believe, at this time, to put out a vote would only result in splitting the ranks of the telephone workers, and if there is anything we need at this time it is unity among those we do have united at this meeting . . . We should perfect our organization by ourselves, by and for ourselves; and once we have perfected our organization, then put the question of affiliation with AFL, CIO, a combination of the two, District 50, UE, or what have you, and remaining independent to the membership, and continue putting it to a vote until such time as you do have a majority of the membership voting one way or another on the several questions submitted to them. I think it would be a mistake to put to a vote at this time the question, for the reason that we only represent some 161,000 telephone workers; and it would be the same as determining when part of your household were away that you planned to move to some other house.

"Let's get them all together, and then put the question, and let's build the organization as we want it. We have the ability and all the other things necessary to accomplish that fact. Then after we have them all together, put the question to them and let the majority of telephone workers determine it themselves, and not a minority of them as we now have."

Jim Sigafoose from Cincinnati argued, "We came down here for one purpose, to establish a strong, independent telephone union of telephone workers, run by telephone people. There is only one way to organize these telephone workers and that is from the inside. We don't need any outside help." Pacific Coast delegates were fearful of the confusion that they believed would follow a referendum on affiliation. As Donald Buckley from California put it, "If this ballot went out before our membership, there would be so much confusion, I doubt if we would ever get out of it." Alberta Cleary cautioned, "We have had a chaotic condition on the Pacific Coast and our people want an independent union at this time. They want a Union of Telephone People. They are tired, sick and disgusted with letters being hurled at them, raiding campaigns—your lunch hours are not pleasant. Your nights at home, the telephone rings, and a big argument is on: why you should belong to the ACA-CIO. Your spare time is taken up by raiding tactics. The AFL has just indicated that they are willing to spend several hundred thousand in the Pacific area to start a raiding campaign. But if we indicate that we wish to build our strength within our own groups, I feel very sure even those independent groups are looking towards CWA, and once we have become a unified group, the chances of us becoming either AFL or CIO would be much better."

Slowly but surely the convention began to swing, settling on a viewpoint perhaps best stated by Joseph M. Deardorff of Idaho: "I think we should get first things first. It was my understanding that the purpose of this convention was to get the Communications Workers of America launched and under way, and not to have the issue confused with the matter of affiliation. While it is a problem at this present time, I think we may be overestimating its importance. I think a lot can depend on timing, as far as the success of the CWA is concerned. I do not know why it is imperative that affiliation be considered such a vital matter at the present time when we haven't even got our own house in order." When the question was called, 71,960 voted for submitting a referendum on affiliation to the membership with 85,055 against.*

*The roll call of the vote on the referendum proposal follows:

DIVISION NAME AND NUMBER	DELEGATE	VOTES	YES	NO	NO VOTE
Indiana Division #1	R.O. Waldkoetter	1700		x	
Florida Division #4	C. V. Wingo	235			x
California Division #7	C.J. Woodsford	1097		x	
Research Division #6	H. Schroder	900		x	
West Virginia Div. #9	T. R. Null	2220	x		
Ill. Traffic Div. #14	A.C. Benscoter	3784	x		
Ill. Traffic Div. #14	Jessie Dillas	3784	x		
Maryland Clerical Div. #16	Helen M. Smith	600		x	
Mountain States Div. #17	T. A. Lambert	6400		x	
Sales Division #18	Louis H. Junker	6000	x		
Southwestern Div. #20	D.L. McCowen	35871		x	
Wisconsin Division #23	Ray Dryer	1067	x		
Wisconsin Division #23	Beatrice Strong	1067		x	
Wisconsin Division #23	D. W. Cholvin	1067		x	

But, as the *CWA News* took care to report in July, the vote was "not a real indication of the sentiment in favor of CIO or AFL affiliation now." Proponents of affiliation were joined by some opponents, who believed that a referendum in 1947 would defeat affiliation altogether, and there were many who favored ultimate affiliation who voted against submitting the question "at this time" for fear of rejection. "We were a prize to both of them [AFL and CIO]," Beirne was to say many years later, "and I had my own ideas, and knew that affiliation had to happen. But when you are leading people step by step, as we did in building ourselves inside first, you

Wisconsin Division #23	Edward Peil	1067	x	
Wisconsin Division #23	Arthur LeFevre	1068		x
Wisconsin Division #23	Harry Johnson	1067		x
Lincoln Division #31	James E. Smith	844		x
Virginia Div. #33	E. L. Evenson	4414		x
Washington Div. #36	H. Robinson	2500		x
Michigan Div. #44	Frances V. Smith	10007	x	
Northwestern Div. #45	R. S. Anderson	1667	x	
Northwestern Div. #45	R. W. Boustead	1666		x
Northwestern Div. #45	J. R. Hill	1667	x	
Northwestern Div. #45	R. L. Rogers	1667		x
Northwestern Div. #45	E. P. Kummer	1666	x	
Northwestern Div. #45	Susan M. Penwell	1667	x	
Cincinnati Div. #46	J. E. Sigafoose	2050		x
Southern Div. #49	W.A. Smallwood	34174	x	
Washington Traffic Div. #50	Mildred Beahm	3000	x	
Indiana Clerical Div. #53	Rosemary Eller	247		x
Equipment Workers Point Breeze Div. #54	R.T. Beveridge	3600		x
N.J. Traffic Div. #55	Mary H. Hanscom	9515		x
Indiana Traffic Div. #56	Mae Mann	3876		x
Genesee Valley Div. #57	John W. Eadie	594		x
Ashland Division #59	J. D. Shepherd	190	x	
Pacific Division #61	Alberta Cleary	556		x
Pacific Division #61	Hazel J. White	556		x
Pacific Division #61	C. M. Good, Jr.	556		x
Pacific Division #61	Oma M. Garay	556		x
Pacific Division #61	Maurice Hebner	555		x
Pacific Division #61	Wm. Lockwood	555		x
Pacific Division #61	D. M. Chisholm	555		x
Pacific Division #61	Donald Buckley	555		x
Pacific Division #61	Geo. Gorman	556		x
(Bloc vote of Pacific Division #61 was cast by Delegate Donald Buckley)				
Equipment Workers Buffalo Div. #63	H. E. Jacobs	500		x
N.J. Acctg. Div. #64	D. H. Plunkett	800		x
Equipment Workers North Carolina Div. #65	C. Love	300		x
	TOTAL	71,960	85,055	235

know how long that takes. Then you very carefully think through when they are going to be ready for the next step. And in 1947, in my judgement, they weren't ready for it. But the shock treatment was there, and I recognized that."

Beirne liked to say, afterwards, that TWOC "never went any place except back into CWA." Still, the remark covers a real hurt. TWOC never did really take off, despite CIO support, bearing out Beirne's judgement that telephone workers were not quite ready for affiliation. "You had to first hurdle . . . the two big trade centers, AFL or CIO? Well, both of them were in pretty solid shape. Our plant boys didn't like IBEW because of what IBEW had done over the years. But for our traffic girls to join that 'communistic CIO' would be quite a gulp. These were part of the factors in the equation in front of us . . ." One must add, too, the general mood of the country at the time. Over four and a half million workers marched on the picket lines in 1946, and such was the public temper that President Harry S. Truman, after the government seized the railroads during the rail strike, secured the passage of a bill in Congress to draft strikers in an emergency dispute by a vote of 306 to thirteen. Fortunately, when tempers cooled, the bill was allowed to die quietly, but the episode pointed up the prevailing political winds blowing through the halls of Congress and in the state legislatures. Champions of "reform" cried out against "monopolistic labor," and succeeded in securing the passage of the anti-labor Taft-Hartley Law over President Truman's veto in June 1947. As CWA president Beirne noted in the *CWA News*, big business propagandists and reactionary politicians "persuaded a lot of people, *including some of our own members* (my italics), that organized labor and particularly the leaders of unions, had no regard for the American public. That unions were almost anti-American, being run by either racketeers or Communists. Workers in unions were either rabble or the innocent pawn of conniving officers."

The initial refusal of CIO officers to sign the non-Communist affidavits required by the Taft-Hartley law gave credence to the charge of "communistic CIO," a belief reinforced by struggles over the question of Communist influence then taking place within CIO unions. The struggle had its roots in the disillusionment created by the Stalin-Hitler Pact of 1940. Papered over by wartime unity, it broke out again when Communist-influenced unions attacked the Marshall Plan and, subsequently, endorsed Henry Wallace, the 1948 Progressive Party presidential candiate. The CIO finally moved against the Communists in 1949, ultimately expelling eleven unions as Communist-dominated. Meanwhile, the accusation, "communistic CIO" worked against CWA affiliation.

Though the CWA came out of its first convention with an annual budget of $485,007, paying salaries of $13,200 to its president, $10,200 to its vice president and secretary-treasurer and $9,000 a year to its directors, it was far from being the one union dreamed of first by Tom Twigg. Seventeen of the former NFTW unions did not come in, most remaining independent and the rest joining TWOC by the end of the year. Naively perhaps, the union leadership assumed that such recognition that the Bell System had acknowledged would carry over from the NFTW to the CWA. Sometime before the Miami convention, Beirne had called AT&T president Cleo Craig to inform him of the pending change. "I told him that we were going into this transition, that there was no change insofar as the union's relationship with the company was concerned, insofar as the contracts were concerned; that the only change we were making was in the internal machinery of our union which we felt, and still feel, is our right to do without any comment or concern on the part of the company." Suddenly, even though Bell System companies had signed new agreements with CWA divisions, dues were impounded by some companies; others refused to participate in agreed upon grievance-settlement machinery. Claiming that the CWA divisions were now really different unions, Bell System companies demanded that they submit fresh proof of their members' allegiance. Companies insisted on documentary proof that the members of a division had voted by a majority to join CWA and/or to submit dues deduction cards covering fifty percent of the workers in a bargaining unit.

TWOC proceeded to snipe at CWA; AUTW and ACEW sued for their shares of the assets of the dissolved National Federation of Telephone Workers. Allan Haywood exploited his considerable number of acquaintances within CWA, exploring the possibilities of breakaways to TWOC. Mrs. Madge Giles, then a steward in Washington traffic on loan to CWA for an organizing drive in Maryland, tartly told "Mr. CIO . . . over my dead body would I ever be a part of CIO!" James Mahady, CWA Louisiana director, recalls Haywood visiting New Orleans twice, "and twice we sat down with him and explained to him what we were trying to do, that our delegates from Louisiana, the majority of them, would vote for affiliation with the CIO; we could assure that. But if TWOC entered the picture, that this was liable to cause a split in our delegation, and we would not be able to assure [Haywood] that we would go CIO. We may defeat the CIO and stay independent." Haywood got essentially the same message in Michigan, as Mrs. Berthalot recalls. "When the TWOC started, Allan Haywood came to see us in Michigan, and Gus Scholle, who was the state president of the CIO at that time, came with Allan Haywood, and he and Fran [Smith] and Allan Haywood and I met in that hotel, and Allan was trying to persuade us to come in with TWOC. And we said, 'Look, you can't do it from the outside, and our people are not yet ready. You must let us do it from the inside. We'll join you, but we have got to do it in our way and in our own time, and let us alone. You will put us back many years if you force the issue now.' Well, Allan just looked at Fran, and I can remember Gus saying,

'Allan, you don't have to sell these girls. They know, they understand. Just listen to what they are saying to you. They are telling you the truth.' So, he let us go home."

Others delivered the same message. Margaret Weiss, who led Maryland traffic into TWOC and later out of CWA-CIO, called Mrs. Audrey Patterson of the Maryland clerical group to a meeting. "When I walked into the room expecting to meet with her and maybe some of her girls, I see fifteen guys sitting there. One I recognized as Phil Murray's adopted son, Jim Murray, who I knew was organizing for CIO, and several members of the shipyard workers' union, CIO. I got the pitch real fast that they were going to work on me and try to get me to bring the accounting-commercial workers into the Organizing Committee. And I told them that I thought we belonged in CIO and that that's what I was working toward, but that I was coming into the CIO with all the telephone workers; that I didn't believe the splinter group was accomplishing what should be done."

To strengthen TWOC, Haywood arranged the transfer of Northern California Traffic, with about 12,000 members, and the West Coast Toll Testboardmen and Repeatermen, roughly 1,200 members, out of the ACA-CIO. Jim Massey, then with ACEW and TWOC, tells how it was done: "I came into Washington on the meeting representing Ernie Weaver who was sick. And Joe Sellers [ACA official] made this statement, 'Over my dead body will they come out of ACA.' And DeMartini [Marie DeMartini Bruce], who was heading up that group [West Coast operators], says, 'Well, you might as well lay down because we're coming out.' So Haywood recessed the meeting and took Sellers down to his office. And when he came back, Sellers wasn't there and the move was made."

TWOC launched organizing drives in West Virginia, Oregon, Southern California, New York, New England and in Ohio. "We had our first battle in West Virginia in October," Farrell Beaver, who came out of South Carolina to give CWA a hand, recalls," where CWA and TWOC squared off on representation of the West Virginia telephone workers. These West Virginia telephone workers were one of the unions that pulled out of the NFTW at Miami. And TWOC went in there immediately. June McDonald was on one side of the fence and I was on the other. I came out of the South for CWA, trying to convince people to stick with CWA and then lets all go into the CIO." Miss McDonald, later a Des Moines CWA District Representative, came out of Illinois Traffic where she had served as secretary-treasurer and education director. When she failed to convince her people to go CIO, she left to join TWOC's organizing staff. Mary Hanscom, Tommy Jones, Bob Pollock and Mrs. Berthalot, among others, pitched in for the CWA in West Virginia. Mrs. Berthalot recalls commuting between Detroit and Charleston, West Virginia, every week for about two months. "We really were doing very well. For some reason or another, we were all pulled back at the same time, and we lost West Virginia." CWA was hard-pressed financially and was unable to match TWOC's strength in this instance, twenty-eight CIO organizers and over $125,000. The National Labor Relations Board poll showed 1,650 votes for TWOC and 1,379 for CWA. TWOC also won in Oregon, and fended off a CWA attack on Maryland Traffic. In Ohio, Bob Pollock and Flossie Graham labored mightily on behalf of CWA but in the 1948 election, with CWA as *the* issue, Pollock lost the presidency to a proponent of independence. Independents held their ground in New York and in New England. But the CWA came out on top in Washington-Idaho accounting and successfully drove back the TWOC in Southern California. For all its success, TWOC was unable to make any significant inroads among telephone workers. As for the CWA, even though it lost members, showing a drop from 161,699 members at the time of the Miami convention to 148,998 the following spring, it remained the leading labor organization in the field. It had centralized its structure and the old NFTW unions were now integral subdivisions. CWA represented some forty-two percent of the Bell System's nonsupervisory employees. TWOC represented about fifteen percent, while nonaffiliated independents represented about thirty-five percent, mostly in Pennsylvania, New York and New England. The IBEW represented about four percent of the system's workers.

Though CWA clearly led the pack, the telephone unions were in considerable disarray. And Ma Bell seized the advantage, dividing and conquering where she could. Before the 1947 strike most telephone unions, after years of planning by the NFTW leadership, had achieved fairly uniform contract expiration dates. After the strike most of the unions made year-long agreements, but they were made at different times and this, together with the drawn-out arbitration procedures, invoked in several states scattered termination dates all over the calendar. Taking advantage of CWA-TWOC rivalry, the companies undertook to scramble the dates even more. Union leaders were fully aware that they were bargaining in 1948 from weakness, not strength. As a *CWA News* editorial bluntly put it, "Following last year's phone strike, many phone workers went on another strike of their own, against their union—and against themselves. Dissatisfied with the wage settlement they got after six weeks of pounding the pavements, many of them withdrew from the union. Many others remained but lost interest and enthusiasm for union activity. They became card carriers rather than real union members.

"Instead of getting mad at the company for the inadequate treatment in last year's wage settlement, they got mad at the union, their own union.

"But they did even worse than this. They adopted a Casper Milquetoast attitude toward the word 'strike' and screamed to high heaven whenever the word was mentioned."

CWA's 1948 bargaining goals were worked out through a series of extensive meetings, beginning with a meeting of the chief division negotiators in Washington, D.C., over six days in January. The executive board announced the program two weeks later, calling for "a wage increase demand," job protection provisions in accordance with seniority, termination pay clauses, pension improvements, union shop, and fringe issues related to localities, type of work or where present conditions were below prevailing industry standards. No specific wage increase was put forward because, as Beirne explained, exact wage formulations "cannot be determined until negotiations are more nearly at hand, when last-minute changes in economic conditions facing the members and the latest available statistical material can be considered." Dial conversion raised the specter of mass layoffs—Sylvia Gottlieb, CWA research director, estimated that the Bell System would require around 100,000 less telephone operators than presently employed—and prompted job protection demands and termination pay. Long dissatisfied with pensions, the union sought (1) to eliminate the company practice of deducting one-half of the social security benefits, (2) provisions for employee representation on benefit committees, and (3) pension eligibility at employee's option after twenty-five years of service for those displaced because of technological improvements. The divisions were also authorized to negotiate for shortening of apprenticeship periods and for the narrowing of town and city wage levels.

CWA's bargaining strategies for 1948 were shaped by the realities as the union's leaders found them. "There will be no national bargaining this year," Beirne acknowledged. "Each of our divisions will carry on its bargaining with the aid and assistance of the international and in accordance with a general program. . . . This year we will bargain, negotiate, meet, discuss. Then bargain, negotiate, meet and discuss some more. Our theory is to bargain and bargain until we have a contract." By spring, nothing much had happened; Bell managements made no offers, and in May CWA announced that it would allow contracts to be extended, in Beirne's words, "to provide more time for orderly collective bargaining." This action, he states, was "consistent with the policy of bargain, bargain and bargain," but he also warned, "extension can't go on forever."

Meanwhile, union negotiators had met with Cleo Craig of AT&T in an attempt to discover what Ma Bell had on her mind. In Aesopian language, Craig indicated, as Beirne informed a Senate Hearing in 1950, "that the companies, the Bell System and the management of the AT&T could not look on with much favor upon improvements in the wage conditions in the industry for the reason that at that time, in 1948, there were no major agreements negotiated nor was there any pattern, so called, established. They were interested also, we were advised, in a type of contract for a period longer than one year."

Just before the Spokane, June 1948, CWA convention, District 50, Washington Traffic, signed an agreement that set the tone for the year, the so-called three-two contract. The wage question was deferred in a three-year contract that provided for two wage reopeners—the first being at any time over the first twelve months at the request of either party. If no settlement on wages occurred, the contract could be canceled at the end of the year. If, however, an acceptable wage settlement was made, the contract continued for another twelve months, at which time it could be reopened on wages. It could then be canceled or extended for the third year on the basis of a new wage settlement. Ten CWA divisions signed three-two contracts, others simply let their existing agreements run on from week to week.

It was, indeed, a bleak settlement, a bleak prospect. But there were no immediate alternatives. TWOC's Jack Moran, bluffed some, threatened a nationwide strike by Long Lines for a thirty-cent an hour wage increase, but he had to settle on near-identical terms. Long Lines only gain, if it was a gain, was a twenty-one month contract with one wage reopener. TWOC was not exactly flourishing and the CWA, as Beirne said, was "broke." In that grim light, signing the three-two contracts made sense. Once signed, as Beirne explained to Senate inquirers later, the CWA divisions "did not have the worry of the loss of recognition, the loss of the grievance procedure, the loss of time off for the union stewards to do their business, the loss of income due to the withholding of payroll deductions . . ." Moreover, as the CWA weekly *Newsletter* pointed out at the time, the agreements contained "tremendous improvements in seniority provisions, force adjustment, and termination pay clauses. These items are of particular concern to workers in the traffic department, which will bear most of the brunt of the Bell System's accelerated dial-conversion program."

CWA, Beirne further explained, "decided to approve long-term contracts, three-year contracts, with two wage reopenings, for the simple reason that 1947 left the union of the telephone workers rather prostrate insofar as finances and organization were concerned . . .

"In addition to that, we were bargaining with a new structure. We had been operating under the new structure for only a matter of some few months. We were faced with no wage increases. We were faced with canceled contracts. We were faced with no grievance procedure, no dues deductions for union functioning, no recognition of the type that is normal and spelled out. We would be back where we have been in more than one instance, of having an organization that was fighting again for its existence against the onslaught of a company that at [the] time has no scruples when it comes to fighting the union.

"Our judgment was to avoid that. We felt the telephone workers should not be confronted in 1948 with the same kind of decision that they had to consider in 1947. The prospects of a nationwide strike in 1948 were not enticing to any responsible officer of the union."

Nonetheless, CWA leaders were not exactly happy with the three-two contract. D.L. McCowen, whose division was still bargaining at the time of the Spokane Convention in early June 1948, bluntly termed it, "a defeatist approach to the problem." The bargaining program, he added, "has been rather difficult to follow . . . for the reason that the executive board on the one hand had the authority to develop and direct the program, yet the responsibility for carrying it out was left to the divisions. It makes nearly any problem difficult to handle when you have the authority at one place and responsibility at another." By the time of the 1948 convention, however, the question of the three-two contract was moot; they existed, and the real question was one of timing a wage demand. Delegates from Western Electric Sales, Division 18, still in negotiations, argued for an immediate reopening; as Butch Novotny put it, "Now is the hour!" W.F. Kelley pointed out that "the pattern is being set in industry—the General Electric this week, and in New York they have accepted an eight percent increase . . . Westinghouse has made an offer. General Motors has settled. Chrysler has settled. It is my belief that the company will expect that immediately following this convention the delegates will be coming back at least looking for a wage increase . . ."

Arthur LeFevre, Wisconsin Division 23, however, believed that the divisions who had already signed three to two contracts were "in no position to resume negotiations . . . We don't think, some of us, that the time is appropriate to resume negotiations." And Miss Cloma Sartori of Washington Traffic Division 50 wanted to know, "We couldn't get money on May 7—how could we get it now?" Beirne and Watts both expressed the view that a convention was the wrong place to adopt bargaining *strategy*. And the delegates agreed with McCowen that it was "wiser to leave it to the executive board, to determine, after some study, when the time is ripe."

Delegates laughed when Bill Smallwood found himself agreeing with the chair on bargaining strategy; it was, as he said, "a strange position for me to be in because usually . . . we are arguing over something." Smallwood had been battling for over a year what he considered "foot-dragging" over affiliation, and, appropriately, his agreement with chairman Beirne was brought about by the Bell System's hard line on bargaining for it was this adamancy that was driving the CWA into the arms of the CIO. There had been all along, of course, pressure within CWA for affiliation. Undaunted by their defeat at Miami, CIO's adherents pressed their cause. At the September 1947, CWA executive board meeting, Walter Schaar of Michigan plant, T.R. Null of West Virginia, Bob Pollock of Ohio and Smallwood petitioned the board, urging it to go on record as favoring the CIO and to call a special convention in December to vote on the issue. At the time, the CWA executive board pointedly rejected the idea, and instead, in the words of the *New York Times*'s labor reporter Louis Stark, "virtually declared war on the Congress of Industrial Organizations." Michigan CWA officials, in December, 1947, broached to Haywood the idea of calling a convention of CWA, TWOC, AFL telephone workers and the independents for the purpose of forming one union. Haywood was favorably inclined and passed the idea on to Beirne. It was discussed at a CWA board meeting prior to the Spokane convention but no action was taken. However, Ma Bell's refusal to bargain, to grant any wage increase at all, and her deft exploitation of CWA-TWOC rivalry worked to bring telephone workers together.

At Spokane, Beirne put the issue bluntly to the delegates, saying, "This convention cannot dodge a decision on the matter of affiliation . . . We should no longer maintain that the telephone workers are reluctant to be a part of either the AFL or the CIO. The thousands of dollars we have spent in combating the encroachment of both these organizations, and the thousands of telephone workers who have joined both of them within the last year, are facts which cannot be overlooked . . . I believe the workers of the country require a strong labor movement. I believe this because I have witnessed the gangster tactics of industry representatives as they spread their gospel of profits and private enterprise. I feel certain there is little brotherly love in the hearts of some of the rulers of America.

"I believe a strong movement will only be attained when there is a single movement. The division between the two major national unions is based in part upon greed and lack of brotherly concern on the part of a few labor leaders. It is a crime that workers are divided in so many union camps. I am convinced they are kept apart by their leaders. I feel certain there is room for all 'in the house of labor.' I think, however, a new house is necessary.

"I believe telephone workers can make their contribution to the erection of a mansion for labor by being joined with either the AFL or the CIO. I think the time has arrived for us to submit the question to our members so that they can establish, in a free manner and by secret ballot, what their thoughts are on this question."

At the time, however, Beirne refused to commit himself, "I know there are some here who would want me to say that I favor remaining independent. I favor CIO, I favor AFL. I am not going to make any such statement. I believe it is necessary for us to determine where we would stand in the AFL and in the CIO before any of us can truly recommend to the members what to do." The convention itself was deeply divided; there were ten roll calls during the week-long convention, and the two with the narrowest margins concerned affiliation.* The delegates were in a fractious mood with

*Actually, the roll-call vote with the narrowest margin was on the motion to endorse President Harry S. Truman for reelection. CWA was the first labor organization to do so, and

D.L. McCowen's Southwestern Division with 34,209 votes on the opposite side of almost every question from Bill Smallwood's Southern Division with 25,080 votes. (Both held to the positions on affiliation taken in Miami a year ago—McCowen against; Smallwood for.) The delegates refused a proposed dues increase—from twenty-five cents to fifty cents per capita—but did compromise on thirty-five cents. And by an early vote on Tuesday afternoon, 76,019 to 58,617 on the roll call, they amended the constitution so that a simple majority of those voting in a referendum could decide affiliation. But they did not get around to the full discussion on affiliation until Friday afternoon, and the delegates would take the extraordinary step of extending the convention well into Saturday afternoon in order to finish the business before them.

While the lines of argument for and against affiliation were roughly those set out a year before in Miami, there was a new note of bitterness rising from CWA-TWOC rivalry. Helen M. Smith, Maryland Commercial, expressed it in a letter to the delegates. "It isn't logical to suppose that CWA could get a charter in view of TWOC-CIO, and before I would sign a card to join up with those double-crossers, better called skunks, I'd take to a corner with a soap box to defeat Maryland Commercial becoming a part of such a nefarious group." Arne Gravem, Western Electric Sales and active in organizing drives on the West Coast, framed the question of affiliation in the light of the West Coast campaign against TWOC. "What are those people going to think when we have our board coming out and asking us to affiliate with CIO . . . ?"

The executive board, too, was divided with eight favoring affiliation, and of that number four voted for the CIO, and five opposed.* John Crull feared a three-way split in the event of a referendum, while Slim Werkau was of the opinion "that we should devote our time and energies in CWA to the organizing activities, which will in the end result in our representing somewhere in the neighborhood of 400,000 telephone workers. We [should not] go with our hat in our hand, trying to bargain with a powerful labor union when we don't have a sufficient majority of telephone workers numbered among our membership." Beirne reiterated his stand for affiliation, but declared that he would oppose it "if all the AFL and CIO has to offer us is the TWOC and the IBEW." Tommy Jones made an impassioned plea for solidarity, "The convention might just as well ask me the simple question,

---

the President, in a surprise visit, spoke to the convention, which was another "first." But the narrowness of the margin is explained by the timing, the endorsement was made *before* the Democratic and Republican conventions and many delegates opposed endorsing a candidate before the political parties had made their choice.

*Beirne, Fran Smith, Mrs. Hanscom, Junker, Dryer, Deardorff, James Smith and A.T. Jones favored affiliation, with Jones, Deardorff, Junker and Fran Smith speaking out for CIO; DiProspere, Dietrich, Hebner, Werkau and Crull were opposed to affiliation.

'Do you believe a telephone worker ought to join a union; and my answer would be, 'Yes.' . . . I believe that we should affiliate with a major labor union. I am not too opposed to AFL, except . . . that they are flat on their posteriors. I think their top leadership is somewhat stagnant and controlled by two giant organizations, the Teamsters and the Carpenters. With an international charter, and by those two exceptions, I wouldn't mind an AFL charter. But with the way things stand, I favor CIO."

Late Friday afternoon, the delegates thumbed down a motion to "affiliate with a major labor union" which was made by Herman Shelton, Michigan (Plant) Division 44, and seconded by James Shelby, Southern Division 49. The roll call recorded 77,857 against and 70,604 in favor. That night, Bill Smallwood talked to Miss Helen C. Carmody, a New Jersey Traffic delegate, and asked her, as she later recalled, if she thought the people had a right to vote, "which I said I thought they did. And he said I should give them that right." New Jersey Traffic, as it turned out, was the swing vote (roughly 9,115 votes needed to turn the convention around). Miss Carmody moved the next morning to reconsider the vote on the question of affiliation. (She had voted against the motion.) The question was carried 76,143 to 66,113. "Butch" Novotny proposed that the convention instruct the CWA executive board to explore affiliation possibilities with the AFL, the CIO and the United Mine Workers. Glenn Watts introduced a substitute, incorporating Novotny's suggestion, based on a formulation first advanced by Ray Hackney during the debate the day before. Beirne was empowered to appoint a committee of five "to investigate the status which would be accorded to CWA by the AFL and the CIO," and the executive board, after a study of the committee findings, was to conduct a referendum on the question of affiliation. D. L. McCowen expressed himself as satisfied, and the resolution was passed without a roll call.

Back home from Spokane, delegates discovered rank-and-file pressures building up for more money in the pocket. The two to three contracts served admirably to concentrate worker dissatisfaction on wages, the one matter that could be opened for negotiations. Wage settlements were reached in auto, steel, oil, rubber, coal, electric and the building construction industries but still Ma Bell remained adamant. Both CWA and TWOC announced that contracts would be reopened. Inexorably, telephone management's refusal to make a wage offer forced the rivals to act jointly. Beirne and Haywood called a meeting of telephone unions in Washington, D.C., on August 20, to consider plans for a cooperative assault on the no-pay-rise policy of AT&T. Fifteen unions, including CWA, TWOC, the Connecticut, Maryland, Pennsylvania and Ohio Federations, joined in the drive for a "third round" wage increase. The unity achieved was tenuous, but it did precipitate a break in the Bell logjam. Illinois Traffic won an average wage increase of 8.8 cents an hour, and during late 1948 and the first half of 1949, nearly all the Bell occupational groups gained wage increases of eight to ten percent.

CWA and TWOC resumed their feud. Nonetheless, Beirne proceeded with affiliation. He named the fact-finding committee in December 1948, asking Ed V. Peil of Wisconsin, George E. Gill of Southern, Lloyd La-Chapelle of Michigan, John T. Walsh of Southwestern, and Beatrice Smith of Northwestern to serve. As A.T. "Tommy" Jones, then Southern Regional Director, put it in the February *CWA News,* "We should follow the pattern set by millions before us. We should affiliate. We have made great strides in the past few years and nothing should distract [us] from it. We have fought the good fight. But most of our fighting has been an attempt to 'reach the pattern' on wages. That pattern in the three post-war rounds has been set by large CIO industrial unions. We have contributed little or nothing to settling those patterns. We have attempted to ride on one set for us by organized labor. For all our fighting we haven't yet equalled one. The Bell System faces us with its billions, with its tight control and its anti-labor bias . . . And the independent companies follow right along. Everybody knows the wages of any community are higher according to the degree of unionization of the community. So the organized efforts of other unions directly affect the wages proposed for us by our employers. For our own good we should see that all industries are organized. We can best contribute to their organization by leading our support through affiliation." Pointing out that "a myriad of unions" spend much of their time and money fighting each other in the telephone industry, Jones argued that the best chance telephone workers had of unity was through affiliation. "Whenever we get into trouble," he continued, "one of our first questions is, 'How much help can we get from the AFL and/or the CIO?' We usually get some . . . but how long will we continue to ask [for] their help without contributing [to] their support?" CWA should affiliate, Jones concluded, with one or the other of the major labor federations. "Then we should work as part of one or the other for a merger of the two. When we do that, we can hold our heads high as a vital, full-fledged partner in the labor movement of this country."

After hearing the report of the fact-finding committee, the CWA executive board recommended affiliation with the CIO and ordered a referendum to start on March 7 and to close sixty days later. Jack Barbash, in *Unions and Telephones,* ably sums up the reasons for the CWA choice: "First, CIO's terms were more favorable in keeping telephone workers together as one international union. The AFL, on the other hand, could offer CWA only status within an existing international union, the IBEW. The second reason was that CIO made a greater appeal to telephone workers as an imaginative and fighting organization. The impression that the pro-affiliation group, at any rate, had of AFL was of craft unionism and stodginess.

There did not appear to be any aggressive AFL sentiment in the CWA; even those who opposed CIO did not seem to favor AFL. Third, CIO stood for industrial unionism, and this had a significant appeal to most CWA people." The IBEW subsequently requested that its name be withdrawn from the referendum ballot, charging that "a hoax [was] being perpetrated on the individual CWA members." In the referendum, which authorized application for a CIO charter, CWA members voted 71,312 for affiliation to 34,419 for remaining independent.

The next step, naturally, was amalgamation with TWOC. A CIO charter was granted to CWA on May 9, 1949, but the details of amalgamation were still unresolved. While Beirne got along with Allan Haywood, his old relationship with Jack Moran was hardly reestablished. Bill Dunn, then Beirne's assistant, however, did have a close relationship with Moran: "We were each widowers, and married cousins as a result of being together here in Washington." So Dunn, "through being an errand boy, if you want to call it that, between the two," brought the two together in a relaxed atmosphere. "There were four people present . . . I brought Moran, and Beirne came with Haywood . . . And on a piece of paper that I have someplace . . . just two or three pages of yellow legal-sized paper—were the criteria that . . . would lead to the merger committee that would lead to the merger. It was quite a meeting." Dunn and Moran had managed to remain friends throughout the CWA-TWOC rivalry by agreeing, within the family, that the subject was taboo. Then, says Dunn, "I became communicator . . . It was a very informal meeting, just sitting around my living room . . . Joe was fighting for the fact that TWOC was only a committee and CWA was a union, an established union then within the house of CIO; that the creation of [a] new union by another name would serve no useful purpose; that we were the dominant group, and that TWOC should lose its identity and the affiliates should come in as a division of CWA. I think that was the biggest point he won. The biggest point Moran won was that out of TWOC would come the one-union concept of an international union and locals, and not the three-level structure that we had. He was able to get committments from Joe that Joe would work toward that end. Joe was in agreement that we should have a two-level union. But Jack wasn't for waiting for ten years for this to evolve. He wanted Joe's endorsement and outright support for it right from the beginning . . ."

For CWA, Ray Hackney, Mae Mann, John Klopp, George Walton and William Gruwell, and for TWOC, Dick Long, Norma Naughton, Robert Creasey, James Massey and Margaret Weiss, sitting as the Amalgamation Committee, worked out the details of the merger finally approved in Chicago at the 1949 convention, June 13–17. TWOC affiliates were duly seated, and the joint committee recommended that the convention, among other things, approve constitutional amendments: 1) to eliminate departmental groups and group directors as an arrangement which had not served its desired purpose, and 2) to increase the number of vice presidents to three. This enabled the convention to carry out another understanding—the election of Beirne as president, Werkau as secretary-treasurer, John Crull, from CWA, as a vice president, and Jack Moran, from TWOC, as a vice president. The third vice-presidency was "up for grabs;" and in a contest Tommy Jones won out over Ernest Weaver and Norma Naughton. Mary Hanscom, Ray Dryer, Ray Hackney, and Joe Deardorff were elected, respectively, eastern, central, southern and western directors.* The Ohio Federation, which had voted on affiliation before the convention, joined. CWA-CIO now had 228,000 members; 54,000 formerly with TWOC.

The CIO pledged $350,000 for organizing, prompting someone to ask, "What does the CIO get out of the deal?" Slim Werkau replied, "A good right-wing union with intelligent union members who exercise their brains for the benefit of all." It was an excellent answer. The labor movement, too, gained an advocate in CWA of an AFL and CIO merger.

*Frances Smith of Michigan could have been CWA's first woman vice president, but fate decreed otherwise. She was nominated by Mary Gannon of Washington Traffic, but Mrs. Smith was not at the convention, being engaged in NLRB hearings in Detroit, contesting Michigan Bell's attempt at de-recognition. She asked Genevieve E. Pashak, head of Michigan (Traffic) Division 44 to decline the nomination on her behalf, citing her reluctance to move to Washington should she be elected. And, it would have been difficult; she had two children in school, was building a home and her husband held a good job in Detroit. However, she was already ill and she died of cancer, at 39, in 1951.

X

Two Level

When CWA went CIO on May 9, 1949, the Bell System promptly coun-terattacked, launching a "cold war" that would last well into the 1950s. With remarkable alacrity, acting on the basis of newspaper accounts, and *before* any sort of notice had been given to the system by the union, and in concert, the Bell companies instituted a wave of recognition withdrawals. Virtually all the companies petitioned the National Labor Relations Board to conduct representation elections. Dues already collected and owed to the union were impounded, and Bell management announced that all future dues would be impounded until the issue was resolved.

It was, tactically, a shrewd move, although something of a gamble. Management apparently believed that they had the union's leaders up against the ropes with a good chance of knocking them out of the ring altogether. Failing that, there was the possibility of greatly weakening the new CIO union, especially for the bargaining round due in 1950. In the event, Bell executives moved to exploit what they perceived to be an opening created by the recent CWA-TWOC rivalry. Expressing "doubts" that their employees wanted representation by CWA-CIO, Bell managements' claimed, as J.N. Stanberry, a vice president of Illinois Bell, later put it at a Senate hearing, "Our company had no proof that the employees in Division 14 wanted to be represented by the CWA-CIO." Stanberry quoted a letter to G.S. Dring, assistant vice president of AT&T's Long Lines department, from CWA president Beirne, issued in the heat of the CWA-TWOC conflict, to the effect that "the character of the union had undergone a change" when the Long Lines group joined TWOC. And Stanberry also cited another CWA document that stated that the company had a "perfectly legal demand," that Long Lines employees prove in some acceptable fashion that they want TWOC-CIO, or CWA, or an independent union to represent them. George C. Gephart, vice president of Southwestern Bell, cited results of the affiliation referendum to shore up his "doubts." Bulletin-board notices, he said, showed in eastern Missouri and Arkansas 2,735 votes for CIO and 2,989 for remaining independent; in western Missouri and Kansas, 1,571 for CIO and 3,000 to remain independent; in Oklahoma, 1,585 for CIO and 875 against, and in Texas, 5,474 for CIO to 3,658 for remaining independent. Totals for the division were 11,365 for CIO and 10,512 for independence.

That these votes were an internal matter and had nothing to do with representation did not bother Bell management. It was, or so it appeared to them, a legal crack worth prying open. The affiliated Bell companies informed their respective CWA divisions that the divisions would be required to sign up a majority of their respective employees on dues deduction cards or else to submit to NLRB representation elections. CWA countered dramatically. As Joe Beirne put it, "In two of our divisions [Washington Traffic and Indiana] we went out and signed fifty-one percent of the cards in no time flat, just to show the company it could be done if we wanted to do it that way." Since the companies canceled contracts, under a clause allowing for expiration on a sixty-day notice, with Southern Division 49 and New Jersey Traffic Division 55, the two divisions promptly agreed to representation elections. In the earlier affiliation referendum, some 20,000 Southern Bell workers had voted CIO; in the NLRB representation election, with members as well as non-members voting at the company's insistance, 26,000 voted for CWA-CIO. Out of 11,000 people eligible in New Jersey, 8,000, non-members and members alike, voted for the union. As for the rest, CWA's officers took the principled position that affiliation or no, it was an internal matter and none of the Bell System's business. "We advised every single one of the companies," declared Beirne, "including the AT&T, that there was no change in the character of our organization and no change in its jurisdiction and no change in its people, and we felt that it was not necessary to supply new evidence."

The companies promptly filed thirty-five representation petitions with NLRB regional offices and invoked the costly practice of impounding union dues deducted from member's wages, stopping collective-bargaining processes where underway, and suspending all grievance machinery. Sensibly, the NLRB decided on a pilot case to expedite settlement of what appeared to be a thorny issue, holding that the arguments advanced in one would apply to all. Michigan was chosen, and after hearings, the Michigan NLRB director dismissed the case. The board, in upholding the Michigan case, vigorously asserted that "the record in the instant case is barren of any evidence that the affiliation of the CWA with the CIO has had any effect upon the structure, functions, or membership of Divisions 43 and 44, CWA, the local contracting unions . . . There has been no schism in these unions, and no other labor organization intervened in this proceeding to challenge their representation status.

"In these circumstances we perceive no reason for not regarding the 1948 collective-bargaining agreements between the employer and Divisions 43 and 44, CWA, which have a substantial period yet to run, as bars to a present determination of representation." While reasonable men might expect Bell management to give in gracefully and withdraw their cases elsewhere in the light of the July 21, 1949 Michigan decision, reasonable men do not reckon the depth of management passions. Nor do they reckon the value of delay to the companies, and the cost to the union. Each company waited until its case was dismissed by its respective NLRB regional office before renewing union recognition. Money was withheld and grievances were allowed to pile up. Ma Bell was that kind of woman. As Beirne graphically phrased it, "The Bell System is the country's best example of the iron fist in the velvet glove. It is a past master in rigid supervision, the speed-up, and other methods for the exploitation of the workers. Traffic operators are timed to stop-watch limits and unfortunate is the poor little operator who is caught using the wrong phrase in answering a customer or taking too long to perform her operating routines. Quantitative and qualitative result studies are constantly being made in connection with construction, installation, repair, and maintenance work of all kinds. Every operation is observed and timed. Even in commercial offices, ink wells and other devices serve as microphones so that trained observers can catch every word uttered by either the employee or the customer who is being served."

One of Ma Bell's public faces was that of a kindly, older woman, a woman-who-lived-in-a-shoe-kind of person, generous though perhaps a bit flustered by all her kind offerings. As *Fortune* magazine (March 1950) described Bell labor relations, "AT&T has worked earnestly to instill a feeling of loyalty- and opportunity-consciousness among its employees. The company has offered not 'jobs' but 'positions,' not a 'livelihood' but a 'career.' Thirty-seven years ago AT&T established a system of non-contributory pensions, and shortly after World War I expanded its welfare program." That program, by the late 1940s, was far from adequate. But pensions, in particular, were a sore point with telephone workers, largely because they were not sufficient and also because the companies refused to bargain pension issues. Encouraged by the U.S. Supreme Court upholding in 1949, and a NLRB decision that "wages" and "conditions of employment" as used in the National Labor Relations Act included pension and insurance benefits as mandated collective-bargaining issues, CWA divisions once again pressed the Bell companies for pension benefit increases. Routinely, CWA bargainers were politely told by company officials that the $50-minimum pensions were adequate and that management could see no need for a change "at the present time." Over the weekend of November 18, *all* of the associated Bell companies miraculously changed their minds. D.L. McCowen, whose Southwestern group was bargaining, seeking pension changes as well as other gains, was asked to meet Southwestern Bell vice president Gephart early Monday morning on November 21, and was solemnly informed that the company was increasing minimum monthly pensions for those over sixty-five from $50 to $100, less Social Security benefits. Identical meetings were taking place that morning all across the country, and Bell company vice presidents offered the same explanation as the one given McCowen. AT&T had changed its pension plan on November 16, and the Southwestern Company then found itself in the position of having to make similar changes or else to have a different plan than the other companies, which was "not desirable" for tax, accrual and other reasons.

The normally unflappable McCowen was furious, an anger widely shared by telephone unionists. Ma Bell had contemptuously slapped the union in the face and defied the law. CWA countered by filing unfair labor practice charges against the company in all the NLRB regions where CWA units had bargaining rights for Bell workers. "If a company has the right to improve pensions unilaterally," Beirne stated at the time of filing the charges, December 6, 1949, "it also has the right to decrease those provisions. If it can capriciously modify pension benefits up or down, it can do the same for basic wages, hours of work or other conditions of employement without consideration of the union representing the employees. If allowed to go unchecked, such actions would mean the complete destruction of collective bargaining in America." NLRB General Counsel Robert Denham, considered by many labor people as leaning towards management, dismissed the cases on the tenuous grounds that the union and its locals were not in compliance with the non-Communist affidavit and filing provisions of the Taft-Hartley Act *at the time the alleged unfair labor practices were committed.* (A handful of local officers in out of the way places just had not gotten around to filing the proper forms.) The NLRB general counsel also held that CWA was not in compliance since the CIO had not completely fulfilled all requirements as of December 1949. CWA, however, persisted, and the unfair labor practice charges remained a thorn in Ma Bell's side.*

Meanwhile, CWA prepared to confront the Bell System in 1950 when contracts were up for openers of one kind or another. The union was in a poor bargaining position as were most unions that year. Unlike the auto and steel unions, which could play one employer off against another in negotiations, CWA faced, as Aaron Thomas "Tommy" Jones pointed out, a system "where there is *no* deviation, *no* faltering, and *no questioning* of unified action at every level of management." As for CWA, Jones continued, "our

---

*All unions under contract with the Bell System filed unfair labor practices charges as a result of management's unilateral pension action. These, too, were dismissed on the same grounds of non-compliance with the non-Communist affidavit provisions of the law. The independent United Telephone Organization, representing Downstate New York plant, was ruled out of compliance when a Manhattan local officer who had been on vacation returned to work and signed his affidavit and just happened to hand it in right after the unfair labor practice charge was filed!

contracts were spread from *one end of the calendar* and *one end of the map* to the other. This was the situation we faced, *forgetting* for the moment the difference in make up and outlook of our various divisions, as we faced up to Bell System bargaining in 1949–50. We had to pay grudging tribute to an anti-union job well done by the Bell System. And we had to pay through the nose." Given that situation, said Jones, *"not a single one* of our experienced division leaders felt that a successful strike would be possible in 1949 or 1950. Many professed fears that even the taking of a strike vote among their membership would result in the decimation of the division." Unquestionably, finances and morale were "at a low ebb." When it was suggested that some of the stronger divisions call work stoppages to protest Bell's violation of the law in acting unilaterally on pensions, division leaders were reluctant and some refused outright, and so the plan was dropped.

CWA's bargaining posture, as well as that of other unions, was undercut by a general softening of the economy then taking place. America's output of goods and services fell from $262.434 billion in 1948 to $257.400 billion in 1949, and gross private domestic investment was off even more sharply, from $45.008 billion down to $34.700 billion. Unemployment rose sharply, as a consequence, from 3.4 percent in 1948 to 5.5 percent in 1949, hitting the 4.684 million mark in February 1950, the highest level since August 1941. Mechanization, the conversion to dial telephones, and a so-called economy drive cut overall Bell employment from 656,000 at the end of 1948 to 593,000 at the end of 1949. Despite unfilled orders for 900,000 telephones, AT&T projected even further layoffs and an extension of "part-timing." Anne C. Benscoter, who headed up CWA's Dial Conversion Committee, estimated that conversion would see 100,000 operators displaced over the next five years.*

Small wonder then that telephone workers were skittish about strikes and deeply concerned over the outcome of bargaining in 1950. CWA marshalled all the skills at its command to do the best it could with a bad hand. In Tommy Jones' pithy formulation, "We had to devise strategy to insure bargaining gains through *maneuvering,* rather than a straight-out contest of force." Divisions with so-called bear-trap wage reopeners, providing for a thirty-day notice with thirty days bargaining to follow, ending in a take-it-or-leave-it situation, were told to sit tight. Around the others, CWA

*In March 1950, *CWA News* reported the impact of dial conversion on Royal Oak, Michigan, the largest remaining manual office in the country, which employed 507 before the cut-over to dial. After conversion, only 212 traffic employees remained; 107 were shifted to other offices, 212 were either laid-off "or forced out in other ways."

According to the CWA, 20,000 telephone workers were displaced during the first nine months of 1949, while the number of telephones in service increased by 1,500,000. As of the end of 1948, there were 31,364,493 Bell telephones in service and Bell Operating companies employed 546,723. Nine months later, the number of telephones was up to 32,850,583 while employment was down to 527,056.

leaders were "determined to drum up considerable furor concerning the possibility of strike action." Beirne appealed to fellow CIO members to make "all the telephone calls they can" in the event of a strike so as to overwork strikebreakers and overuse equipment. On January 30, 1950, Beirne announced that CWA divisions in a position to do so would strike on February 8. Cyrus Ching, director of the Federal Conciliation and Mediation Service, asked for a postponement of the strike date, which was agreed upon, to February 24. Then President Truman arranged another "truce," this time for sixty days. As Tommy Jones later explained, "The strategic value to the union of these truces cannot be *overemphasized.*" It brought the various divisions closer to a common termination date, which would greatly strengthen the union should it be forced to strike.

CWA hopes for a presidential fact-finding board as a means of publicizing the union's case for a wage increase (see table for an example of what might have been done) were dashed by AT&T's blunt refusal to appear before anything other than a statutory board. The companies during this period were also calling in their employees for "friendly conferences" about bargaining. CWA officers were accused of being "greedy for power" and not working in the best interest of telephone workers. In Jacksonville, Florida, telephone workers were told, "Employees who go on strike might as well look for new jobs, and in small towns, workers were told they could get increases, "if only the union didn't want one for large cities," and city workers were told just the opposite. The Bell companies also carried on an intensive and extensive propaganda program aimed at the public, using so-called public service advertisements carrying uniform "messages" though imprinted with the respective company names. These advertisements were tax-deductible and so paid for by the taxpayer.

Just as the presidential truce expired, a Western Electric installers' grievance exploded into a walkout that nearly precipitated a nationwide telephone strike at exactly the wrong time. Some divisions had conducted strike votes, some carried and some did not, and others had not as yet polled their members on the question. Towards the end of April, the operating fund of the union showed a book overdraft of $400. "That's $400 in the red," Jones emphasized in making his point. Those with "bear-trap" reopeners were "living on borrowed time," and the union had to settle or strike by midnight of April 25. The day before, 10,000 installers walked off the job to protest the handling of a South Bend, Indiana, grievance. Nine installers had refused to cross muddy, impassable fields to install equipment in a new television tower and were docked for lost time. This simple grievance ballooned. The installers refused to return to work until they had been paid the lost time, and when the company informed them that if they did not return by Monday, April 24, they would be considered as having "resigned," the rest of the Western Electric group stopped work. The CWA

Last On The List

Phone Workers Need Wage Increases Now

INDUSTRY	INCREASE SINCE 1939	
	AMOUNT	PERCENT
All manufacturing	$0.747	118.0
Durable manufacturing	.767	109.9
Nondurable manufacturing	.709	121.8
Blast furnaces, steel works, rolling mills . .	.803	95.0
Agricultural machinery	.853	119.1
Automobiles	.778	83.7
Bituminous coal mining	1.046	118.1
Boots and shoes	.603	119.9
Class I steam railroads	.604	84.6
Construction	1.001	107.4
Cotton manufactures, except small wares .	.722	185.6
Electric light and power	.670	77.1
Electrical equipment	.770	106.6
Food	.665	109.6
Machine tools	.761	101.2
Machinery	.782	108.5
Petroleum refining	.905	92.9
Retail trade	.570	106.3
Rubber products	.779	103.3
Street railways and busses	.707	99.0
TELEPHONE	.501	60.9

Source: U. S. Bureau of Labor Statistics

THESE FIGURES taken from the report of President Truman's fact-finding board in the steel industry dispute show how telephone-worker wages have fallen behind since 1939. While average wages for the industries listed have increased by 76.2 cents per hour, those of telephone workers have risen by only 50.1 cents. In plain language, it would require an increase of 26.1 cents per hour to bring telephone workers up to par.

Between 1939 and 1949, there was an increase in real national wealth of fifteen percent. Real wages in terms of purchasing power have kept pace in most industries. Telephone workers are the only major group in the nation where real wages have dropped. In terms of equivalent purchasing power, average wages in the telephone industry are six cents per hour below 1939.

Study these figures carefully. They highlight CWA's wage case. They show that even retail trades workers—a highly unorganized group—have fared better than telephone workers in wage increases.

AT&T always mouths pious phrases about comparable wages. Here's proof positive that telephone wages don't compare.

Source: *CWA News*, March 1951, page 3.

leadership sought to isolate the installers; the walkout was neither condoned, nor authorized. Picket lines were not set up so the possibility of a general strike did not materialize. The dispute was resolved and the installers returned to work on May 1.

Nonetheless, CWA negotiators experienced a few bad moments as they traveled to New York City to meet with AT&T brass at the University Club. There, Beirne, Jones and Bill Dunn "negotiated" with "certain top officials," notably vice president W.C. Bolenius, then in charge of personnel, who promptly informed them that there would be no way of reaching an agreement if CWA persisted in its demands for a general wage increase or in pushing the unfair labor practice charges still pending before the NLRB. After some discussion, Bolenius raised the possibility of shortening progression schedules as a means of getting some money into the pockets of telephone workers. He suggested a reduction to seven years from the prevailing eight year norm; the union countered with five years. And so the discussions proceeded. Bolenius later denied "negotiating" in testimony before the Senate subcommittee probing labor relations in the Bell System. "I indicated to him [Beirne] that I could do no bargaining whatever, that I could come to no agreement whatever, that all I could indicate in any way was what I thought I could possibly *advise* the companies as to my own personal view of any of these matters, if they were to ask me about such matters." (My italics.) As it happened, the union leaders asked "what assurance we could have that he would give such advice." And Bolenius was much put out, angrily demanding if they were questioning his integrity. They were not, but wanted to be certain, for as Beirne later wryly said, "Experience has convinced us that advice is an order, that advice is direction; that once the advice is given, it will be followed."

Though Bolenius insisted, at least to the inquiring Senators, that as far as he was concerned there was no meeting of minds and no agreement was made, the weary CWA spokesmen left the University Club at 6:30 the next morning with "reason to believe that our collective bargaining with the Bell System across the country would be resolved." Progression schedules were shortened to six and one half years, with the money "feathered back" into the shortened period. Cities and jobs were reclassified upward and there was an understanding that Western Electric workers would gain comparable benefits. And the South Bend grievance was to be settled with no loss of jobs. CWA agreed to withdraw all standing unfair labor practice charges before the NLRB. It was no bad bargain in a bad year.

Still, there was flak from CWA members, many of whom were disturbed by proposed changes in the constitution slated for the June convention, by the handling of the South Bend incident, and by the ups and downs of the negotiations. Maryland Traffic Division 38 signed a separate agreement with the Chesapeake and Potomac Telephone Company, and broke-away from CWA. Petitions for the recall of the officers were circulated at the Cleveland 1950 convention and various charges were leveled against the leadership in so-called rank-and-file letters which were given wide circulation at the time. The job of defending the administration fell to Tommy Jones who had served as bargaining coordinator during the negotiations. He made a remarkable speech. Even in print, it evokes a controlled passion with rhetorical flashes of insight and ample evidence of an analytical mind at work. With a theatrical assurance Jones set the stage for a slashing critique of the union's outstanding weaknesses. He never let his audience lose sight of the enemy, "An industrial empire where *mortal man* is crowned as *King* and *God* . . . an organization where every management representative at whatever level must toe the mark with unswerving and unquestioning loyalty to the Bell System party line—*must* toe the mark, or vanish . . . We need to remember that the continuing bargaining relationship with the Bell System amounts to a *grim* and *dogged* industrial *war, which* goes on year after year. We need to approach this collective-bargaining matter from the point of view of opposing *armies.* And we need to remember [that] each year's bargaining program and its outcome is synonymous to a battle in a *major shooting war.* We need to remember those things because that's the way Bell System management views them and that's the way they deploy their labor relation's forces."

Then Jones developed his critique of the union. "Sometimes our own outfit acts like a Mexican army, where everybody is a general. Some of our Mexican generals design their own medals, cut and color their own campaign ribbons, and literally besprinkle themselves with both, according *to their own ideas* of their honor and glory. Sometimes the secondary leaders in our army won't fight unless they know all of the battle plans and then won't fight unless they approve them. Some seem to forget that our fight is with industry management and they spend most of their time and energies seeking to sow *suspicion* and *distrust* of our general staff." Spelling out the structural weakness of the union, Jones began weaving an intricate account of the 1950 negotiations into a story of a union building its defenses as best it might, struggling against odds to win a modest victory and gaining thereby a new maturity. "Our strength has been conserved for use in the job of future building and strengthening of the union."

The speech was received with mixed emotions. As F.P. Lonergan, a Southwestern Division 20 delegate, responded, "I think the negotiations of our own division, and from all the other divisions that I have seen, were lousy . . . the membership didn't do a good job and therefore their negotiators couldn't do a good job." When Jim Sigafoose of Cincinnati moved that the report be accepted with a vote of thanks for a job well done, D.L. McCowen moved to delete the words "well done," explaining that while he believed that the job was well done by Jones, "I think that there is a possibility of it being interpreted that the telephone workers are satisfied, and I don't think that part of it is correct." McCowen's amendment carried.*

Dissension over the contract negotiations affected debate over proposed constitutional changes to create a new two-level structure for CWA. The semi-autonomous divisions were to be eliminated with the locals directly chartered and responsible to the international union. Dues were to be divided between the two. Convention delegates were to be elected by locals rather than by the divisions. Geographical districts, financed by the international, would service the locals and otherwise administer the union but would no longer have policy-making functions. The idea was not new, of course, for as D.L. McCowen said, "When we went CWA initially, we only took a half-step in the right direction." But CWA was born of a compromise and it took affiliation with the CIO and merger with TWOC to give further impetus to the natural development of the one-union concept.

The 1949 convention had endorsed the idea, and ordered the executive committee to appoint a special committee to draw up the necessary constitutional provisions. Under the direction of its chairman, Ray Hackney, committee members Richard Long, Mae Mann, James Massey, Norma Naughton, and Glenn Watts working with CWA counsel Charles Koons and Southern Division attorney Tom Adair, worked for nearly a year on a new constitution. The committee also held a series of meetings throughout the country to discuss the proposed changes. So nearly everyone at the convention was prepared for a major debate; however, tempers were sharpened by the set-to over collective-bargaining perspectives. Western Electric installers and sales people, in particular, were unhappy about the pro-

*The next day, however, the delegates also adopted a motion, proposed by McCowen, giving "a vote of confidence" to the executive board for its efforts "in administering the policy and program of CWA during the past year."

posed dismantling of the semiautonomous divisions. As Beirne told the delegates, "There are two camps in this convention, which is healthy; there are opposing viewpoints, which is healthy." And, there was "confusion."

Ray Hackney, speaking for the committee, did a masterful job in presenting a complex issue so as to dispel perplexities. He began by analyzing the sources of dissatisfaction with the existing structure. "We know," he declared, "that the life blood of our union is in locals first and in the membership, and second we know that our life blood is within the sphere of a bargaining unit." But, as he acknowledged, the international union is "out of touch with the locals. The locals are out of touch with the international." The existing divisions were a buffer and when they failed to implement convention policies, a stumbling block. There were thirty-nine divisions and thirty-nine ways of bargaining, striking, handling financing and holding conventions. Out of twenty-nine division presidents, twenty-seven "were of the opinion that we needed to change the structure." But the simple elimination of the divisions failed to solve administrative and collective bargaining difficulties. So districts had to be established "to service" the members while the bargaining units, whose determination lay in other hands, be maintained. Locals were to be uniformly serviced by the international, through the districts organized on a geographical basis, with the exception of Long Lines and the Western Electric groups, but locals were to run their own affairs. Where division presidents formerly ran conventions and elected CWA's top officers, delegates from the locals would now do so. During conventions, local delegates comprising a given district would meet to elect district officers and while they could not make policy they could make policy recommendations to the convention. Bargaining committees would be elected, though contracts negotiated within a district require the approval of the district director. District personnel, other than the director, would be appointed at the recommendation of the international president by the executive board. This procedure was similar to that in other unions and recommended by the special constitution committee because staff would not be *representing* the membership; they will be *servicing* the membership." The rights of the members were further protected by constitutional provisions for recall and referendum. The committee, Hackney said, worked out these and other safeguards, to ensure "the proper amount of latitude to let people speak their minds, and let them run against whoever they want to, or condemn who they want to."

The report sparked a lengthy debate, which ran for several days. At the urging of D.L. McCowen, whose sense of fair play prompted the action, the convention set aside its rules to allow a non-delegate, Attorney Henry Mayer, to speak in opposition to the proposed changes. Mayer, who represented New Jersey Traffic and several other groups within CWA, was a controversial figure in the union's history. He had been barred from the floor at previous conventions, and though an advocate of CIO affiliation and former counsel to TWOC, now was vehemently opposed to the proposed two level structure; "don't sell them [the members] a one level structure on the pretext that is two level," he pleaded. Much of his speech was a defense of his record, and he had made a contribution to the development of CWA, but his attack centered on what he perceived to be an over-concentration of power at the national level. "Of course you need some measure of centralization of power," he told the delegates. "Of course you needed the obliteration of the division, and I urged that and argued that just as sincerely as anybody in this room. And you need it today. But how can you go out to your people in the field and say, 'We have destroyed the divisions, and we have moved the power out of the divisions.' Where? I say completely to the top . . ." Specifically, among other things, he criticized the absence of a grass-roots policy committee to guide the leadership in formulating bargaining goals. "All of the powers and duties residing in the divisions are moved up," he charged, "not down to the locals."

Ray Hackney rebutted Mayer, reminding the delegates that under the new constitution collective-bargaining committees would be elected. Power, Hackney declared, "has not all been moved up. When we talk of bargaining units, you are not talking of the international and divisions as bargaining units. If you yourselves will get into your heads that the bargaining units, and the powers allocated to bargaining units as compared to the divisions that now exist, you can clearly see that lots of power remains in the membership of the locals, comprising a bargaining unit. It must be that way. We said we didn't want to destroy it, and it hasn't been." Speaking earlier, Beirne had hit out against what he termed "confusion" and "destructive tactics." He also pointed out that Bell management had been holding meetings, analyzing what was going on within the CWA, to prepare plans for combating the union in the period following the convention. "We have now an international going hat in hand to divisions to assist them," Beirne asserted, and always to the same old reliables—Southwestern, Southern and District of Columbia Traffic. "We now go to the CIO and they help us." But, he added, "how long are we going to kid the telephone workers about bargaining when we don't have the union that can bargain for them? . . . We will only get recognition from the Bell System management when we command their respect. We will only command their respect as we build the kind of an organization that can truly represent the telephone workers —a strong, closely knit, well-coordinated organization."

While the convention was clearly swinging towards acceptance of the Hackney committee recommendations, Beirne was convinced that "the whole report could go down unless we could find an answer; a compromise that would bring the balky Western Electric delegates around. The committee was, in Beirne's words, "dead set against districts for sales and installation, and, of course, they had Long Lines in their corner." The latter did not want a separate district for themselves *or* for the Western Electric groups, either singly or in combination (a dream of Ernest Weaver, head of the Installers). The committee, according to Beirne, thought that their proposals would go over but he did not. "The installers and the sales fellows were not only persuasive out there in public on the mikes, but they were also busy lining up votes, and this I respected. I came from that group. I know how they can do it." So Beirne went down on the convention floor, "and got in a huddle . . . with the installers and sales guys, and said, 'Okay, I'm going to join you. Now, how about the rest of it? Can we put this thing over if you get your districts?' And they said, yeah, they'd fight like hell for everything else in it."

The vote that carried the new constitution was 135,000 to 79,000. The delegates also amended the constitution to provide two more districts, Numbers 10 and 11, for the installers and the sales group of Western Electric.* The executive board was instructed to submit the new constitution to a referendum, held in September 1950, and two-level was approved by a three-to-one vote. The transition to two-level proceeded smoothly. Amalgamation of the locals reduced the number from 1,400 under the old constitution to the 634 represented at the April 1951 convention when two-level went into effect. In May 1951, the *CWA News* was able to report, "This is the first time our union has not been tied up for months and months when the structure was changed." Two years later, the Western Electric districts were "dissolved," the locals "redesigned" and reassigned to the geographical districts, and the district directors named national directors effective in 1954.**

---

*Beirne's strategy in handling the question of the two additional districts was, apparently, aimed more at the referendum than the actual convention vote. Ernest Weaver and Louis H. Junker, respectively installation and sales spokesmen, voted against the two-level recommendations in the convention roll call but did not campaign against it in the referendum.

**Long Line National Bargaining Unit and Non-Bell National Bargaining Unit directors were not members of the executive board, nor were the directors of Western Electric Installation and Sales Bargaining Units after 1954. The elected leadership of the union remained constant throughout the immediate period following adoption of two-level. Elected in 1951 and again in 1953 were:

J.A. Beirne, president
John L. Crull, vice president
J.J. Moran, vice president
A.T. Jones, vice president
C.W. Werkau, secretary-treasurer
Mary Hanscom, director District 1
Glenn E. Watts, director District 2
W.A. Smallwood, director District 3
Walter Schaar, director District 4
Ray F. Dryer, director District 5
D.L. McCowen, director District 6
J.R. Hill, director District 7

In March 1950, *Fortune* magazine, the nation's most prestigious business journal, noted, "If the Communications Workers of America (CIO) win their showdown with the Bell System, the largest private employer in the U.S. (600,000), the final step in the transformation of a white-collar, middle-class-minded group of employees into a security-conscious, tight-knit trade union will have been completed—and a significant demonstration of the organizing potential of similar groups of workers will have been provided for U.S. labor." Reviewing the recent history of telephone unionism, *Fortune* also noted that, "Broken and dispirited, the union might have fallen apart if it were not for its president, Joe Beirne (pronounced Burn), and his outstanding talent—salesmanship. Handsome, black-haired, and Jersey City Irish—Beirne toured the locals, sold himself and them on the need for a strong centralized organization—which resulted in the CWA."

CWA did not quite win its "showdown" with the Bell System in the spring, but the union's leadership was greatly encouraged by the adoption of two-level. In terms of morale and strength, the union was in a better position to grapple with the industry in the fall of 1950 and again in 1951 negotiations. When the Senate subcommittee on labor management relations proposed looking into Bell Telephone System labor relations, the CWA seized the chance to place the telephone workers case for improved wages as well as for recognition before the public. Beirne made a masterful presentation, detailing the history of telephone unionism, illustrating the manipulative role of AT&T, and stressing the importance of collective bargaining in a democratic society. Moreover, testimony—"out of their own mouths," as the *CWA News* declared—from high company officials bore out CWA's chief contention that "AT&T holds the ultimate life and death power over the managements of the associated companies."**

CWA's case for a wage increase in the fall of 1950 was given a certain

---

LaRoy H. Purdy, director District 8
Joe Deardorff, director District 9
Ernest Weaver, director District 10*
Louis H. Junker, director District 11
Long Lines National Bargaining Unit director, Carl W. Peters
Non-Bell National Bargaining Unit director, J. Curtis Fletcher

*Ernest Weaver died on August 14, 1953 of a heart attack in Greensboro, North Carolina. He was on a visit to a local union at the time. He was replaced by James Massey as unit director of the installation group.
**Witness the following exchange:
MR. BOLENIUS: Mr. Murdock, I think the question of control, if that is what you are inferring, is a question of fact and really not a question of theory. Literally, theoretically through stock control, the AT&T company could completely upset the boards of directors and the officers of a company; to my knowledge I never remember of any such occurrence having taken place.
MR. FREEHILL: Is that because there has been no necessity for it?
MR. BOLENIUS: Yes; I suspect that is true.

urgency by the outbreak of the Korean war. Prices had already begun to rise and, in anticipation of economic controls, the country's unions prepared to defend worker interests. The North Korean Communist forces crossed the thirty-eighth parallel, a United Nations demarcation line imposed as a consequence of the settlement of World War II in the Far East, to attack the Republic of Korea.

The United Nations rallied to resist this act of aggression. Congress passed the Defense Production Act on September 1, 1950, and a few days later President Truman issued an executive order setting up an Economic Stabilization Agency with an Office of Price Stabilization and a tripartite Wage Stabilization Board. Beirne would serve as a member of the Wage Board but as of late 1950 a wage policy had yet to be formulated. In September, the CWA executive board authorized negotiations for voluntary wage increases. "During the past ten years," the *New Republic* observed in November, "the real wages of telephone workers (what the paycheck will buy in terms of today's purchasing power) have remained static. In 1939, telephone workers ranked sixteenth in hourly earnings among 123 major-industry wage earners in this country. Today they rank sixty-seventh. The average hourly earnings of telephone workers are $1.40, while average wages in the automobile industry are $1.75; in steel, $1.70; in coal, $2; in gas and electric utilities, $1.61 an hour." (See chart.)

In response to union pressures, Chrysler, Ford, the Aluminum Corporation, General Electric, Westinghouse and other major corporations negotiated wage increases. But, not Ma Bell. "With a unanimity typical of the Bell System," a CWA *Newsletter* reported, "company managements throughout the country last week refused to move on wages through voluntary contract reopeners." Ma Bell cried poverty, pleading an "inability to pay." Beirne promptly punched a hole into that line of argument, "Telephone business is booming," he said. "Bell System profits have gone up sharply. The company made $110-million more in the past twelve months than they did in the same period a year ago. Profits for the third quarter of 1950 showed a steady increase." AT&T then adopted what Beirne aptly described as a "divide and rule" strategy, seeking to tempt non-CWA independents into below par settlements by dangling wage offers and hoping to use such settlements as pace setters in negotiations with CWA. But CWA countered with an imaginative strategy of its own, a hit-and-run technique that proved to be effective when Western Electric and Michigan Bell were struck on November 9.

CWA's tactical problem, as strike director Robert Pollock pointed out, was to achieve "maximum effectiveness with the forces at hand while imposing as little hardship as possible on the non-striking members." The idea was to hit Bell where it was most vulnerable, then move on before management had a chance to recoup. "Picket lines were established according to plan," the *CWA News* explained after the strike ended. "The technique involved the placing of picket lines before different exchanges each day and then removing them . . . Key in the hit-run strike were the mobile roving picket squads of CWA Divisions 6 and 18, composed of Western Electric installation workers employed in key exchanges and of repair house workers. These workers picketed the buildings in which they [were] employed. Operating company workers employed in the exchanges honored lines in virtually every location picketed." This hampered management scabbing and the use of strike-breakers for by the time management rallied around one location, the pickets were off elsewhere.

Bell management countered with injunctions in Louisiana, Alabama, Virginia, New Jersey, and Cincinnati and Des Moines among other places. It tried to initiate back-to-work movements, telling New Jersey operators, for example, that "they were pulling somebody else's chestnuts out of the fire." Operators who refused to agree to work "regularly" were locked-out. These tactics failed, and at the height of the 11-day strike, as many as 150,000 telephone workers were off the job. Long distance and manual services were badly crippled and even dial service was slowed down. Management finally got down to cases on November 19 when contracts were negotiated for Western Electric after twenty-five hours of continuous bargaining. A contract settlement followed in Michigan, within an hour. Seventeen thousand Western Electric workers obtained average wage increases of 11.3 cents an hour and Michigan workers won increases ranging from $3 to $5 a week. Reclassification of area differentials raised wages by as much as $9 a week in some areas.

"Quiet and persistent" bargaining would characterize the next year when negotiations took place under the eye of a watchful government. The new mood was signaled by rapidly-breaking developments in CWA talks with the Chesapeake and Potomac Company concerning "voluntary" wage agreements. "Hurried," Tommy Jones later told CWA delegates at the 1951 convention, "is not quite an adequate word—these negotiations were literally galloping." In his years of bargaining with the Bell System, Jones had never seen anything like it. "In their philanthropy," he said, "they were just breaking their backs, trying to give away their money." Wartime labor shortages were having an effect, as Jones indicated in a wry comment. "Of course, the fact that a wage freeze was imminent and that they couldn't hire anybody at their scandalously low wages had nothing to do with the matter." Before they were finished, the Chesapeake company agreed to a ten percent wage increase for traffic employees. Despite a wage freeze, imposed on January 25, 1951, the ten percent "wave" would wash over most of the telephone industry. Strike votes were taken quietly and without fanfare, providing a cutting edge to talks between CWA president Beirne, vice president Jones and various Bell System companies' officials in a CWA

Phone Workers State Their Case

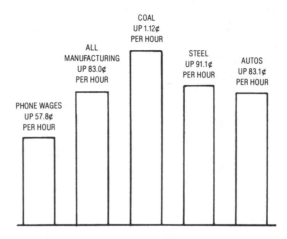

COAL
UP 1.12¢
PER HOUR

ALL
MANUFACTURING
UP 83.0¢
PER HOUR

STEEL
UP 91.1¢
PER HOUR

AUTOS
UP 83.1¢
PER HOUR

PHONE WAGES
UP 57.8¢
PER HOUR

This chart, based on Bureau of Labor Statistics data and prepared by the Communications Workers of America, shows that telephone workers' wages have lagged badly on a cents-per-hour basis.

effort to smooth the way for more realistic negotiations. By the end of June 1951, contracts covering 150,000 Bell workers in eight companies, including Long Lines, were concluded on the basis of the ten percent wage increase formula. CWA had won the absolute maximum allowed under wage stabilization. Revised town and job classifications made for additional wage gains. As Beirne remarked at the close of the 1951 bargaining wave, "Proof positive of the success of our new structure is already here in the pockets of our members."

For all of the "galloping" in 1951, the Bell System was in no hurry to truly recognize CWA. Nor, for that matter, was the system fully open to needed improvements in working conditions and welfare benefits. (See Budget.) As late as 1950, the Bell System, the nation's single largest employer of women, imposed cruel limitations on the rights of their employees to a full and normal life. When Ruth Wiencek visited operators at home during the course of a CWA organizing drive in New England, she discovered, "a rather amazing thing. The key to women's status was whether she was a MT or regular. MT meant 'married temporary,' . . . that she had become

Operator's Budget

NO ENTERTAINMENT, NEW CLOTHES

HERE'S THE budget of New Orleans operator, Quntella C. Hulsey. It shows why phone workers have so badly needed a wage increase.

Salary $35 per week for four weeks—$140 plus Sunday time $6.00. Total $146 minus income tax and social security deductions, making total take home pay less than amount required to cover the barest minimum needed for living expenses.

EXPENSES:	PER MONTH
Rent	$ 50.00
Groceries	$ 45.00
Lights and Gas	$ 7.00
Telephone	$ 2.00
Car Fare	$ 4.20
Taxi Cabs	$ 2.80
Lunches	$ 12.00
Laundry and Cleaning	$ 10.00
(Clothing, Amusement, Doctor Bills, Offering to church, Donations to charity), necessities but insufficient funds.	
Miscellaneous	$ 5.00
TOTAL	$138.00

Source: *CWA News*, June 1951, page 3.

married and she lost her seniority rights. And older single women whom I visited were marked on the organizing cards as 'regular.' And there were obvious signs of men being around the house. Sometimes I'd encounter them ... Finally, when I got to these girls, it was evident that they had been living with these men. Many of them had worked as long as twenty years, twenty-five years, and didn't want to surrender their seniority rights." Deeply religious women with a strong sense of family were forced into either lying or living in sin. And when a married woman had a child, there were no maternity leaves, she was often fired, or in company jargon, she "resigned."

Hit-and-run walkouts flared up in the early 1950s as a consequence of what Tommy Jones termed "management arrogance and duplicity." In part, the idea was to dramatize a particular grievance as when 600 operators walked out of the Dallas exchange during a heat wave to point up the inadequacy of electric fans blowing over tubs of ice as a means of air conditioning. Sometimes a simple "gimmick" would suffice as when Bill Webb rented an ambulance to park alongside a Memphis exchange where Mrs. Gene Cox still worked in her ninth month of pregnancy and had been refused a maternity leave.* A photograph of the ambulance and Mrs. Cox was reprinted all over the country and helped to win maternity benefits in negotiations that year. But often strikes were necessary, as against Pacific Telephone and Telegraph Company in 1951 to force bargaining to a conclusion. And a major strike was necessary to win concessions in 1952 from the Michigan, Ohio, New Jersey, Pacific Bell companies and the Bell Telephone Laboratories and Western Electric. The walkout began on April 7 when Western Electric employees quit work and spread quickly until 31,000 Bell System workers in forty-three states were out. According to *Business Week,* "Up to 200,000 other workers respected the strikers' picket lines." The 1952 strike was short, lasting a few days except at the Tonawanda Western Electric manufacturing plant where it ran twelve weeks, and ended on terms averaging a gain of 11.3 cents an hour.

The increase in strike activity pointed up CWA's greatest weakness, the lack of money earmarked to protect members out on strike. As Jones remarked in his bargaining report to the 1952 convention, "we might observe that self-examination is still needed before some of our units are ready for that 'national bargaining' which practically all profess to desire. Our present centralization is about as close as we can get it, short of the real thing. And yet we find dogged resistance to even-handed direction in some quarters, with all shades and hues of reasons." There will be national bargaining one day, Jones added, but "you can't whip the Bell System" without financial aid. "In terms of desperate financial need, unity is subject to stresses and strain, spirit sags, and no amount of savvy can substitute for real material aid." The debate at the convention was over the kind of defense fund, not over the principle. The majority report favored a fifty cents per member fund administered by the international; the minority favored a fifty-fifty split with half of the money going to the local unions. As June M. Dale, a delegate from Local 9580, put it, "The question seems to be how the money will be handled. It would take us years to accumulate any sizable amount of money; and in my local's opinion, to have money divided into hundreds of locals would be a step backward in the progress

---

*Bill Webb likes to recall that the young lady in question nearly upset carefully laid plans by riding up to work, as she did every morning, sitting side-saddle on her husband's motorcycle. Fortunately, she was headed off by a fellow unionist, who reminded her that that picture would be the one to land in the newspapers and not the one they wanted of the ambulance and the distressed young woman.

of CWA." F.J. "Butch" Novotny, Local 1104, New York Western Electric Sales, however, argued that the locals needed the money, "we still feel now that we were discriminated against . . . This, to me, is nothing but a tragic joke because I know that the locals today with the $3 dues structure are just about getting along, and they cannot stand any additional expenses without increasing their dues." But after two days of hectic debate, the majority of the delegates came to agree with Vincent B. DeMaio, Local 9505, Southern California, who argued, "In the coming crucial years we should not hamstring our union. Strike at your international and you strike at the very core of your union. We are an embattled army. We are an embattled army fighting the smoothly coordinated operating companies. We must also have smoothly coordinated control of our ammunition, smoothly coordinated control of our leadership." By a roll call vote, the delegates voted 133,047 votes in favor of the majority report and 101,883 opposed.

The fund proved to be of almost immediate use. Though "first cluster" bargaining opened in the spring of 1953 with two "harbinger" agreements reached without a strike—Ohio Bell and New Jersey—walkouts broke out during the "second cluster" round of bargaining. Over 5,000 workers at North Carolina Western Electric Radio Shops were out for six weeks in the spring, protesting a substandard wage offer from the company. New Jersey traffic observed picket lines mounted by an unaffiliated plant union, successfully forcing the company to the bargaining table after three days out. A series of hit-and-run stoppages in South Bend, Michigan City and Culver, Indiana, began on July 21, and quickly spread throughout the state. Seven thousand strikers remained out until September 19, despite court injunctions, the use of high school girls as scabs, and the beating of pickets by "goons." The Southwestern strike in August ran twelve days before the company fell into line. CWA spent $766,000 out of the defense fund, most of it for groceries, house rent, coal, clothing, school books, hospital and doctor bills, medicine, and for soup kitchens.*

CWA negotiated more than eighty contracts in 1953, including sixteen out of twenty-one Bell operating companies, five Western Electric manufacturing plants, sales and installation, Bell Laboratories and AT&T Long Lines. "In the main," John L. Crull, who was in charge of overall negotiations, declared, "we accomplished our objectives. We secured pay hikes

---

*The *CWA News,* October 1953, gives the following breakdown of defense fund expeditures:
Indiana strike $450,000.00
North Carolina Radio Shops of Western Electric 215,000.00
Southwestern strike 75,000.00
New Jersey Sympathy strike 26,000.00

TOTAL $766,000.00

which averaged about six and one-half cents an hour from the Bell System. Our gains in the independent portion of the industry were even greater. We shortened progression schedules in most contracts. We reclassified a number of towns and jobs."

The "stall," evasion and procrastination characterized Bell's bargaining stance in 1954. "Our legitimate jurisdiction is the entire communications industry," the delegates to the 1953 convention asserted. That convention had also set bargaining goals for the year, placing at the head of the list hospitalization and surgical benefits as well as improvements in pension benefits.* Yet, by mid year, the *CWA News* would report, "With almost monotonous regularity, CWA contracts with independent companies are negotiated with less trouble, often with greater improvements than with the Bell System." The independents were not out of line with settlements being negotiated within the Bell System, roughly increases ranging from $1 to $2.50 a week at basic wage levels; in some instances they were below, but, in many cases, they were above and included health insurance coverage. "Last year," John Crull pointed out to the 1955 convention, "many companies in other industries reached agreements with their unions, which added hundreds of thousands of workers to the evergrowing list of those receiving these company-paid-for benefits. The Bell System and many of the independent telephone companies are still dragging their feet, lagging far behind the parade in this very important employee welfare field."

"Honest, good-faith bargaining with our union is missing," Beirne declared at the end of 1954. Unnecessary delays, he pointed out in another year-end statement, "were encountered. These could have been resolved more quickly had these [Bell System] companies bargained more maturely." CWA, however, had fended off a major attack on union seniority in a 146-day strike at Western Electric's Tonawanda plant near Buffalo, New York. Moreover, Beirne could cite agreements, "which in the whole were on a par with those secured by most other major unions," obtained "in [the] face of increased unemployment and rather unstable business conditions."

---

*The eleven-point program stressed:
  1. Hospitalization and surgical benefits to be paid for by the employer.
  2. Establishment of pension plans in contracts where such do not now exist and improvement in minimum pension payments in existing plans.
  3. A general wage increase.
  4. Shortened wage progression schedules.
  5. Short tour hours
  6. Six after-six traffic tours (six-hour tours after 6:00 P.M.)
  7. Reclassification of clerical wage rates in all departments.
  8. Job descriptions for all departments.
  9. Elimination of area differentials.
  10. Such local bargaining demands as may appear to be critical.
  11. Elimination of merit systems in Western Electric and Bell Laboratory bargaining units.

It was no mean achievement wrested from an autocratic company. Yet one contract remained unsigned at the end of 1954, though bargaining had been going on, interminably it seemed, since mid summer. Though few knew it, a major confrontation was brewing in the South for as Joe Beirne once warned, "the management of any autocracy cannot indulge in give-and-take based upon facts and reason, but can only revert to dictatorial practices . . ."

XI

A Down South Strike

To imagine the South existing outside this continent, as W.J. Cash observed in his perceptive book, *The Mind of the South,* would be quite impossible. Yet, for all its quintessential Americanisms, the South is, in poet Allen Tate's phrase, "Uncle Sam's other province." Or, so it surely was in 1955, a turn-around year in southern history when blacks took to walking rather than riding in the back of the bus and when telephone workers struck so that they might walk tall beneath the southern sun.

For some time, in the early 1950s, within the CWA the feeling was growing that someday the union and the Bell System would have a show-down. What galled telephone unionists was AT&T's refusal to recognize the union, but perhaps even more irritating was a certain coyness, an off-and-on-again touch to their relationship with the company. The Beirne-Craig agreement of 1946 implied a *de facto* recognition that was un-ceremoniously yanked away a year later. The Korean War with concomitant government regulation imposed bargaining parameters on the industry and created hopes that a true bargaining relationship might, after all, emerge as it had in other major industries following World War II. With an assist from the timely death of Joseph Stalin, President Dwight David Eisenhower ended the war in Korea but failed to manage the transition to a peacetime economy with like success. Dial conversions and the further mechanization of telephone communications intensified the bite of the Ei-senhower recession for the industry, and Ma Bell quickly seized the advantage.

A fifty-nine day strike against the Indiana Bell Telephone Company cost the union $450,000 and twenty workers their jobs. (They never were rein-stated although the CWA did manage to find employment for them else-where.) A six-week Western Electric strike cost the union's defense fund $215,000, another increment of budding bitterness. When Western Electric management at the Tonawanda plant near Buffalo, New York, sought to take away fundamental seniority rights, the union fought back for 146 days on the picket lines over the summer and into the fall of 1955. Over the same time, negotiations were dragged out by Bell management almost intermina-bly even though the final settlements clearly formed an acceptable pattern from the first. Ma Bell seemed to be searching for a weak spot, testing union resistance here and union determination there. Ominously, the weight of the system's opposition to unionism began to settle on the Southern Bell bargaining unit, where negotiations had been underway for nearly six months.

In retrospect, the reasons for this choice are clear. For all its famed hospitality, the South had been hostile to organized labor. After an initial success at the turn of the century among coal miners and iron and steel workers in Alabama, unionism had been crushed by the growing power of the giant corporations rising in the industrial South. The national unions were too weak at the time to come to the aid of beleagured southern unionists and there was no Wagner Labor Act to provide some measure of federal protection. Once won over to the union cause, southern workers were intensely loyal, but they were also fiercely individualistic and deeply religious. This explains the intensity and bitterness of the textile strikes of 1929 and late 1930s, and such anomalies as the Grover, North Carolina, textile local that surrendered its charter after it had gained recognition from the mill owners, on the ground that after looking into the matter it had concluded that unions were incompatible with Christianity. Ben Porch recalls that when he was in the first grade in Alexander City, Alabama, the workers of the Avondale Mills blockaded the roads with cotton bales and, armed with shotguns and a machine gun, stood guard "to protect the city *from the CIO.*" (My italics.)

With the passage of the Wagner Labor Act, the labor movement made some inroads. After World War II both the AFL and the CIO mounted drives to organize workers in the South, and by 1947, the CIO claimed 28,000 new members and the AFL 330,000 in the region. But the Taft-Hartley Act laid the way open for the passage of so-called Right to Work laws in the states, and most, if not all, of the southern states quickly adopted such legislation. Labor's southern drives, in the words of historian Philip Taft, "quietly expired." By 1955, the South was the home of the runaway shop and a mere fifteen percent of the southern labor force carried union cards. Ominously for CWA, a 1954 strike against the independent Alabama Telephone Company in Reform, Fayette and Haleyville counties ran for almost one year. Seven of the fifty strikers faced jail sentences for "abusive language" on the picket lines. An operator of a non-union mill told his employees that he would fire them if he caught them even speaking to the striking telephone workers. Within the South, nonetheless, CWA was a major trade union beachhead, covering nine states with 126 locals reaching into more than 600 southern communities. "Working together for their own protection and welfare," as Lee White reported in the *CWA News* (December 1951), the 32,000 men and women organized in CWA District 3 had "helped the South, too. . . . Telephone workers, like their fellows in other CIO affiliates, have become community-conscious as the years went by.

They have broadened their concept of the role of the union member in community life. They are making themselves heard in the Community Chest Drive, in the bond drive, in political activity and in civic affairs." This activity would stand them in good stead in the struggle that lay ahead.

By the end of September 1954, when CWA first withdrew "temporarily," its notice of contract termination—an unprecedented step—to allow negotiations with Southern Bell to continue, a majority of Bell companies (twenty-three) had acceded to the year's pattern, withdrawing demands that would have weakened already-won rights and granting four to seven cents-an-hour increases. The Southern Bell bargaining committee, chaired by Lonnie B. Daniel with Ed Hayden, Bessie Kerr, A.B. Long and Margaret Roepke, had reason to be hopeful. They had proposed a package that ought to have broken the log-jam, including proposed wage increases, town reclassifications, schedule shortening, short-hour tours, and changes in the arbitration procedure. The union indicated its willingness to sign a statement of recognition of obligation to process grievances through an improved machinery of settlement. This was designed to meet specific, and to some extent justified, management complaints about wild-cat walkouts. The company countered with some concessions on wages, town classification and short-term tours, and a movement towards the settlement pattern appeared to be underway.

Then Southern Bell opened a cold war front. It circulated the story that the union was holding up a wage increase "the workers are entitled to receive," even though it was the company that had refused to put proposed wage increases into effect, a proposition amenable to the union. It soon became clear that the company had not introduced a no-strike clause as a matter of strategy—as several other Bell companies had done, later withdrawing the idea. Southern Bell remained adamant, insisting that "the parties agree that there shall be no lock-out, strike, slow-down or other interruption of service during the life of the contract." No-strike clauses are not exactly unheard of in labor-management agreements and they exist today in most CWA contracts. But they are accompanied by the arbitration of differences and by the union-shop or some other type of union security. Southern Bell flatly refused to agree to expansion of arbitration and fell-back on southern states right-to-work laws, which outlawed the union shop, to avoid the guarantee of security.

Relations between the Southern company and the union were turbulent. Fred Turner, Southern Bell president, was a boss of the old school; paternal when he could run the show but obstinate and hostile when workers asserted their rights. During the past year there had been about thirty quickie strikes and between 1947 and 1955, according to George E. Gill, then assistant district director of the region, "we had more than a hundred wildcat strikes." Workers struck "over things that they had been putting up with for years; they all of a sudden decided that they couldn't stand it any longer." Women were sitting at the switchboard, in Georgia director Earle Moye's colorful phrase, "with not a dry thread on them, wringing wet with perspiration . . . We had the girls start wearing shorts to work. Then the company would send them home, see . . ." These strikes often worked, and the workers learned something about solidarity. Outside repairmen, Gill says, "learned from the '47 strike the spirit of unity, you know, solidarity. And they made the determination that they weren't going to cross anybody's picket lines because they knew how it felt. So we had a lot of cases where the company would suspend the guy because he refused to cross the picket line, and then the favorite answer to that was to call the local out on strike and tell them: When you let him go back, then we'll go back."

The worker's right to respect another's legitimate picket line is crucial to the labor movement, and especially so to the CWA where a strike, say, of one bargaining unit is immensely strengthened by the refusal to cross picket lines by Western Electric installers and Long Lines workers, or vice versa. Southern Bell's "no strike" demand aimed at the very heart of the union, and in more than one way. As CWA president Beirne pointed out, "Under the Southern Bell 'no-strike proposal' almost any action on the part of the worker may be construed by the company to be a work interruption—or slowdown—at which point a supervisor could discipline or discharge a worker without the slightest danger of answering responsibility for an unjust action. Under their proposal union officers or selected groups of individual workers could be disciplined or discharged by the company without fear of the company having to answer for their action." The potential for union-busting need not be spelled out, but an example given by District 3 director W.A. Smallwood illustrates the danger. A grievance was settled at a high company level, not long before the strike, but then management flatly refused to live up to the company's pledged word. When reason and logic failed to move the company, the workers took matters into their own hands and walked off the job. At that point, the company agreed to live up to its written promise. Such cases, Smallwood declared, "let us to believe that the company has a motive in its demand which is far beyond anything involved in the question of work interruptions. We frankly admit that the union has a responsibility to share in this connection, but we have proved that the problem can be controlled by any number of ways short of placing a club in the hands of the company . . . the question goes deeper than anything the union has yet faced in its dealings with the Bell System." As Lonnie Daniel, head of the bargaining committee, succinctly put it, the company "thought that with a good fracas, they could just tear the union asunder."

CWA had been patient, as Beirne observed on the eve of the strike, but that patience wore thin as the company remained adamant, stretching out the talks month after month. Finally, after filing a sixty-day strike notice, as required by law, and securing a strike authorization from the national union, the Southern Bell bargaining unit set a strike date. At midnight, March 14, the nine states walkout of 50,000 telephone workers began, including several thousand Long Lines, Western Electric sales and installation workers. The official call had been set for 3:00 A.M., but many workers left their jobs earlier. Picketing at the telephone exchanges on the first day was described by the *New York Times* correspondent as "generally peaceful." Within a few hours, the first cable was mysteriously cut. At 4:45 A.M., according to W.A. Thompson, Alabama manager of the company, 100 pairs of wires in the Birmingham-New Orleans toll cable had been "severed" somewhere southwest of Birmingham. "It was no accident as far as we can determine," Thompson said, charging "deliberate sabotage." Southern Bell promptly organized "security patrols," allegedly aimed at preventing further line-cutting. Within the next forty-eight hours, the company charged that it had been "sabotaged" forty-six times in three states. Rewards totalling $10,000 were immediately offered to anyone providing evidence leading to the conviction of the saboteurs. District strike director George E. Gill promptly declared that the vandalism "is none of our doing. We neither initiate nor condone such action." And Henry H. Bolin, president of the Birmingham local, echoed the feeling of CWA when he said, "We are resentful that the company would even conceive of us performing such acts."

There is evidence that Southern Bell was well prepared for the strike long before it took place. As CWA vice president and national strike director A.T. "Tommy" Jones pointed out, Southern Bell maintained "an army of professional strike-breakers" in supervisory ranks. "Supervisors consistently do the work of nonsupervisory personnel," Jones noted. "The company has, by their own figures, one supervisor for every five workers." *Business Week,* on March 19 at the start of the strike, tipped the company's hand, reporting, "Their [the strikers'] jobs were taken over by supervisory personnel and other company employees, *many pre-trained in handling switchboard jobs.* " (My italics.) To supplement its own supervisory force of 10,000, the Southern company imported scabs drawn from the supervisory staffs of the "other" Bell companies. And, according to James E. Youngdahl, an assistant regional director of the Amalgamated Clothing Workers, "a well-planned effort . . . underway for some time before the strike began" succeeded in recruiting "several thousand students from colleges and universities all over the South who proved willing to cross picket lines." Just as Harvard students were used to break the famous 1919 Boston police strike, students from Georgia Tech, the Alabama Polytechnic Institute at Auburn, and Louisiana State were aksed to perform the same service in the 1955 telephone strike. "Nearly 300 Tulane students," Youngdahl reported, "maintained manual switchboards in New Orleans. Football players led crowds of Mississippi Southern students across the lines, jeering the pickets."

The jeering students actually turned out to be an exception. No other strike in southern history has ever drawn such broad popular support. In Americus, Georgia, pickets were invited to use the home of the mayor, next to the telephone building, as strike headquarters. In Slidell, Louisiana, a local merchant put up an awning to protect the strikers from the hot sun. When Reverend Cantebury of Sunflower County, Mississippi, heard some of his members en route to church yelling, "Communists," at picketing telephone operators, he tossed away his sermon notes and preached that the brotherhood of man is in trade unionism. "He had people coming out and apologizing to those girls," Mississippi strike director Bill Webb later reported. When the ladies of Corinth, Mississippi, gave a wiener roast for CWA members and their families right next door to the telephone exchange they had a bonfire to cheer the dark night-picket line. Company officials summoned the fire department and the police and two pumpers and three squad cars showed up, sirens screaming. But instead of the expected arrests and dousing of the fire, the firemen and the police joined the festivities. As for the Mississippi Southern students, they scarcely lasted the day at the Hattiesburg exchange. When telephone workers massed in front of the building, demanding the students be sent back to the campus, Chief of Police Hugh Hering also showed up to keep the peace. At this point, more often than not in the history of strikes, the police would have shepherded the scabs, especially so in right-to-work states. But when Hering made it clear that he was going to do his job—and nothing more—the company quickly caved in and the students were sent packing under the cover of darkness.

"We had no idea when we went on strike March 14 that such terrific support would develop from other labor organizations and from the public," W.A. Smallwood told Youngdahl. "Somehow our strike caught the imagination of the people." Elected officials often cooperated with CWA officers. As James L. Mahady, Louisiana strike director, later pointed out: "The police almost never interfered in any strike activity except where they were called by the company, and even when they were called by the company in some places, they were irritated as hell at being called. They didn't want to get involved at *all* one way or the other and they resented being called." Mahady believes that the "personal contact that goes on every day between Joe Doaks, the local installer repairman, and the power structure of the community" explained this phenomenon. "If the city is big enough to have a fulltime mayor," Mahady explained, "some telephone worker, not management but worker, is in the city hall . . . almost every day and on a first-name basis, and talks to them that way. And when the telephone company calls to make a complaint, they [city officials] say, 'Now look, Joe

Doaks don't go running around with bombs blowing up people. I know him."

Thomas Adair, legal counsel to CWA District 3, makes the same point, townsfolk "look on the [CWA] member as being a fellow townsman, who perhaps goes to the same church, uses the same doctor, or has coffee with them, puts in their telephone and chats with them." Adair also adds that the very nature of telephone work is that these citizens of the town who are also telephone employees are voters and they are in most all of the towns and communities throughout the South, and I think there's recognition on the part of the public officials that there is some political weight there that makes them hesitant to mistreat the telephone worker who is a member of CWA." Drawing upon his experience as a labor attorney, Adair notes that the treatment of labor in the South varies with the size, location and character of the city or town. "Mistreatment," he says, "was the rule for other unions in the southern half of Georgia, Alabama, most of all Mississippi and in Northern Louisiana," but "it was not as bad for CWA members." A factor in this difference, Adair believes, "is that CWA as an organization has emphasized community activity, and in many locations there are members and local officers of the CWA locals that are very active in the community chest drives and in Boy Scout work and church work and various other community endeavors. And this tends to identify them with the community and with the leadership in the community and with those people who are trying to do things for the general betterment of the community." Moreover, the telephone company was often seen as an outsider, somewhat removed from local concerns, and not intrinsically linked to the economy of the community. As Adair points out, "Many of the manufacturing plants in textile and other fields that have moved into southern communities have been heavily subsidized by those communities, either giving them tax exemptions, or buildings being built for the manufacturing concern, or stock being sold locally with some ownership. In this type of situation, if there is an active labor dispute or an attempt to organize by a union such as UAW or the textile workers, the community immediately becomes defensive and fears that whatever they've invested may be lost, and these employers quite often are able to convince the community that they will have to move the plant or close the plant down if a union comes in, because they could not afford to meet the demands of the union." With Southern Bell this was not the case.

While local community support was vital to the success of the strike, it was sometimes embarrassing. On seeing a telephone lineman climb a pole, a Georgia farmer was so incensed that he tried to knock the man off by hitting the pole with his pick-up truck, and he wasn't much mollified when he discovered that the hapless lineman worked for a local independent company and was not on strike. Local youth discovered a new sport, testing their markmanship by shooting down telephone wires at night with their hunting rifles. "Our cause cannot be served by vandalism," W.A. Smallwood found himself pleading more than once during the strike-torn seventy-two days. "Our enemies know that and we trust that our friends, wherever they may be, will know and remember that we are striking on matters of high principle and we desire intensely to keep the strike on the same high plane."

CWA members, too, were often cheeky, difficult to discipline. In Hattiesburg, a short, scrappy plant man showed up everyday for the picketing and when a supervisor came out and started up the street, he would get right behind him and "kick his butt about every other step," putting on a show for his fellow workers. "I remember visiting the local office one afternoon," Bill Webb says, "to meet with the defense fund committee and all at once I heard a guy yell out—he was calling out to a scab named Black there, the notorious scab, I think the only man in the plant building. He was saying, 'Come on out the door, Black, and I'll blow your guts out,' you know. And there he stood with an automatic shotgun cocked. So one of the local officers runs down and gets the gun away from him and brings it back upstairs and gives him some money and tells him to buy some fish bait or something and go fishing, get out of their hair. 'You're going to get in jail.' So the guy agrees and disappears, and I guess forty-five minutes passes and we hear him again. We look down and he's gone and gotten another shotgun. So they had to go and take it away from him a second time and take him home. I think that he was drinking a lot."

"We had more militant members," George E. Gill acknowledged. "They weren't really afraid of what was going to happen to 'em . . . This made the '55 strike impossible to control and difficult to lead. This caused people to do things outside the policies of the union, against the advice of the officers and the staff." The strain on the staff was considerable.* "Strike activity on the part of a staff man is always more maintaining morale of the striking members than it is anything else," according to area director W.W. Brown, who covered South Carolina, Georgia and Florida to do just that. "You do a million things. You work with this committee and that committee and

*Field staff at the time consisted of area directors W.W. Brown (South Carolina, Georgia and Florida), R.B. "Ben" Porch (Kentucky, Tennessee and North Carolina) and Sam Sims (Alabama, Mississippi and Louisiana) and a strike director for each state:

Florida	Roy Armstrong
Georgia	Earle Moye
Kentucky	W.C. Sigler
Louisiana	James L. Mahady
Mississippi	James W. Webb
North Carolina	L.L. Bolick
South Carolina	T.J. Volk
Tennessee	W.E. Buttram
Alabama	J.M. Van Houten

help solve little details; suggest that 'This is where you carry your work out' and that kind of stuff. Talking to individuals and to groups, trying to keep the spirit alive and morale high more than any other one thing." Sam Sims "traveled extensively from town to town, state to state, local to local, addressing meetings mainly because most of my time was used in doing that." Selina Burch gave James L. Mahady a hand in directing strike activities in Louisiana, but "she stayed right here in New Orleans. We didn't think it was a good idea to have a woman traveling over the state during this period," Mahady recalls, "at all times of day and night, and everything else." Margaret Kennedy assisted Bill Webb in Mississippi, and all the strike directors put in countless hours marching on picket lines. "We kind of lived in automobiles," Bill Webb says. "In the last portion of it I was reluctant to travel alone, fearful I might be accused of some violence or something like that. The company had lots of detectives hired and things like that, so I had these meetings every night, strike meetings at different locations and many times [had to drive] back to Jackson at night. So I made sure I took somebody with me, you know, that wasn't involved in anything during the meeting."

Roy Armstrong, who directed the strike in Florida, gives us some idea of what it was like to be on the road almost constantly. "It's some 700 miles from Pensacola to Miami and I was covering the whole state. I drove night and day and slept very little and ate less, but I visited the picket lines, I held meetings daily in one town or another. I was trying to coordinate whatever programs [were] going on during the strike, various types of activity such as getting relief for the people that [weren't] working, seeing that the picket lines were conducted properly, without any involvement with outsiders or the company, and trying to keep it [as] cool as possible because it's during such times as that, after so many weeks, tempers do get rather frayed. Sometimes you get someone to promise you to do something to keep cool and a few minutes later he's pretty warm about something if somebody hits him wrong. Trying to locate people and select people that would watch these things and keep our picket line moving without any violence or any bad effect from the public. I was moving from one group to another, and I would meet until a late hour with one group, and then I would start traveling, maybe sleep a few hours after I got there in the morning, then I would start holding meetings until the wee hours, and I just kept repeating this, not eating at the right time or not eating at all. I'm one of these people that can go without eating a long time. In fact, I have a reputation of starving everybody to death that rides with me anywhere. Consequently, I lost a considerable amount of weight, but all in all I think that we had a cool, successful strike . . ."

There were frustrations. While the five-member CWA bargaining committee worked night and day, searching for a solution, the company remained adamant. As the *CWA News* reported late in the second month of the walk out, "Management negotiators haven't changed their position in any respect since the strike began." President Beirne reported in the same issue, "They have said to us—Yes, we are part of the scheme which results in Western Electric, Long Lines and other groups in CWA having contracts expiring in different months of the year. Yes—we are part of the management team in the Bell System who directly affects decisions in the Western Electric and Long Lines. Yes—we know we can refuse to reach agreement in Western Electric and Long Lines just as we are refusing to reach agreement in Southern Bell. *Yes—we are deliberate when we tell you to drive your own members through your own legal picket lines.* . . .

"Behind the whole dispute is the Bell System management. They have detailed written plans of operation and they act like the Chiefs of Staff in the military establishment. Does anyone honestly believe that thousands of management people were voluntarily shipped into the Southern area? They were ordered to scab—or else. It is that simple when one has the power of economic life or death. . . . While they worry and spend countless hundreds of thousands of dollars on maintaining service and while they play games in public print, they could settle the matter at less cost to the public if they worked half as hard to settle with the union—which one day they will have to do anyway."

Commenting on the current state of negotiations, or to be correct, on the lack thereof, Beirne stated, "Impossible conditions attached to the company's no-strike pledge demand—while refusing union demands for unlimited arbitration of employee grievances as a substitute for strike power—can be taken in only one way. We can't help but view it as a move to bust up the union. The company is asking us to commit hari-kari, and we're not planning to do that."

The lack of movement in Atlanta meant a lack of knowledge out on the picket lines. Rather plaintively, Mahady reported, "I think it had a very reassuring effect on them to see somebody from staff, you know, come out there and share their lack of knowledge . . . They didn't know anything, they weren't hearing anything, neither were we." Such uncertainties were compounded by the inability of the strikers to truly shut down Southern Bell. "Telephone service," Thomas Adair conceded, "was not completely disrupted and you were still able in most places to get a long distance call through; the company utilized its management personnel, including, for instance, its whole legal department." Under such circumstances, the temptation to sabotage may have been too great for some telephone workers, especially since it was in maintenance and repairs that the company remained vulnerable. Where dial telephones had been installed, service—short of a breakdown of equipment—was virtually uninterruptible and scabs sufficed to keep up some level of long-distance service. As Adair noted, "Although people could get a long distance call through, it was not handled with any real efficiency . . . Of course, the company stopped altogether doing routine servicing and putting in new installations, continuing with construction work and that sort of thing."

As great as the temptation may have been, and it arises whenever strikes involve automated production, equipment or services, the union could not condone sabotage. In an exchange with CIO president Walter P. Reuther, CWA president Beirne made this clear. Reuther had expressed concern over the almost daily stories in the press reporting damage to company property, saying "Your union, I am confident, recognizes that malicious damage to property should have no place in the industrial-relations sphere." Beirne did not deny that here and there misguided workers may have damaged company property, but he did point out other possible culprits: friends of the strikers, enemies of the company, even enemies of the union seeking to discredit it. "We do all we can to prevent such damage," the CWA president declared. The union was willing to arbitrate all issues, he added, and acceptance by the company of arbitration would surely end the costly strike. "We feel that peaceful picketing, plus continued negotiations across the conference table, plus publicity of the union's position, should ultimately bring about a settlement of the strike."

At the staff level, according to Jim Mahady, the union urged its members constantly, "For God's sake, don't resort to violence because we're doing fine. We're getting a good press . . ."

The union, however, was not entirely without resource. To harass the company's scabs and otherwise interfere with telephone service, it launched Operation Zilch. It started when Tommy Jones urged strikers to tie up long-distance lines with person-to-person calls for "long-lost uncles," such as "J.P. Zilch." To set-up a telephonic picket line, the union published a list of 770 numbers to call, referring calls "in chain fashion from one number to another." As one strike leader told *Time* magazine, "We can keep the ones who are working so busy it won't be easy for them to make money for Bell Telephone." From Salisbury, North Carolina, a typical Zilch-caller asked for Joyce Scoto at a Birmingham number. The operator calling that number was told that the party could be reached at another, and so it went for twelve times in all and for sixty minutes. To curb the "nuisance," the company sought an injunction and $60,000 in damages from ninety-nine Georgia unionists. "And all we were doing," said one, "was just using the telephone."

Still, there was some fraying at the edges as the strike stretched out. Here and there some people would drift back to work. Visiting one of the few hostile communities in Louisiana, Jim Mahady discovered that nearly everyone had gone back to work. "Two of our plant boys were sitting in front of the office playing mumblety-peg," and one told him, "These people just can't stand the pressure." When Mahady asked why the two plantmen had not gone back, one said, "Well, we believe in what we're out here for or we wouldn't have come out in the first place if we didn't believe it. Going to stay until the bitter end." In Sardis, Mississippi, a fast-talking chief operator talked all the operators into going back to work, but when Mary Calthorp, a local officer, returned from a regional meeting she stormed over to the exchange, shouting in through the entrance, "Get yourself out of that office. How dare you?" And the young women walked out and stayed out to the end of the strike. When the local president in Orlando, Florida, wanted to return to work, shaken by the confession of a member that he had slashed six cables, the union held a mass meeting. Roy Armstrong recalls what happened with a note of awe, "This guy got up and said he'd had a *dream* that told him he ought to go back to work. And he was going to follow the dictates of that dream. So he gets up and starts out of the meeting [saying], 'Anybody else that want to go back, let's go.' Well, there was one guy who was shakey anyway [who] got up, a toll test board man, got up and walked out with him—out of two, three hundred people. And there was this little girl, who is now in supervision down there, girl named Polly Merritt, boy, the fire flew out of her eyes, and she said, 'This strike is not over by a *damn* sight!' And you ought to have heard that hall. Something shook those people up to see that guy turn around like that, and they were more determined from then on than ever to hold the line because their leader, the local president, defected on them."

As the strike dragged on into that "cruelest month," April, the company intensified its attack, pressing for arrests, seeking injunctions and threatening discharges. "As time went on during the seventy-two-day period," Adair later recalled, "we had *hundreds* of local cases—criminal charges— and that sort of thing pending—and dozens of injunction cases." In some cases, injunctions were issued *ex parte,* that is without notice to the union and without a hearing. In Louisville, Kentucky, the company secured an injunction against picketing, and, "we decided that we would ignore it." And Miss Mabel Cooney, the traffic representative, added, "So they came down and hauled a lot of us to jail." Repeatedly, Birmingham police broke up peaceful telephone-worker demonstrations, Police Commissioner Robert Lindberg proclaimed a state of emergency in the city, and the sheriff of Jefferson County (Birmingham) requested National Guard intervention. (Governor James E. Folsom wisely refused to intervene, saying that he "couldn't possibly imagine why troops would be needed.") Two thugs forced their way into the Chattanooga, Tennessee, CWA offices, where one held Local 3802 president W.A. Carmichael at gun point while the other broke up the furniture and yanked out telephone wires. A private detective, who later confessed that he had been hired by the telephone company, appeared at the home of E. Seaborn Tibbitts, vice president of the Atlanta local, waving brass knuckles. He had been assigned the job of "roughing up" Tibbitts, but apparently his heart was not in it for he was easily subdued despite being armed with a pistol. Tibbitts called the police and the southern Sam Spade spent sixty days in the county jail.

Forty policemen with an assist from the local firemen hosed down demonstrators outside the downtown Miami telephone exchange on April 23. Telephone workers had gathered to protest the use of scabs. Someone threw some paint at the police and the hoses were turned on, knocking strikers to the ground. Seven men were arrested and charged with "disorderly conduct." Speaking for the Miami local, Howard Walton denounced the police action as "one of the most disgraceful acts I have ever seen." When strikebreakers showed up in Holly Springs, Mississippi, driving a telephone repair truck, three local members went over to talk to them. And after they had explained what the strike was about, the "scabs" joined the union and left the company truck sitting there. The company retaliated by filing charges against the three CWA members under an old statute barring interference with "a man's lawful vocation," which carried a penalty of three years in the penitentiary. In Tupelo, Mississippi, prodded by the company, the local police arrested fifty-two plant men while they were at church, charging them with the crime of "threatening to breach the peace and tranquillity of the community." Telephone unionists wrung a bit of wry humor out of some arrests, as in "the case of the double-barreled spitter." A young lady, on the Gulf Coast of Mississippi, was arrested for spitting through a cab window at a scab. There were two scabs in the taxi, and each testified in the court that they had been spat on in one spit, so to speak.

A big city mayor issued "shoot to kill" orders against "vandals." A Pensacola, Florida, justice of the peace released a gun-toting strikebreaker, berating CWA members who had complained. Four weeks later, the same man struck a picket captain over the head with the butt of his pistol, then stuck the gun into the stomach of Local 3109 member Cecil Bragg and pulled the trigger. (Though the bullet grazed Bragg's kidney and spine, he survived after transfusions given by his fellow unionists.) Several exchanges were dynamited during the course of the strike, cables were cut and other equipment damaged. Florida Local 3112 offered a $500 award—a lot of money for a small local—for the arrest and conviction of whoever dynamited two exchanges in the West Palm beach area. The company filed a complaint against CWA with the National Labor Relations Board charging the union with mass picketing, abusive language, violence and damage to company property. James Shelby, an assistant to CWA vice president Moran, and Charles Perry, president of Local 3511, and two other CWA members were charged with a conspiracy to damage Southern Bell property. Before the strike ended, Southern Bell discharged 249 strikers for offenses ranging from alleged "verbal abuse" to alleged "sabotage. It also claimed $5 million in property damage—3,000 instances of "major damage"—in a post-strike suit against the union.

Long strikes are costly strikes. As James L. Mehaffey of Local 3403, reminded fellow delegates at the 1955 CWA convention, "Our grocery bill in our little town of Baton Rouge amounted to $3,000 a week to feed our people. It was ten weeks. Now you can figure that easy. Three times ten . . . You have to buy special diets for some children. You have to have a quick cash emergency for someone who is in an accident, and the hospital demands cash on the barrel before they take them in. You cannot leave your people on the street bleeding to death." During the course of the seventy-two-day strike, the CWA Defense Fund spent $4,313,212.98. CWA members contributed $350,000 to the fund and another $75,000 to the Communications Workers' Relief Committee. Gus Cramer, fresh from an identical job in the Towawanda strike, recalls overseeing the Georgia strike fund. "I wrote checks totaling almost $1 million, of which ninety-three cents of every dollar went direct to the members or their families for food, shelter and clothing and the other necessaries of life that without which the employees would have certainly been whipped to the ground." It was a touchy job, as Miss Martha Moudy, who handled the defense fund for South Carolina, has remembered. "Some of the locals did real well in handling the defense fund. Other locals did a miserable job in handling the defense fund and made people mad, and they went back to work." And Earle Moye recalled that "some people weren't getting anything; others were getting too much . . ." Still, considering the amounts of money as well as the number of people involved, there were very few complaints. The successful operation of the Fund was essential to the strike, and indeed, had not various CIO unions come through with a loan totalling $1.25 million at a crucial moment the fund might have gone under and with it the strike itself. The United Auto Workers advanced $500,000 as did the Steelworkers while the Amalgamated Clothing Workers stood security for a $250,000 loan from the Amalgamated Bank.*

Public pressure for a settlement mounted in the face of Southern Bell's refusal to negotiate or submit to arbitration dispute issues. The union had proposed arbitration but increasingly felt that some outside intervention was needed to get Southern Bell to accept or to get moving toward a settlement of some kind. Various feelers were out when, in mid-April, Bill Webb received a call from the governor of Mississippi, Hugh White, asking Webb to meet him at the governor's mansion. "His assistant had been in

---

*When CWA paid back the money, according to vice president John Crull, the auto and steel unions returned half of it. Crull quotes UAW president, Walter P. Reuther as saying, "Here take this back and use it for organizing. You *need* it now that your strike is over." And, Crull added, "the Steelworkers couldn't be beat by the Auto Workers, so they said, 'We'll do it, too.' "

college with my brother, so I knew the governor, and my daddy knew him well, you know." Governor White told Webb that he wanted to intercede, and Webb replied that he had best talk with district director Smallwood. "I couldn't call on the phone because the scab operators were listening in, you know, to everything. So I had to arrange this where I gave a predesignated pay station number, you know, and Smallwood had Lee White, his P.R. man, call me at that number and I related to Lee what the situation was with the governor and to get clearance from Smallwood as to whether or not we wanted to try and go through with this. They all very definitely wanted to try to go through with this." A conference of the southern governors to discuss means of ending the telephone strike and the concurrent Louisville and Nashville Rail Road walkout was proposed. The governors of the thirteen southern states met in Nashville where they issued a statement demanding that the communications and rail strikers return to work immediately. The statement added that "every consideration of economic justice" would require that if the strikers agreed to go back, the employers should pledge arbitration in the railroad case and special negotiations in the telephone strike. The governors also appointed a sub-committee of Governor White of Mississippi, Governor James Folsom of Alabama and Governor Marvin Griffin of Georgia to meet with company and union representatives. The three governors did so on April 23 in Atlanta.

While nothing much came of the governors' settlement attempt, the Atlanta meeting did focus public attention on CWA's willingness to arbitrate its differences with Southern Bell and on the company's callous inflexibility. The three governors met with both company and union officials but, unfortunately, according to Adair, they agreed beforehand that any recommendations had to be unanimous. Georgia's Governor Griffin, Adair adds, "neither understood arbitration nor did he understand *any* position that some outsider should tell a company what it had to do with its own money and employees." Governors White and Folsom, however, strongly favored arbitration but were hamstrung by their prior commitment to unanimity. Once back home in Alabama, Governor Folsom did blast the company's position as unreasonable. Folsom termed Alabama's right-to-work law a "right-to-wreck" law, adding, "the telephone company is the largest, dominatingest, most monopolistic corporation in the world. When a corporation gets all-powerful as AT&T it should become some sort of public corporation." And he expressed the feelings of a growing number of southerners: "They are trying to make the South a guinea pig in a test tube. They are trying to run over the workers and make them work for low wages and I resent it."

Southern Bell president Fred J. Turner reiterated the company's opposition to arbitration, and advertisements were placed in the major newspapers proclaiming that "Arbitration is Not the Answer." In a letter to Senator

Estes Kefauver (D., Tenn.), Turner claimed that the issues involved in the strike were "fundamental" to the operation of the company and should not be submitted to arbitration. Senator Kefauver—with Senator Russell B. Long (D., La.), concurring—replied on the floor of the Senate, where he contrasted CWA's repeated willingness to arbitrate with the company's refusal, by saying, "This is, it seems to me, a dispute that could be arbitrated. When negotiators cannot agree after ten months to serve all the people then it is time to call in neutral outside parties to settle the differences." When President Eisenhower in his May 5 press conference declared that "the prospects of a settlement are bright indeed," which was news to the hard-pressed union negotiators, CWA president Beirne requested that the White House propose "full public arbitration" of the dispute and that the President name the arbitrator. Pointing out that CWA's efforts at settlement had been met by "arrogant indifference," Beirne wrote, "In the past four years our union has brought over 3,000 grievances before the company, some of which involved flagrant contract violations. Because of the company's refusal to include fair arbitration procedures in the contract, we found ourselves without adequate peaceful means to obtain just settlement of these grievances. Now, the Southern Bell Telephone Company is demanding inclusion within the contract of a tight 'no strike' clause. Mr. President, we have agreed to accept such a clause, provided the company will accept standard arbitration procedures for resolving any disputes arising from the application of the contract. This the company has refused to do."

A company spokesman issued a blast against the union, charging that its arbitration proposal was "a calculated attempt to gain from an arbitrator what the union has not been able to justify through the process of collective bargaining." If Joe Beirne hadn't been so angry, he might have laughed at the company's nerve for, as he immediately pointed out, in collective bargaining there is supposed to be give and take and with "the telephone company it is all take and no give." President Eisenhower waffled, and his legal counsel informed the union that there was no national emergency that would justify intervention. The President, persistently questioned by the press, cautiously endorsed arbitration and announced that the federal mediation service was "working" at achieving a settlement. When asked, "And therefore the pattern of arbitration [it had been accepted by both parties in the railroad strike] will be just as useful?" the President replied, "In my opinion, yes." The movement towards settlement had quickened.

On May 25, 1955, after seventy-two days on the picket lines, the strike weary Southern telephone workers returned to work. They did so after approving a one-year contract with basic wage increases ranging from $1 to $4 a week for all employees in the bargaining unit, about 50,000. (The company had wanted to exclude 5,000 low seniority workers.) The contract also provided for arbitration of suspensions and discharges, of disputes over job vacancy fillings and selection for training. Work tours for operators were reduced with the six and one-half-hour tour cut to six hours, seven-hour tours ending after midnight cut to six and one-half hours, and eight-hour tours ending at 10:30 P.M., cut to seven hours. A total of twenty-five cities were upgraded by at least an additional $1 a week while the upgrading of several hundred assignment men by one step added $3 to $4 to their weekly wage. On the central issue, the union won a major concession, a contractual right to respect legitimate picket lines. It was, as Bill Smallwood put it, "a ringing victory for union principles." The essential clause read: "The company agrees that it will not discipline an employee for violating any provision of the agreement solely because he refuses to cross an author-ized picket line established in connection with a lawful strike at premises where such striking employees are working." The company could no longer force telephone workers to cross picket lines, whether manned by fellow telephone workers—Western Electric installers, sales or Long Lines—or by fellow workers in another industry. It was no small gain for so long a strike.

One issue remained sticky to the very end of the two-day, around-the-clock settlement negotiations: What to do about the 249 workers discharged by the company during the course of the strike? The union was still smart-ing over its inability to reinstate the twenty strikers fired in the fifty-nine-day struggle against Indiana Bell.* The company agreed to submit each case individually to arbitration in the expectation, as a company attorney told Adair, that "if you win five percent of them, we'll be surprised. We think we used the right standards and we think we have the proof, and we don't expect you to win five percent of them, and maybe none." As a consequence, CWA became engaged in what labor historian Philip Taft termed "one of the largest arbitrations in the history of American labor disputes." Four arbitrators were selected, and meeting as a group, they decided on the procedural rules. Single arbitrators held hearings in the localities where the alleged misconduct took place. Arbitrators were empowered to sustain, set aside, or modify the penalty and to order back pay. Over the year-long proceedings, that company, in the words of CWA General Counsel Charles V. Koons, "was very picayune and very, shall we say, vindictive." As Bill Webb described the proceedings in Mississippi, "If you left home with a case of eggs in the back seat of your car and you went out to the picket line and passed them out to everybody that was massed in front of the company and yelled, 'Throw the damn things,' the arbitrator would uphold your discharge. [That was 'malice with forethought'] . . . If you were just in the crowd and someone stuck an egg in your hand and yelled, 'Throw it,' you know, that was 'animal exuberance' and you would get suspended a week,

---

*CWA found jobs for these workers but was unable to get them reinstated.

maybe, but you would get your job back." On May 18, 1956, the company announced that in 200 out of 245 cases that had been submitted to arbitration, forty-three discharges had been upheld and another eighteen had not been contested by the union. Among the remaining 139 cases, fifty-two had been reinstated with full back pay and eighty-six had suffered some loss of pay and were reinstated by the company without further arbitration.* The company paid about $200,000 to meet back pay claims upheld in arbitration. The $5-million suit against the union was settled by a $215,000 payment.

To rebuild the CWA defense fund, sadly depleted by the Southern strike, the delegates to the 1955 convention in St. Louis voted to assess each member one day's pay. It was a draconian step, especially so since it is extremely difficult to discipline members who refuse to pay up. Members could be expelled for failure to meet the assessment but, as Miss Mabel Cooney, the Louisville traffic representative, pointed out, "Usually we decided it was wiser to get their dues than it was to kick them out." Miss Cooney's recollections afford a glimpse of how collection may have come about in many places. ". . . The stewards would try to collect. As I remember we had a holiday right after, and we were supposed to pay that. I said, 'Well, I got double time for that holiday,' and I'd just give them one half of it, and that would be my day's pay. So I went right ahead and paid mine right away." Considering the difficulties—as Bill Smallwood pointed out right after the strike, "Our members in all parts of the country are being subjected to a brainwashing campaign from management on the Southern strike"—the assessment campaign did remarkably well, raising over $1.5 million within a year.

The roughest part of a strike, especially a long one, is often its aftermath. George E. Gill, who became District 3 director shortly after the strike when Smallwood became CWA secretary-treasurer, has recalled that period with particular clarity: "The '55 strike . . . brought about a three-year period of cleaning up. It took about that long to clean up the legal questions, arbitrations, and the relationship with the company which, of course, was almost destroyed by the '55 strike . . . We had in that unit some very, very difficult years: collective-bargaining table, rank-and-file membership—we lost—we were down below the fifty percent membership mark shortly after the end of the strike. When it got down to fifty percent, I quit publishing the figures.

*CWA District 3 attorney Thomas Adair made this observation in 1970: "It might be surprising that many of these employees who were discharged in 1955 as being completely unfit for having engaged in misconduct are now members of Southern Bell management and South Central management. I don't have the exact numbers, but the last case . . . I tried . . . one of the chief witnesses for the company was their district plant manager whose case I had in 1955, where he was accused of blowing up a telephone pole."
It is an interesting sidelight into labor relations in this country.

Didn't tell the locals, didn't tell anybody. The company never knew for certain how many we had because I let them believe that we were collecting some cash dues members so they would not be able to check on it. They were never certain. But I think if the same man had remained president of the company, we might have had a decertification election a year after the strike, and we might have lost it. We could have. So we had some very dangerous, dangerous years for about two years. It shook the staff. It caused a substantial turnover among the local officers, which was good because the new ones began to build it back from the wreckage . . .

"The company, in the meantime, had changed officers. They had changed presidents, they had changed the personnel vice-president who was really responsible for labor relations, the key man from their point of view. And they began to recognize the mutual advantage of some sort of decent relationship. In the meantime, the local unions turned very, very strongly toward the community relations part of their work because they recognized also that to just go out and strike was going at it the hard way. It was just only a part of a union's work. They've done a great job of turning the thing around."

It was a long strike. It was a rough strike. And what is truly remarkable is that it was a strike over principle. Increasingly, during the 1950s, labor's struggles were economic in character. Yet, as Joe Beirne told the delegates to the 1955 convention following the Southern strike, "Here came our members in the south. Here came our members from states with eight out of those nine states having right-to-work laws on their books. Here comes members from that area in America where the press and the opinion makers have continuously said it is an anti-union part of America. Here in the face of that picture, against the largest corporation in the entire world, our people fought for the most basic of union principles: The right to strike or respect picket lines . . . permitting us to help others." Out of this developed a new momentum, a certain force that placed the weight of the organized telephone worker against that of a corporate giant. The hinge of fate had begun to turn.

XII
A Pattern Emerges

On Saturday, November 10, 1951, Mayor M. Leslie Denning of Englewood, New Jersey, dialed a three-digit code, then dialed a seven-digit local-call number. While he waited briefly for an answer, a "circuit sniffer" found an idle trunk, a local connection was made, and in Alameda, California, Mayor Frank P. Osborn answered his telephone. As the mayors chatted, "Little Audrey," went into action, recording the calling number, the called number and the time span of the call. By the time the call was completed all the essential information for recording and billing was punched on a tape. The "99.9 percent pure," untouched by human hands except for the free labor provided by the customer, long-distance telephone call is today a commonplace. In 1951, however, that ceremonial call, as the *CWA News* phrased it, may well have "sent shivers down the spines of telephone workers." As well it might, for that call set the parameters for CWA's struggle over the next decade with the Bell System for recognition and stature.

Automation has become the catch-all word used to describe a process that has its beginnings in the industrial revolution when work was first subdivided and then simplified in order to substitute the machine for labor. This process is largely responsible for our material progress over the last century or more. That drudgery should be eased or replaced by mechanical means is an attractive idea, especially so to working people. Joe Beirne, put it this way: "Why should we, as human beings made in God's image and likeness, be required to work if we can get machines to do that work for us?" Ideally, as Anthime Corbon, a worker and vice president of the French Constituent Assembly of 1848, noted, "As the system [of mechanization] is extended to its extreme limits, the worker's function becomes increasingly intellectual. This ideal attracts me greatly." But, as Corbon was quick to add, "The transition period is a hard one, since, until the new machines are created, the worker is himself made into a machine by the simplification of his work, and suffers the unfortunate effects of a debasing necessity," including that of possible unemployment.

Such possibilities were very much on the minds of the delegates to the 1955 convention. CWA's potential membership within the Bell System in 1953 was 358,000, but by 1955 it had dropped to 343,000. The union barely managed to hold its own with its membership at 252,218 in October 1954, and at 252,707 in March 1955. The long and costly Southern Bell strike adversely affected membership recruitment. "In internal organization," as Jack Moran pointed out a year later CWA "definitely [is] subject to the law of diminishing returns . . . the assessment [imposed to rebuild the defense fund after the Southern strike] raises the problem of how we can recruit back into the union those who have resigned or been expelled because of refusal to pay the assessment." (7,745 were expelled, as of March 1956, for non-payment of the assessment; CWA membership went down to 249,269 as of the same date.) In financial straits as a consequence of the Southern strike, CWA cut back its organizing budget for the fiscal year 1955 by $50,000 to $291,000. With an organizing staff of ten, four men and six women, the union was hardpressed to meet the demands for organizational aid from its local unions. "Because of the difficult situation with which we are confronted in the area of external organization," Moran recommended that "we must recognize that our best bet for an increased membership in the next year or two lies in internal organization." According to Moran's estimates, the union enjoyed a 73.6 percent "development" in membership prior to the Southern strike.* Local organization, in his view, would strengthen the union immeasurably.

Lack of money, of course, was not the only obstacle to CWA organizing. "CWA strikes are 'played up' out of all proportion," Moran told delegates to the 1955 convention, citing one instance where one so-called independent fended off a CWA drive with the slogan, "Sixteen Years Without a Strike and the Lowest Dues." While condemning "the fallacy of supine 'we-will-never-strike policies,'" Moran did point out, "we do have to reckon with the often unfounded fears of other telephone workers, as well as cheap dues,

---

*Moran's report to the 1955 convention shows the potential for "internal" organization district by district:

"I should like to review very briefly with you the non-member problems, district by district:

In District 1 there are about 9,000 non-members.
In District 2—about 9,000.
In District 3—about 14,000 at the start of the recent strike.
In District 4—about 11,000.
In District 5—about 7,000.
In District 6—about 10,000.
In District 7—about 5,000.
In District 8—about 4,000.
In District 9—over 20,000.
In Canada—about 250.

"Our highest development by district is District 6, which has about an eighty-two percent development by our figures.

"Our lowest development is in District 9—with about a sixty percent development.

"But what I want to show is that in every district there is room for improvement. By and large, it is up to the staff—and the locals in each district—to do the job."

In 1956 Moran estimated, "we have over 100,000 non-members" in the Bell System.

when we organize." The Taft-Hartley Act enabled employers to openly advocate independent organization. Cloaked by President Eisenhower's amiable cheerfulness, anti-labor Republicans dominated the National Labor Relations Board. When the CWA succeeded in winning over ten of the eleven executive board members of the New York Telephone Company independent employee group, the company seized upon the lone dissenter and created a new organization around him. Despite CWA's many gallant supporters, company propaganda carried the day when the company-dominated outfit nosed out CWA by ninety-one votes in a 1955 representation election. As Moran poignantly remarked, such defeats "are hard to take."

Some idea of the state of the union at the time may be glimpsed in a study of a mid-west Long Lines local carried out by Professor Joel Seidman, chairman of the Social Sciences Department of the University of Chicago. Of about 2,450 non-supervisory employees just half were union members in 1953 when Seidman first looked into the local's affairs. As a result of intensive organization and the winning of important grievance cases, membership rose over the next few years to roughly eighty percent. As a group, the telephone workers were better educated and came from homes with slightly higher social status than did other worker groups studied by Seidman. Many of their fathers had been small businessmen or white-collar workers or skilled workers. The telephone workers had on the average almost twelve years of schooling and many had some college training as well. (For all Americans, the median years of school completed in 1950 was 9.3 and in 1960, 10.6.) All the workers interviewed were native-born whites, half of whom had had parents born abroad. Except for the equipment technicians (375), the employees were all female. On the average they were thirty-five years of age, with eight years of experience with the company; half were married; half either single or widowed, and most of them were Catholic.

Telephone workers, at least in this local, were a good deal more chary of strikes than other unionists. A very young operator reacted, "No, I wouldn't want to picket. I wouldn't want to walk up and down outside the place. I'd feel like a big jerk. I thought it was the union's job to picket— I mean the stewards and the officials." Another operator admitted to not liking to picket, "but I figure if I don't go nobody will go, and where are we going to get without it?" Despite their relative newness to unionism, however, most of the telephone workers shared the general view of trade unionists that the picket lines of others ought to be respected. "It's our code," said a young operator, "it's the principle of unionism—stick together even if it's your union or not." Nonetheless, Seidman concluded, "The telephone workers had perhaps the narrowest concept of the proper scope of union activities of any of the groups studied." There was widespread objection to union political activity on the ground that this was "an area for private decision, beyond the scope of the union's proper function." There was, too, some feeling that political discussion would create dissension within the union, which "had enough to take care of" in collective bargaining. (Perhaps paradoxically, many who opposed political activity also favored union lobbying for favorable legislation.) Internally, the union was felt to be democratic and local elections, held every year, usually saw opposition for all offices. (These were not full-time jobs and what compensation there was hardly covered expenses.) Though friendly candidates supported each other and sometimes ran as slates, there were no organized factions and no caucus meetings. Personalities rather than issues dominated the local elections. On balance, Seidman felt, telephone workers do not look to the union as an avenue for self-advancement. The steward's job carried little prestige, and the union was often viewed as being marginal to the life of the worker. Other workers criticized the union for being too aggressive toward the company—for asking for too much money, for calling strikes, for attacking the company too often and too bitterly in its publications." Telephone workers were still influenced by Bell System paternalism.

Yet, for all the workers' favorable view of their employer, the boss remained the union's best organizer. As one operator put it, "Well, it's the supervision. Always walking up and down in back of you saying, 'don't talk to your neighbor, sit just so, pay attention to the board'—it's terrible, worse than any job that I know of. They treat you like children." Another added, "Those sneak observations—that's awful. The chief operators can go to any section of the roon and plug themselves in to listen to the operators. They just want to see if you are monkeying around, but they could see that from the outside."

Joining the union was a voluntary act since "no legal and very limited social pressure could be brought upon non-members." Moreover, non-union members received all the benefits of the union contract, except representation in the case of a grievance. Since the telephone workers as a group, according to Seidman, had a favorable view of their employer, "the most important consideration leading them to join the union was the desire to have some form of protection available in the event it should be necessary." As a young technician put it, "If you're on the carpet from the lower echelons of the company, then the union will take your case to the higher echelons." An operator with twenty-one years experience said, "Well, [the union] got us better working conditions . . . The supervisors are not allowed to yell at the girls like they used to be able to do. They used to tell the girls off, but now a girl has a right to turn around and tell her, and if she is dissatisfied she can go to the union and complain about it, and the union will make an adjustment . . ." As other technicians elaborated, "If the union wasn't there they would be pretty tough on the men. The supervisors had to take a little more human approach to the employees in general. Today you get your own choice about hours on the basis of seniority. They can't throw you back on a dirty job and forget you. They can't keep on picking for the same men in the premium-pay jobs. It has forced them to give a bit more human thought to the employees."

CWA continued to make strides in forcing the Bell companies "to give a bit more human thought to the employees." Cluster settlements came a bit faster after the long Southern strike, and by the end of 1955 fifty contracts were negotiated covering some 332,564 workers employed in thirty-four Bell units. In the operating companies, the pay hikes for 1955 averaged 8.5 cents an hour for all workers, plant, traffic, accounting and commercial. In Western Electric and Bell Laboratories, the increases averaged 10.5 cents an hour. Fringe benefits, including town and job reclassification, improved holidays, increased traffic and plant evening- and night-differential payments, shorter tours and the like, added $6.9 million to the value received in 1955. In addition to the Southern strike, workers in northern California and Nevada struck for two weeks; Haverhill-Lawrence manufacturing plant for sixteen days, and three other units for shorter periods, involving a total of 114,049 workers. Fewer strikes and more gains marked the succeeding year as CWA probed for a "pattern" behind the "cluster" settlements. Hourly wage raises averaged 10.2 cents in a $72-million 1956 package for 341,549 Bell workers in forty-six states. (Pre-contract wages, according to the Bureau of Labor Statistics, averaged $1.86 an hour.) Negotiations were marked by three strikes and several short stoppages. The longest strike—against the North Carolina radio shops of Western Electric—lasted sixty-four days and ended with the longest contract, a three year agreement. (All the rest were for one year.) The Haverhill-Lawrence plant went out again for thirty-two days and Duluth telephone workers struck for nine. All three strikes followed company attempts to weaken arbitration provisions or to worsen working conditions.

While CWA searched for a "pattern," or for a responsible way to resolve disputes, telephone management probed for the union's soft underbelly. In truth, CWA faced a dilemma: on the one hand strikes and the willingness to strike were useful as a way of catching the public's attention and as a form of psychological pressure against the companies; on the other hand, automation enabled the companies "to take" a strike, forcing workers out for long and costly periods of time. The frustrations created by a strike that failed to interrupt service were in sharp contrast, say, to an auto strike that actually stopped assembly lines or a steel strike that shut-off furnaces. Strikes, in short, that cost management as well as workers, made it frighteningly easy for telephone management to provoke sabotage and violence.

And sabotage and violence often alienated the very public support the union needed to win.

The union's dilemma was etched in a bitter seven-month strike against the Ohio Consolidated Telephone Company, an independent replay of the 1955 Southern Bell strike that pitted the fast-growing General Telephone System against CWA. CWA Locals 4372, 374 and 375 had enjoyed good relations with Ohio Consolidated, a company based in Portsmouth, Ohio, which operated in twenty-four eastern and southern counties for fourteen years. Its contract provided for a union ship and the bargaining unit included service assistants, senior clerks and "head men." The company had been owned by Theodore Gary & Co., owner of a chain absorbed by General Telephone late in 1955. General management was in the process of integrating Ohio Consolidated company into its other Ohio operations when the CWA contract expired. At that point, the expansionist General Telephone Company decided to teach CWA a lesson, one that it hoped would not be lost on other employees, some of whom were already CWA members.

General management proposed, by union count, seventy-six "retrogressive," union-wrecking contract demands. *Fortune* magazine later reported that the new company president, Clare Williams, "recoil[ed] at the idea of union membership as a condition of employment," and the elimination of the union shop, union security, was, as *Fortune* phrased it, "the big one, certainly for the company." In addition, the company demanded a no-strike clause, a time-limit on the presentation of grievances to arbitration, a new title, "occasional operator," and the removal of all service assistants, senior clerks and "head men" from the bargaining unit. With mechanization in the offing, the latter two demands would mean a sharply reduced membership for the union as workers could be technically elevated into "supervision." After months of fruitless negotiations, CWA members voted 304 to four to strike; the walkout began on July 14, 1956. As Curtis Fletcher, CWA's non-Bell national director, stated the issues, "Unions are not in business to lower working conditions. They are in business to improve them. That's what we intend to do at Ohio Consolidated."

Portsmouth, Ohio, a strong union town, population, 40,000, with its steel mills and railroad shops, respected CWA picket lines and hoped, as most union people do, for a short strike, for workers often count a long strike as a lost strike. But out in the counties, as 584 CWA members walked on picket lines, there were disconcerting signs of trouble ahead. Ruth Rauscher, a Titlonsville operator, was roughed up by three men delivering a refrigerator to the exchange. She was CWA's first victim. The company hired a team of private detectives to "watch" its property but, as they later testified, they were given other assignments. "We did surveillance work on routes 139 and 140 as instructed," one detective later stated in an NLRB hearing. "On September 2, at the Scioto Motel in the city of Waverly, Ohio, in Room 22, we had a meeting with Mr. E.C. Kimble and Mr. August Purpura. At this time we gave a report of our activities and Mr. Kimble expressed dissatisfaction. Mr. Kimble also advised us at this meeting that we were to put out of the way a Mr. Hipple, Mr. Cook, Mr. Sheperd or Mr. Bush in any way that we saw fit. He further instructed us that a way this might be carried out would be [to] run these individuals down in an automobile or run their cars off the road or any way that we saw fit. Upon being asked what would happen to us if any trouble resulted, he advised us that we would be taken care of by the telephone company and its attorneys." These particular detectives were dismissed a few days later for not producing, but the company had set the stage for violence.*

America, the noted Catholic monthly, termed the Portsmouth strike "one of the longest and most violent walkouts since the dog-eat-dog days of the late 1930's." And the nation's press certainly played up every act of sabotage or violence that conceivably could be blamed on the strikers. However, little or no mention was made of the long foot-dragging days of peaceful picketing, or of the trailers where pickets could warm up or grab a cup of coffee, that the city fathers of Cadiz, Cambridge, Dillonvale and Baltimore allowed the union to park at the curb just outside picketed exchanges. No one reported the chief operator who taunted one young woman until she could bear it no longer, until she just hauled off and smacked her tormentor in the mouth with her purse. Nor was anything said of the company's hiring of 120 new employees, "replacements" allowed under the Taft-Hartley act as a means of firing strikers and strike-breaking.

Management intimidation did not always work. When the bosses snapped photographs of strikers on the picket line, union officials secured cameras for each picket, who then took photographs of everyone entering and leaving the exchanges. Community support remained strong, and was indeed at times vigorous. When coal miners in Baltimore heard that a management man had arrived from General Telephone in Texas to operate the local exchange, they got some lumber and boarded up the exchange. After three days, he called out, "If you let me out of here, I'll leave town and *never* come back." And so they did, and the man from Texas caught the first train out of town. Frank Thernes recalls how the Columbus, Ohio, CIO came through at Christmas time to boost CWA morale. "They had had

*NLRB trial examiner C.W. Whittemore dismissed complaints lodged against the union by the company because the company did not come before the board with clean hands. He acknowledged that there had been some acts committed by union members but he said that the company had committed the first act, showing "its contempt for the rights of its employees ... by (a) threatening its employees with physical violence, (b) conspiring with hired investigators to engage in violence against certain strike leaders, and (c) engaging in actual physical violence against striking employees."

The strike leaders threatened in the above instance were: William Hipple, strike director; Russell Cook; Norman Bush, and Gene Shepherd, all CWA activists.

a strike the year before," Thernes said, "and they had four truckloads of toys that had been contributed to their members, sitting in a warehouse . . . bicycles, tricycles, dolls, electrical toys, and they sent those trucks down here for distribution to our members and their children. As one member told me, 'My child will never have that many toys if he lives to be a hundred and is a baby all the time.' " What might have been a dismal Christmas, turned out to be a beautiful one.

The strike, however, turned nasty, brutal. Earlier the company had claimed 112 separate acts of violence against its personnel and property. Cable cutting crippled telephone service; by mid October vandals had slashed 290 cables. Ohio Consolidated president Williams ordered the switches pulled on Columbus Day, and 17,428 telephones did not ring for sixty-one days. A shouting mob of 500 threw rocks, beer bottles and telephones yanked from pay stations at the Portsmouth exchange. Governor Frank T. Lausche (elected to be a senator in November) asked the state legislation for legislation to authorize seizure of the silent telephone facilities, but the law-makers refused to comply. The Portsmouth city council declared a state of emergency and authorized the city manager to call for the National Guard if necessary. The area around the Portsmouth exchange was sandbagged and the company restored "vital" service, leaving about seventy-five percent of service shut down. Cable cutting, however, continued, and, ironically, the day before the strike dragged to its bitter close, the Portsmouth exchange was again totally silenced. The new governor, C. William O'Neill, ordered a National Guard unit into the area to maintain emergency telephone service. Federal mediators finally managed to get company and union officials engaged in a marathon, twenty-five-hour bargaining session and emerged with a new agreement. Three days later, union members ratified the agreement by a vote of 207 to 186 and returned to work on February 28, 1957, after seven long months of strike action.

CWA claimed no great victory, but it did protect its members. The union gave up the union shop but secured a maintenance-of-membership clause. The members that the company wanted ousted from the bargaining unit were allowed to remain unless the NLRB ruled otherwise. The no-strike clause sought by the company was modified so that strikes were not prohibited when the company refused to arbitrate a grievance or over grievances that were not arbitrable. Before the strike, Ohio Consolidated workers averaged $1.25 an hour and under the new agreement they would get raises averaging 4.74 cents an hour. Under the Taft-Hartley Act, the company could keep 120 "new employees" and dismiss the "replaced" strikers. But the union forced the company to restore all 120 to their jobs. Of the nineteen members fired for alleged violence, eighteen wanted to return to the company and their cases were submitted to arbitration where the union won back ten jobs. Work elsewhere was found for the remaining eight.

Cable cutting in the Portsmouth strike obscured a lesson later made clear in a four-day September strike of Western Electric installers: Telephone workers may strike but dials continue to work.* This had become increasingly so as local areas converted from manual stations to dial operation but final conversion to long-distance dialing seriously undercut the union's "last resort" power to interrupt the system by striking Long Lines or Western Electric installers, with other workers observing picket lines. "Out of all this strike activity," CWA vice president John Crull concluded, "we have learned a lesson, particularly as the telephone company has become more and more automated: [that is] that the telephone company . . . with about sixteen to twenty percent of the total work force being supervisory . . . together with those people who are strictly opposed to strikes can do a pretty good job of keeping the telephone service running whether there is a strike or not." Mel Bers, a CWA researcher, demonstrated that the telephone company actually made a higher rate of profit during a strike because of the money saved by not paying wages while customers kept paying their bills. (The wage bill was approximately sixty to seventy percent of telephone operation. It is lower now.) As Joe Beirne so graphically put it, "Striking was like throwing a rock at the *Queen Mary* as she sailed down the harbor."

This is not to say that the union was powerless. No organization with a quarter of a million members or more ever is. But the limited effectiveness of the strike weapon in an automated or highly mechanized industry does pose crucial union problems of strategy and tactics. Debate within CWA over such problems, whether couched in the language of finance, the question of area/regional differentials, or the formulation of collective bargaining policy, was as yeast to bread in the union's internal life. New faces appeared on the executive board, in part as a response to this ferment within the union, as well as to the normal change of generations, or as a consequence of clashing personalities. At the 1955 convention, Louis Knecht was elected director of District 9, W. "Duke" Smith, of District 8, and James Smith, District 7. Elaine Gleason became bargaining unit director for Long Lines, and J.E. Dunne, of Western Electric installation.** Slim Werkau

---

*The 1957 installers' strike, however, went well for the union. The 23,800 striking technicians maintained picket lines around the country which were observed by operators and other members of the CWA. Before strike wages ranged from $1.39 to $2.80 an hour, and the union won increases ranging from six to twelve cents an hour and an increase in travel allowances and other benefits. The agreement provided for a two-year contract, a new development in Bell System bargaining, in line with the lengthening of contracts being agreed upon in other industries at the time and earlier.

**Directors were elected by their regions and, in 1955, the elections were by acclamation in Districts 2 and 6 and in Western Electric Installation, Western Electric Sales, and Non-Bell. The results of the 1955 elections were as follows:

died shortly after the 1955 convention and vice president Crull took on his tasks until the CWA executive board named W.A. Smallwood secretary-treasurer in September 1955. George E. Gill followed Smallwood as director of District 3. Jack Moran retired in the fall of 1956 and was replaced by Ray Hackney, the CWA's constitutional architect.

Sometime in late 1954 or early 1955, divisions over policy sharpened and opinions began to crystallize around two of the union's leading personalities, CWA president Beirne and vice president Jones.* Initially, as often happens in intra-union fights or, for that matter, in struggles within most other institutions, there was a tendency to paper over differences. Jones had been feuding with secretary-treasurer Werkau and, in 1955, convinced the executive board that it should name an auditing committee to look into the union's books. As Walter Schaar, chairman of that committee, recalled its sessions, "It was Jones on this side of the table and Werkau over there. And I'm here to tell you there was some awful bitter stuff that went between those two in committee." The audit committee found nothing seriously wrong; the issue had to do more with the manner of financial reporting than it did with its substance. By convention time, Jones reported, in response to a question from the floor, "those problems have been solved." A break

---

President—Joseph A. Beirne
Vice presidents—John L. Crull
J.J. Moran
A.J. Jones
Secretary-treasurer—C.W. Werkau
District directors:
District 1—Mary Hanscom
District 2—Glenn Watts
District 3—W.A. Smallwood
District 4—Walter Schaar
District 5—Ray Dryer
District 6—D.L. McCowen
District 7—James Smith
District 8—W. "Duke" Smith
District 9—Louis Knecht
Bargaining unit directors:
Long Lines—Elaine Gleason
Western Electric Installation—J.E. Dunne
Western Electric Sales—Louis Junker
Non-Bell—J. Curtis Fletcher

*The first indication of a public break occured at the 1955 convention. A Jones quarrel with Werkau had been simmering for some time. According to Beirne, "Tommy and Slim never did get along . . . And we had a bad year in '54 financially. Tommy . . . went after Slim Werkau." Both LaRoy H. Purdy, a Beirne supporter, and Ben Porch, who backed Jones, agree that Jones pushed the Southern Bell strike while Beirne had reservations about the wisdom of striking at that time. (Both men backed the strikers solidly once the decision was made.) "I'm not sure," Porch has said, "that his [Jones'] motives weren't, at that time, to get himself established and be in a position of running against Joe at some subsequent convention. This is purely an opinion." Beirne believed that Jones wanted to be secretary-treasurer but "finally I began hitting him and forced him to run for president."

between the principals over the question as to how best reduce area and regional wage differentials was averted by a convention move to remove area differentials from the national bargaining program. Despite many tense moments, Beirne felt free to state at the close of the convention, "For the first time in a long time we had political fights. And in America political fights are misunderstood by most of our people. I hope that they are not misunderstood here by those who engaged in them. I hope the political fight, as a political fight, ended for the next two years, and that we go out of here with the firmest of determinations to honestly and sincerely try to make our resolutions, our principles work."

By the 1956 convention, however, the Beirne-Jones quarrel was out in the open. In retrospect, Jones seems to have picked a rather odd issue to wage a major fight over. The passions aroused by the Korean War, which ended in 1953, and by Senator Joseph McCarthy's demagogic play upon legitimate fears of totalitarian Communism had quieted down. The senator's popularity had washed out beneath television klieg lights during the 1954 Senate hearings on his attack against the U.S. Army. Yet Jones picked bones over a union decision to take to arbitration Wisconsin Bell's dismissal of Stephan L. Kreznar, president of Milwaukee Local 5502, as a security risk. (After his dismissal, Kreznar resigned.) The company contended that the dismissal was justifiable and for "cause," basing its position on a letter from the Industrial Personnel Security Screening Board which alleged that Kreznar was a member of the Socialist Workers Party. (American adherents of the late Bolshevik leader, Leon Trotsky, murdered in Mexico in 1940 by agents of Soviet dictator Joseph Stalin, organized the Socialist Workers Party in the late 1930s.) Kreznar admitted attending SWP meetings in the past and reading Trotskyite literature but denied, on oath, being a member. CWA argued that a denial of security clearance based merely on a government letter, unsupported by evidence, was insufficient cause for dismissal. Earlier the union had proposed that Kreznar be transferred to a nonclassified job, but the company rejected the request.

Jones opened his attack at the 1956 convention, about half way through his report on his duties as a vice president responsible for strike activity and collective bargaining. He charged the executive board with an attempt to purge from the staff two of his supporters, and briefly criticized a proposal for making Ohio and Michigan into separate districts. Jones then sailed into the Kreznar case, crying out, "Never before has CWA's International Executive Board voted to align itself sympathetically with a known supporter of Communism or with Communism in any form and let it be never again." After a passionate condemnation of Communism, Jones claimed that should the convention fail to repudiate the executive board decision to uphold Kreznar's right to arbitration, "that very failure would open the door to a flood of spies, subversives, sneaky, slippery, slimy creatures who crawl in the dark of the night." Kreznar, Jones charged, was a "known supporter" of a Communist organization. "In these times anyone who knowingly supports and participates in the activities of such a Communist organization knowingly engages in activities inimical to the security of the United States by definition of our government." Ending with a rhetorical flourish, Jones asked the delegates, "If those CWA members who fought and died in the Korean War could be here as delegates to this great convention, if they could know of their union's needless defense of a known Communist supporter, if they could rise to a point of personal privilege, might they not walk to a microphone and simply ask why—why?"

The debate that followed was sometimes acrimonious, but on the whole it was a thorough-going examination of the issue. The delegate from Milwaukee, David G. Roche, reported that while his members did not "condone or defend" Kreznar's political beliefs," they did defend the arbitration request. "If our contracts are to have any meaning at all, we must take the companies to arbitration when a contract is wilfully violated, or eventually our contracts will be meaningless." Convention rules were suspended to allow president Beirne to state the executive board majority's view. He commended Jones for presenting a "very good document on the subject of communism" but added that that was not the issue before the delegates. "Stephen L. Kreznar is and was a member of the Communications Workers of America," Beirne continued. "He was fired by the telephone company of Wisconsin on January 25. The only reason given by that telephone company was that they had received a letter from the government which denied clearance for classified work to Stephen L. Kreznar. Nothing else. There never was; there is not now anything else which the Wisconsin company has. On February 17, the union processed a grievance to get Stephan Kreznar placed on non-classified assignments where clearance was not needed. The company refused. The company refused to tell us how many employees have been checked for clearance. The company refused to tell us whether or not all jobs were classified or if there were some that were non-classified on which Kreznar could work." Kreznar, Beirne reported, informed the union that the government accused him of being a member of the Socialist Workers Party and that he had falsified his personnel security questionnaire. And he also denied such membership under oath. "Now," Beirne declared, "we may set ourselves up to consider whether a man lies or not, and if we do that, based upon only our own conclusion, we are no better than that totalitarian who says, 'You are an enemy of the state. I have said so. Line up to the wall.' And you are shot. We are no better than that. But ours is the Anglo-Saxon Law. Ours is a law that says, 'You are innocent until you are proven guilty.' Let us always hope it will be that way." Jack Moran pointed out to the delegates that Kreznar had been a member of the union for fifteen years, and so must have worked for the telephone company during World War II and the Korean War. He also reminded them that "all the arbitrator is going to decide is whether or not the company has the right to fire a member on the basis of a letter from the government." The delegates upheld the executive board's decision to back the Kreznar arbitration by a five-to-one vote.*

The Beirne-Jones fight roiled through the union over the next year. The executive board was divided with the vote often running eight to five against Jones. District 7 was said to be a Jones district and the South reportedly was running "two to one for Jones." Jones also had some support on the West Coast among the installers and Long Lines. D. L. McCowen, who sometimes backed Jones on specific issues, said, "I personally felt Tommy was more wrong in more respects than Joe, even though, as I said, it wasn't all black and white." Glenn Watts backed Beirne and Louis Knecht soon declared his support. E. J. Follis, a Jones backer, sized up the two men this way: "Perhaps the point is that they were both completely different types of people, Joe and Jones. Jones was more of a detailed walking encyclopedia. Joe was more of a salesman. And finally, Beirne was much more of an effective person and had twice the political savvy of Jones." The struggle between the two men came to a head when Jones declared himself a candidate for president of the union in the spring of 1957.**

On the second day of the 1957 Kansas City Convention, Tuesday, June 18, George Milne and James A. Sanders, delegates respectively from Beirne's home Local 1196 and Jones's home Local 3411, placed the contenders in nomination. After the seconding speeches, the vote was taken and Beirne won handily—137,077 to 83,937. John Crull and Ray Hackney were re-elected vice presidents unanimously. W. A. Smallwood was re-elected secretary-treasurer unanimously, too. James Massey, an installer from the South nominated to run against Jones for the third vice presidency, won 134,770 votes to 101,410 for Jones.† Jones's defeat created some fears of a

*The arbitrator subsequently upheld the company's right to fire Kreznar.
**George Miller and Esther Woeste coordinated Jones's campaign.
†In what was a rather unusual departure in a labor paper at that time, the *CWA News* carried the following boxed announcement in its June 1957 issue:

Unhappy With Beirne
Jones Offers Himself As Presidential Candidate

A. T. JONES, CWA vice president, has announced his candidacy for the office of international president and was already conducting a vigorous campaign as this issue of *CWA News* went to press.

"purge" among his supporters, a not unreasonable apprehension considering what had happened to "oppositions" in many other unions, but it did not happen. The convention commended Jones for his faithful service to CWA, and he was offered a staff position. (Jones turned it down and

---

Jones has been unhappy over the leadership of CWA for some time, and in his announcement, admits to a "growing rift" between president Beirne and himself.

Beirne describes it this way: "Tommy has been running for the presidency for the past four years. His campaign is now out in the open. Good."

In his announcement, Jones charges Beirne with "defending Communists" and with trying to "force CWA members to purchase group life insurance." But most of all, Jones criticizes Beirne for what Jones describes as trying to "secure my removal from office as a CWA vice-president in the upcoming elections."

Jones says Beirne is doing this "in reprisal for his own blunders and deceit."

He wound up his four-page statement by offering himself as a candidate for CWA president.

The districts elected the following directors at the 1957 convention:

District 1	Mary Hanscom
District 2	William J. Walsh
District 3	George E. Gill
District 4	Walter R. Schaar
District 5	Ray F. Dryer
District 6	D. L. McCowen
District 7	D. K. Gordon
District 8	W. H. Smith
District 9	Louis Knecht.
Western Electric Installation	Joseph E. Dunne
Western Electric Sales	Louis Junker
Non-Bell	J. Curtis Fletcher
Long Lines	Elaine T. Gleason

Glenn Watts, former district director of District 2, became an assistant to president Beirne.

CWA leadership remained constant over the next eight years. Beirne handily defeated Edward J. Ward of St. Louis, 230,227 to 13,281, in 1959, while Crull, Hackney and Smallwood were re-elected unanimously. James M. Massey was opposed by Harold Wright of Akron, Ohio, winning re-election 187,836 to 51,260. When Louis H. Junker, a specialist in labor grading (a long-standing bone of contention within Western Electric), retired on a disability pension in 1960 after serving for seventeen years as the head of the sales group within the union, he was replaced by F. J. Novotny as national director. (Junker died at age 61 in 1961.) William R. Martin replaced W. H. Smith as District 8 director in 1959. Beirne, Crull, Hackney and Smallwood were all unopposed in 1961. Massey defeated James A. Sanders, 154,155 to 69,593. Fred Garrett replaced Martin as District 8 director. John Lax was elected director of the new Canadian District 10. Kenneth Silvers replaced Joseph E. Dunne as Western Electric Installation national director.

When John Lax, the Canadian director died in November, 1961, he was replaced by William M. Dunn.

ultimately went to work for General Telephone in Michigan.) "There wasn't a single one of us who supported him [Jones] who was taken off the payroll," E. J. Follis has since observed. And George Miller later recalled, "I suppose I was probably more surprised than anyone else that Joe didn't move to make it tough. He didn't . . ." And former education director Jules Pagano makes the fundamental point that the Beirne-Jones fight "tore the union . . . down the middle intellectually and conceptually for a while. There were real issues articulated very well by both sides and in great form, but when the final decision was made, you didn't have anybody marching off with his thirty percent or forty percent and try to establish a new union. Tommy Jones just fell by the wayside . . . And all the staffers, some of them who were very close to the Tommy Jones brain trust, are now officers of the Communications Workers [and] are members of the executive board with total loyalty to the institution and no problem about the readjustment once they recognized that they had lost their day. They went on to build the union as best they could within the new framework."

The Jones defeat consolidated the Beirne leadership of CWA and cleared the way for a major change in the formulation of collective-bargaining programs and strategies. Down to 1957, convention delegates decided the priorities and the content of the union's collective-bargaining program each year. There were advantages for doing so in the formative years, as Beirne pointed out. "We talked out our negotiating goals in open convention as a very necessary means of getting to know one another and getting to understand each other's point of view. The good that we received from this open discussion outweighed the disadvantages . . ." But the disadvantages had begun to mount up. Telephone workers were falling behind in the new movements in bargaining—health, welfare and pensions—leading Beirne to conclude, "I think it can be safely said that all of us are not happy or satisfied with the results of our bargaining efforts." Convention discussion tipped the union's hand, inhibited planning over the long range and often forced union negotiators to freeze on what were, realistically, impossible demands. The changing political moods of the conventions, at times, placed the union in contradictory bargaining postures. In 1954, for example, the delegates placed a high priority on the elimination of differentials; a year later, they took this always touchy issue out of the national-bargaining program altogether only to restore it the succeeding year as the second goal of bargaining for 1956. And though D. L. McCowen, a long time advocate of the elimination of differentials, recognized that elimination at "one full swoop" was not practical, the 1956 stand, in effect, made immediate elimination within bargaining units virtually mandatory.*

---

*The resolution admitted to some flexibility but it did tie negotiators' hands more than was perhaps necessary. As adopted, that part of the collective bargaining resolution reads:

To avoid the hard and fast setting of bargaining priorities as well as the revealing of strategies occasioned by the formulation of collective bargaining goals in the convention "gold fish bowl," the CWA executive committee recommended the creation of a collective bargaining policy committee. As a delegate, Marvin Schlaff, Local 9590, pointed out, "The convention by its very nature cannot take into consideration the problems of continuity, and only a committee that is able to plan from year to year, and plan one, two, three and maybe four years in advance in terms of what kind of precedent we are going to establish in bargaining this year and in the future can do so." Each district was to elect members to the policy committee and the officers and executive board were also to serve.* (Similar committees were

---

2 GEOGRAPHIC DIFFERENTIALS

Ultimate objective
Eliminate all wage differentials based on geographical location.

1956 Objective
A. Wage rate differentials based on geographic locations, within the bargaining unit, to be eliminated.
B. Wage rate differentials based on geographical locations, between bargaining units and the industry key towns, to be narrowed.

Principles to be observed
(1) Priority shall be given to the correction of greater inequities.
(2) Initial demands shall be drawn so as to avoid increasing inequities based on geographical wage differentials within bargaining units.

*The members of the first Collective Bargaining Policy Committee provided, as president Beirne noted, "a perfect cross section of the union." The listing below is from the *CWA News*, February 1958, page 5:

Joseph A. Beirne, president of CWA and chairman of the Policy Committee; W. A. Smallwood, secretary-treasurer; John L. Crull, vice-president; Ray Hackney, vice-president; James M. Massey, vice-president; Mary Hanscom, District 1 director; William Walsh, District 2 director; George Gill, District 3 director; Walt Schaar, District 4 director; Ray Dryer, District 5 director; D. L. McCowen, District 6 director; D. K. Gordon, District 7 director; Bill Martin, acting for W. G. Smith, District 8 director; Louis Knecht, District 9 director. Joe Dunne, national director, Western Electric-Installation; Lou Junker, national director, Western Electric-Sales; Elaine Gleason, long lines director; Elma Hannah, representing Canada. John W. Price, Western Electric coordinator.

District 1—Frances E. Stiles, president Local 1000, Don Lansing, vice-president Local 1290; Martin R. Bianco, vice-president Local 1150.

District 2—Orville F. Taylor, president Local 2108, Thomas A. Tribble, Jr., president Local 2202.

District 3—Helen C. Corbitt, Local 3808; James A. Sanders, president Local 3411; P. R. Latta, president Local 3611; Jim Dinkins, president Local 3060; Doris P. Kelly, secretary Local 3511.

District 4—William H. Schwartz, president Local 4103; Norman Mackay, president Local 4000; Ernestine Locknane, president Local 4351; Harold L. Schurr, treasurer Local 4305.

District 5—Stanley V. Swensen, president Local 5090; Lawrence A. Gillingham, president Local 5502; Velma Fultz, president Local 5800.

District 6—Jane Simmons, vice-president Local 6300; Albert Bowles, secretary-treasurer Local 6215; Robert J. Krumm, president Local 6600; A. Kenneth Ferguson,

formed subsequently for each bargaining group—Bell System, the independents, and others.) The work of the committee was reinforced by appropriate conferences of the presidents of CWA locals. Beirne later credited the creation of the policy committee as precipitating what later came to be called "pattern" bargaining. "They were coming up with some pretty good stuff," Beirne said. "We were able to use what they did in '57 as the basis for getting started in '58, really, on what we now can call "pattern bargaining.' " While the new committee was not directly involved in the 1957 bargaining (it became operative in 1958), the Bell System certainly became open to more improvements as well as to speedier "cluster" settlements. Basic $2 and $5 wage hikes were negotiated, without retrogression in other contract terms, and there were no major strikes. CWA also negotiated a historic group insurance plan with Southwestern Bell, a precedent setting development that truly opened for future negotiations a whole range of health and welfare benefits.

The value of the Collective Bargaining Policy Committee was quickly proven. The committee prepared a detailed case for a substantial 1959 wage increase, and for long-needed improvements in vacations and pensions. The first test of the new procedures occurred in Milwaukee, Wisconsin, where Wisconsin director Ed Peil and the members of his committee—Catherine Conroy, Mary Lou Morrisey, Ed Brophil and David Roche—pressed Wisconsin Bell on critical local issues and assistant to the president Glenn Watts and director of research Sylvia Gottlieb outlined national demands. President Beirne and District 5 director Ray Dryer were also on hand to back up the negotiating committee. The union also launched a high-powered public relations campaign, with major advertisements in Wisconsin newspapers, informing the public, "We want you to know . . . that our bargaining demands are in the public interest." Press releases and press conferences stressed the union's theme, the telephone workers' need for substantial wage increase and for improvements in vacations and pensions. A strike vote gave the negotiations a cutting edge, and last minute, around-the-clock talks on January 27, 1959, rounded out the negotiations. At a

---

president Local 6325; Lena Trimble, president Local 6500.

District 7—Donald C. Miller, vice-president Local 7102; Raynor D. Miles, president Local 7505.

District 8—O. John Goodwin, president Local 8103; Billie L. Sponseller, secretary Local 8611.

District 9—James L. Burgess, president Local 9102; William M. O'Kelly, president Local 9211; R. W. Rivers, president Local 9490; Donald G. Matheson, vice-president Local 9590.

Non-Bell—James Booe, Local 9571; manufacturing—Fred E. Vaughn, Local 1162; long lines, Roy Schultise Local 2550; installation—Anthony W. Stein, president Local 7290; sales—Waldo E. Bland, president Local 9595; non-voice—Morton Bahr, president Local 1172; Canada—Mager J. H. Brown, president Local C-1.

membership meeting, where "they were hanging from the rafters, "according to local reporters, president Beirne was able to give the details on the "biggest package in CWA history."

CWA racked up in a five-month contract what the *CWA News* termed "pattern-setting" wage hikes ranging from $1 to $3 weekly for operators and clerks, and from $2 to $5 for plant craftsmen. In addition, four towns were upgraded, giving some workers total weekly raises as high as $7.50. Split tours in Milwaukee were cut to seven hours. A new title—Sr. Plant Records Clerk—was established, providing a new wage differential. In all, the basic wage increase averaged 8.2 cents an hour. Traffic boosts, exclusive of all fringes, amounted to about 6.6 cents an hour; plant, 9.3 cents an hour. Vacations were stepped up to four weeks after thirty years, marking the first major change in the Bell System vacation plan since 1939. While the wage settlement did not set a true pattern, with the rest of the companies falling almost automatically into line, it did set a precedent for negotiations over the balance of the year. But a separate agreement providing a boost in minimum pensions for those over age sixty-five, from $100 to $115 a month, was a pace setter. It was also the first time ever that the pension plan was altered in conjunction with contract bargaining. Since both CWA and the Bell System companies prefer that the pension plan be uniform throughout the system, the pension gains won in Milwaukee were quickly established throughout the member companies. Union negotiators signed similar agreements on pensions with their respective company officials within a matter of days. Visibly pleased, Beirne told Wisconsin CWA members, "We had unity of purpose, and teamwork all up and down the line, for the first time in our history. And now we are beginning to reap the real benefits of such unity."

The bargaining gains of 1959 were surpassed in 1960 by a historic breakthrough in company paid-for medical insurance, improved vacations, higher minimum pensions and increased amounts of company-paid-for group life insurance as well as sizable wage increases. The 1960 pattern settlement—it came in Northwestern Bell early in May—gave employees with twenty-five years service, a five-year reduction in the service period, four week vacations. Pension minimums at age sixty-five were raised to $120 to $125 a month, depending on length of service. Company financed life insurance policies were raised from $1,000 to $2,000. Under an "Extraordinary Medical Expense Plan," the company-paid-for insurance plan covered eighty percent of medical and hospital expenses up to $15,000 a year for employees and their dependents. Wage increases in 1960 CWA-Bell System contracts averaged a little better than seven cents an hour. Increases for operators and clerks ranged from $1.50 to $2.50 a week. For plant craft and related workers, the increases ranged from $3 to $4.50 a week. (The hourly average wage in 1959 was $2.18.) Almost 300,000 telephone workers were covered by CWA-Bell System contracts negotiated in 1960. Total money value of the contract improvements for these workers averaged ten cents an hour. These changes cost the Bell System roughly $130 million annually.

Negotiations with the independent telephone companies secured comparable gains for more than 20,000 workers covered by some fifty-six such agreements. But the process was a good deal more complicated. Separate negotiating committees met with the management of the various companies, some of which were relatively small operations while others employed several thousands. Curtis Fletcher, CWA's non-Bell director, reported that settlements in 1960 were "generally good." Most, he added, "have been equal to or better than the average for the entire telephone industry." Wage increases ranged from a low of 4.2 cents an hour for the workers of the Council Grove Telephone Company to a high of 21.4 cents an hour for those of the North Penn Telephone Company. Ten of the fifty-six contracts were with the burgeoning General Telephone System (GTS), covering some 15,400 workers. Wage increases in the GTS settlements averaged over six cents an hour. General balked at granting health insurance. As Fletcher reported, "In each of these General negotiations, the bargaining committee had to fight endlessly to get the company to agree to the EME [Extraordinary Medical Expenses] benefits. The General system would not agree to one uniform agreement. Each one had to be bargained out separately."

CWA contract gains were scored against a background of increasing automation and rising unemployment. Unemployment rose to over four million, a 5.2 percent rate. The percentage of dial telephones to total telephones (within the Bell System) rose from 75.5 percent in 1950 to ninety-seven percent ten years later. The number of telephone operators, which had peaked at 162,661 in 1950, dropped to 139,045 by 1960. Total Bell employment peaked at 745,629 in 1955, dropping to 735,766. At the same time, the number of Bell telephones in service and system profits rose sharply, from thirty-five million telephones in 1950 to over sixty million at the end of the decade. Bell profits nearly quadrupled, rising from 1950's $358,866,925 to $1,250,055,000 ten years later.

"Old habits of thought and old ways of doing things are luxuries," CWA president Beirne said of the new age of automation. Pointing out that "a period of self-examination has begun, he said, "we have welcomed automation [in the telephone industry] because we see its tremendous potential . . . but we demand measures be taken to prevent the cure of this miracle drug from killing the patient with side effects." In testimony before a House Labor Committee, Beirne acknowledged that not all current unemployment was caused by automation, but he added, "we cannot escape the fact that unemployment and the problems flowing from it have been aggravated by rapid technological advances, for which little or no advance planning was done—either at the private or public level—to cope with the impact on unemployment which inevitably was to follow." Beirne urged a broad-scale attack on the problem of automation, including the creation of a U.S. bureau or commission on automation, passage of aid to depressed areas, higher minimum wages, a strengthened public employment service, vocational training, early retirement, and unemployment insurance coverage, so long as the worker who wants to work is displaced by technological change.

CWA's progress and program attracted broadening support, especially among telephone workers. In the spring of 1961, CWA won representation rights for 24,000 New York Bell plant workers, the largest single group to join the union since the early 1940s. The elections were close: in downstate voting, CWA won out over the unaffiliated union by a vote of 8,156 to 7,700; in upstate voting, CWA defeated the IBEW by 2,526 to 2,484. CWA president Beirne viewed the election victories as "a real breakthrough, perhaps more important in their implications for future growth than in their immediate significance for CWA." It was a morale booster and an auspicious beginning for the 1960s.

XIII

New Horizons

President Dwight D. Eisenhower closed his administration with a warning, "In the councils of government we must guard against the acquisition of unwarranted influence, whether sought or unsought, by the military-industrial complex. The potential for the disastrous rise of misplaced power exists and will persist . . . The prospect of domination of the nation's scholars by federal employment, project allocations, and the power of money . . . is gravely to be regarded." Buoyant and youthful, John F. Kennedy opened his presidency with a call, "Ask not what your country can do for you; ask what you can do for your country." Though hampered at the start with a near seven percent unemployment rate, and tragically cut short by death in Dallas after a thousand days, the Kennedy administration marked the beginning of the longest period of sustained economic growth in modern history.

The union's relationship with the new administration was cemented by an invitation from the President to the members of the Collective Bargaining Policy Committee for a visit to the White House. (CWA had backed Kennedy in the 1960 presidential race.) "Yours is an outstanding Union," the President told the policy committee members, "and I am a great believer in the contribution which the union movement can make, not only in this country in maintaining a progressive economy, but also the contribution which the union movement can make around the world." He also commended the committee for the "responsibility" shown to both CWA members and the American people in meeting their assignment, the drafting of a collective-bargaining program.

Through the 1960s, a decade rich in contradictions, CWA continued to grow in membership, to make economic and welfare benefit gains, and continued its thrust towards national bargaining. Management developed a healthy—if grudging—respect for the union and its members. Lester Velie, writing for the *Reader's Digest,* reported a Bell System Company president as saying, "Beirne and his people are tough negotiators," and a top AT&T official as saying, "Beirne is an honest, aggressive union leader with integrity and a strong sense of human values."

As Glenn Watts has pointed out, "a new breed of management" emerged

211

within the Bell System. Men like Erickson, McNeely, Robert Lilley and Walter Straley, were rising within the corporation, replacing, in Beirne's colorful phrase, "the Neanderthals of the Bell System management." The new breed, according to Watts, "accepts as facts of life the existence of unions in the industry, that they are going to be there, and that they might as well deal with them, and that they'll try to deal with them as honestly as they can without capitulating or giving the business away or giving them the shirt off their backs or anything like that."

In the early 1960s, Beirne initiated meetings with McNeely and Erickson. "I'd just call them up," he later said, "and we began then, for want of a better term, a series of meetings where we just 'philosophically discussed' the ideal situation for the resolving of problems that they were familiar with and that I was familiar with. And we drew on our recollections in different situations, and talked about what the official company view was, and the private company view, and what *our* view was, and how could that be solved."

Still caught up in cluster bargaining, CWA was seeking a way towards true national bargaining. "We ought to have three contracts," Beirne once proposed. "One contract would carry recognition and payroll deductions and grievance procedures, and that should be a contract that would run for five years and thereafter—five years because the law says no more than five. And it would run on and on like a Tennyson poem. Then there should be a second one that would deal with items that are identical throughout the entire Bell System, like our pension plan, like vacations, like progressions schedules, length of progressions schedules; and that second contract AT&T and CWA would negotiate. That would run for three years, negotiated every three years. Then the third contract would be a local contract, and that could run for one year, or for three years, or be identical in length of time and termination date with the national contract, or could be separate. So that you'd at least have established on a permanent basis the relationship, so there would be no question of that. And that wouldn't become a bargaining point that the other side could use and say, 'Well, we'll shut off your dues,' or something like that. You take the threat out of the bargaining arena. And then you identify the things that affect all Bell System people in exactly the same way, and we'd bargain on them on a three-year contract. We'd do that once, one sitting, one contract, to go out all over. Then in the twenty-one places, or the 103 places where we have contracts, or whatever number of contracts we have, those local people could sit down, and they'd just be taking care of their local problems. So you would minimize strikes in my judgment."

Backed by a membership willing to strike for its rights, and with a unified strategy worked out by the Collective Bargaining Policy Committee, the CWA leadership created a pattern out of cluster bargaining that became a precursor of national bargaining with the Bell System. In June 1962, union negotiators broke through Ohio Bell resistance to establish a $2 to $5-weekly wage package that set a pattern for Bell units within the same cluster. Contract re-opener talks, dragging badly until then, suddenly came to life and in a fast and furious marathon Illinois Bell State Area Traffic; New Jersey Traffic; Western Electric, Buffalo; Cincinnati & Suburban, and Chesapeake & Potomac, D. C., fell in line. Michigan Bell set something closer to a true pattern for the Bell System the following year in a package CWA president Beirne termed "without precedent in the history of collective bargaining in the communications industry." The Michigan thirty-eight-month contract provided for an average wage increase of 13.33 cents an hour in the first fourteen months with provisions for a re-opener on wages in 1964 and 1965. Improved vacations of three weeks after ten years service, health- and retirement-benefit improvements boosted the hourly value of the contract to twenty cents an hour. The union estimated the cost of the contract for the 15,000 Michigan Bell employees at $21 million and at $411 million for the 750,000 employees of the entire Bell System in the U.S. and Canada. The pre-contract Michigan wage scale ranged from $71 to $136 a week.

The 1963 Michigan precedent was confirmed in the fall of 1964 when the company agreed in a last-hour re-opener session to wage increases ranging from $2.50 to $5 a week. The authoritative *Business Week* headlined its account, "As Michigan goes . . . so goes the nation." The article continued, "Such is expected to be the pattern now that Michigan Bell has settled a pay dispute with Communications Workers of America." The union, *Business Week* reported, "chose Michigan Bell as its primary target and pattern-setter in 1963 because, it said, the company has in one unit the diversity of situations found in most areas of the country. Terms negotiated in Michigan could be applied widely."

But there was more to the pattern than discerned by *Business Week*'s astute labor reporter. Within the context of a developing "friendly-warrior" relationship with management, the union had to confront and resolve two difficult issues—automation and wage differentials. In a convoluted way, the two issues were related for automation was changing the skill mix within the industry, drawing various parts of the country together and, thereby, rendering even more obsolete the industry's cherished belief in the so-called community wage theory. Stated most simply, the community wage theory holds that a giant nationwide corporation, such as AT&T and its member companies, should pay wages that "compare favorably" with all the other wages in a given local community. When employers were small, family-owned firms, towns and cities infinitely varied in economic conditions, with goods produced *and* sold locally the community wage theory made some sense. But with vast improvements in transportation, refrigeration and mass production, the theory had become archaic. CWA president Beirne was being kind when he observed that "while participating in the dramatic changes in economic thought during the last seventy-five years, they [management] just never got around to asking themselves if their old reliable community wage theory was out of focus." What management overlooked D. L. McCowen was ever ready to point up. "Do not hold me to these figures," he told delegates to the 1954 CWA convention, "but I believe I am safe in saying that in the wage for plant craftsmen, when we compare the wages of plant craftsmen in Weatherford, Texas, with those in New York City, there is some $30 a week difference."

CWA negotiators tried to grapple with the problem, pressing the lowest wage zone into the next highest in every bargaining unit, but with only a limited success. As Beirne conceded, over the years, "the total picture has changed very little." By 1963, according to Beirne, the union had become convinced that both the community wage theory *and* a single rate were "bad economics," which left it in something of a dilemma if not exactly in a dither. "Equal pay for equal work" is a powerful slogan, appealing to workers' sense of equity. Indeed it makes eminent sense when it refers to a woman working on the same job as a man but getting less pay though living in the same job market area. But to give the same wage to a worker in, say, rural Utah as to a worker in metropolitan Los Angeles may create a new inequity—one that goes against the worker living in a high cost of living area. With some idea that this might be so, the union's leaders decided to call in some outside professional help "to search for answers in an orderly, well-reasoned manner." And in January 1965, Robert R. Nathan Associates, a firm of noted economic consultants and statisticians, submitted to the union a pioneering reported entitled, *Geographical Wage Standards*.

Ten specialists had worked for two years to produce the 500-page report. A survey of existing community wage theory practices revealed a hodgepodge of unfair wage rate differences throughout the country. In Albuquerque, New Mexico, for example, where the top craft job paid $125 a week, a "modest but adequate" standard of living cost $159 a year below the New York City standard. Yet Bell paid the Albuquerque craftsman $1,250 a year *less* than his counterpart in New York City. Within the Chicago labor market area, roughly encompassing the city and its major suburban environs which share a common cost of living, the only operators receiving the Zone 1 rate of $87 a week were those working within the city limits of Chicago. Suburban zone rates ranged downward from $85.50 to $77.50, though the cost of living varied little from suburb to suburb. In many small communities, the Nathan researchers discovered Bell companies paying low wages and charging premium rates for service. (They also found the belief that the cost-of-living was lower in small communities than in large cities to be a myth. It wasn't always so. Georgia customers in towns with 26,000 telephones, as an instance, paid an independent residential rate of $4.90 a month, seventy cents more than a customer in a similar town in Michigan. Yet the Georgia telephone worker received less pay than his Michigan brother. "A prevailing wage standard does not meet the ideas of equity held by telephone company employees," the Nathan Report concluded. "Most employees compare themselves to others in the industry and want to know, why the differentials? A prevailing wage standard which puts wage differentials between towns at the mercy of industrial composition, difficult occupational comparisons, and an arbitrary choice of relevant rates cannot be intelligibly explained to employees, much less justified as 'fair.' "

The Nathan Report recommended that the community wage theory be dumped in favor of a more equitable and rational pay system based on costs of living. This meant, as defined by Nathan Associates, the cost of maintaining a specified level of living and well-being which takes into account both *quantity* and *quality* of goods and services that make up that standard of living. In practice, this would mean that while a Laredo, Texas, craftsman might take home fewer dollars than the New York City man, he would have the dollars he needed to buy the same amount of diapers and potatoes that could be bought by his coworkers in New York City. Nathan's experts allocated to labor market areas, roughly analogous to those established by the U. S. Bureau of Employment Security, every one of the more than 2,700 work locations listed in Bell System labor contracts. Tables were drawn up based on the rate of pay for a key job in each of the four major departments of an operating company (plant, traffic, commercial, accounting) in each work location. By using a cost-of-living formula devised by Nathan Associates, the report concluded that the more than 100 wages zones then maintained by the telephone industry under its community wage theory could be reduced to just six wage bands with a wage differential of no more than $4 between each band. CWA's research department estimated that the cost of the introduction of such a simplified wage system would average approximately fifteen cents an hour for some 300,000 Bell workers. Some would receive no increase in their wage rate but others would get as much as $20 more a week. The Nathan Report was adopted by the CWA's Collective Bargaining Policy Committee at its January 1965 meeting.

While the Nathan Report provided the basis for a rational, equitable and just wage policy, it did not—it could not—resolve the dislocations created by automation. Telephone workers, as we have noted, are no strangers to technological change. The "cut over" to dialization begun in the early 1920s had lasted until 1954 when the companies had absorbed most of that great changeover from non-dial to dial service. The value of advance notice was not lost on the union and, on occasion, it saved jobs. In Michigan, for example, the union learned of pending changes in the mid 1940s, some two-and-a-half years before. Lester Velie reported what happened in the *Reader's Digest:* "The union people went to work. They studied every employee who faced displacement. Who would accept retraining for other jobs? Who would accept assignments elsewhere in the Bell System? Who, near retirement, would retire early if offered special termination pay? With union cooperation, about half of the operators were transferred to new jobs. Others took early retirement. Thus, twenty years before West Coast steelworkers and longshoremen worked out their famous 'no-firing-because-of-automation' agreements with employers, Beirne's union and Michigan Bell were able to say, at cut-over time, 'No one has been fired.' "

Nonetheless, telephone companies were not always so co-operative. Pacific Telephone & Telegraph Company, *CWA News* reported in November 1962, "seemed to want the best of both worlds—automated machinery and low pay-scale clerks to operate them." PT&T's accounting department, conveniently assigned G-1, G-2 and G-3 clerks to do G-4 work on newly installed IBM tabulating machines. The union argued in an arbitration case that the women doing that work should be assigned a new title to reflect their new skills, and that they should be paid a commensurate rate of pay; that is, a G-4 scale. The union won, as it happened, but the company tried to slip by by using G-3 clerks and paying G-3 rates, a practice that the union fortunately was able to halt through the grievance machinery. However, the PT&T case was no isolated affair as the Bell System expanded its introduction of centralized automatic message accounting, direct distance dialing, direct inward dialing, computer use for billing and records and a wide variety of advances in switching, installation and repair techniques. The revolutionary transistor was soon replaced by the molecular stamped printed circuit, opening up the possibilities of an all-electronic computerized telephone network. Frederick R. Kappel, AT&T chairman, announced on September 19, 1964, that the changeover to electronic switching in every part of the country would cost $12 billion and take up to thirty-five years.

AT&T publicists spoke of electronic marvels to come—housewives coffee-klatching at the neighbors would be able to turn off the oven at home by touch-telephoning, and calls would be switched automatically from home telephones to host telephones when customers were out visiting—but for the telephone worker, electronic switching boded technological and operational changes of vast import to skills and earnings. Electromechanical switching, for example, required tens of thousands of wires in each telephone exchange and called for an endless process of resoldering and replacement as wires wore out. Mechanical relays switch in thousands of a second but a transistor operates in millionths of a second. An electronic switchboard, it was expected, would replace five or six regular switchboards. The electronic switchboard servicing New York City's famed Pennsylvania-6 exchange, the first installed, handled 7,000 lines using

54,000 transistors but required thirty percent less space than the old switchboard. As a consequence of this kind of technological change—and others—CWA's Collective Bargaining Policy Committee ordered a study of "job structure" covering the "breakout" of plant top craft and other skilled jobs affected by automation. This early study, undertaken in 1962 and 1963 and based on the personal experiences of men and women who work in jobs affected by technological change, prompted the union to look further. CWA president Beirne, then serving on President Lyndon B. Johnson's Commission on Automation, had become impressed with the need to relate CWA's concerns over automation with those of society-at-large. The union commissioned the Diebold Group, Inc., an internationally-known management consultant firm, headed by John Diebold, the man credited with creating the term, "automation," to undertake an analysis of automation's impact on the communications industry and relate it to similar developments within the country.

When the Diebold Report was released in April 1965, the union found it somewhat disappointing. This, one suspects, was a matter of expectations. The Diebold Report did not contain the kind of practical proposal that highlighted the Nathan Report and that could easily be embodied in a collective-bargaining program. Still, it was informative. Beirne noted that the union "does not necessarily agree with all the findings of the study" though it was "gratified" that its conclusions "broadly sustain CWA's approach to the problem of automation." This problem, Beirne added, "is so vast and complex that we need all the facts we can get, all the fresh viewpoints we can find, all the creative insights that are available if this union is to find the answers that will help guide its future policy and conduct."

The Diebold Report was slightly more optimistic than the union's leadership. Earlier, a Department of Labor study, prepared for the President's Committee on Labor-Management Policy, made the following forecast: "New development—including pre-assembled equipment, electric switching, and computers—are likely to have a significant impact on installation, construction, maintenance, and clerical workers. Total employment may continue to fall, although volume and variety of communications service are increasing." This was consonant with the union's expectations and experience. During the period 1947 to 1957, total telephone employment rose about 2.8 percent a year, from 585,000 to 768,000. Between 1957 and 1963, the new phase of automation, employment declined 1.9 percent annually to 685,000. Within this, total significant changes took place in the employment mix. The number of telephone operators decreased by nearly one-third, from 232,348 in 1954 to 161,848 in 1963. (Much of this drop was absorbed by attrition eased by the high-rate of turnover among operators.) Central office craftsmen increased by one-third, from 41,347 in 1954 to 54,749 in

1963. Installation and exchange repair craftsmen increased by nearly one-third, from 47,172 in 1954 to 62,390 in 1963. Diebold predicted that by keeping pace with the "information revolution," employment within the communications industry would *increase* over the next five years and, in the absence of a major national economic downturn, the report also foresaw a "relatively stable work force" in the industry over the long haul. The union, however, remained fearful, believing that current job increases would prove to be only the temporary consequences of expanded construction, the increased manufacture of new equipment, and of new installations. Over expansion could accelerate joblessness later. "Even if the work force in our industry remains relatively stable," Beirne commented, "we are faced with a deficit of jobs since the proportion of jobs in communications relative to the total number of jobs in the economy will fall. A vital, growing industry that fails to supply its fair share of jobs to the total economy brings up questions that are too big for any one group to answer."

Armed with the new analytical concepts and tools provided by the Nathan and Diebold Reports, CWA was all the better prepared to exploit the development of pattern bargaining. The consequences were immediately apparent; as a *CWA News* headline exuberantly proclaimed in the fall of 1965: "14¢ Pattern Sweeps U.S." In the last wage reopener in a three-year master contract with Ohio Bell due to expire in 1966, the union won: General minimum wage increases for all employees in all departments ranging from $2 to $4.50 a week. Raises of $3, $4 and $4.50 were gained in the top grades in all wage scales in all zones. Upgrading brought additional wage increases of up to as much as $8 a week. Job reclassifications for commercial service representatives and all accounting department clerks added $3, $4 and $4.50 weekly to their pay envelopes. Four cities—Akron, Columbus, Dayton and Toledo—were moved into the highest wage zone, formerly occupied by Cleveland alone. Wage zones were reduced in Ohio from six to four in line with the recommendations of the Nathan Report. Although the company issued the by now customary disclaimer—that the Ohio settlement could not be taken as a pattern—the other Bell companies in the cluster (Illinois, Michigan, New Jersey, Wisconsin, District of Columbia's Chesapeake & Potomac) quickly tumbled into line. Beirne credited "painstaking preparation", including the Nathan Report, for the union's success in taking "vast forward strides toward elimination of long-standing wage inequities throughout the Bell System." Though few realized it at the time, CWA was now one step and two strikes away from true national bargaining.

Before the union could take that step, however, it had to re-build its inner defenses, organize the unorganized within the Bell System, and drive off an attack from an unexpected antagonist.

The CWA had been hailed in various magazines as "the union automation built," or "tomorrow's union," sobriquets earned by the union's skillful use of publicity and community support as bargaining power to offset its vulnerability when on strike. But in one respect the union lagged behind other unions. It had no union shop and few maintenance-of-membership clauses in its contracts. Members could instruct their respective companies to stop the deduction of dues at any time the union irritated them, either by being too militant or not militant enough. Lacking the rudiments of union security, the union staff and local officers in particular had to devote much of their time to internal recruitment, leaving little time for the organization of the truly unorganized. CWA secretary-treasurer William A. Smallwood reported to the 1962 convention that the number of CWA locals had grown to 800, thirty-nine more than reported at the 1961 convention, and that membership had reached 278,439, about 18,000 more than the year previous. Vice president James M. Massey told the delegates that the union had participated in thirty-two representation elections of which it had won fifteen and had achieved five recognition agreements without election since the last convention. The internal organization campaign, a major CWA effort, brought 364 locals to the third-year membership goal of at least eighty-eight percent of their potential members; in 1961, 386 locals had reached the second year objective of eighty-five percent.

The AFL-CIO merger in 1955 put a damper on intra-union raiding. The individual unions were encouraged to sign no-raiding agreements, and CWA did so with the IBEW. This foreclosed an avenue of "escape" for disgruntled union members, excepting the unaffiliated Teamsters. (A good deal of the raiding between AFL and CIO unions, especially in the post-war years, consisted of angry or dissatisfied members, in effect, shopping among unions, playing one off against another in an attempt to get the best deal.) CWA played a key role in the merger of the two national labor organizations, and Beirne was credited by *Business Week* with preventing the breakup of the merged federation in 1962 over the no-raid issue. "After a night-long attempt to draft a no-raiding pact had brought tempers to a boil," *Business Week* reported, Beirne "lectured AFL-CIO council members on their responsibility for the continued existence of a merged labor movement. Witnesses say he sounded like—without quotation marks—a labor statesman." Beirne also played a leading role in the expulsion of the powerful Teamsters union from the AFL-CIO on charges of corruption and racketeering. But he earned the undying enmity of Teamsters' president James R. Hoffa when he urged the AFL-CIO to "form a rival Teamsters union and lure Hoffa's members away from him." (James B. Carey, president of the International Union of Electrical Workers, joined Beirne in making the plea for the formation of an AFL-CIO truckers' union.) "Some of Hoffa's bluest language is in reference to the two men," *Business Week* reported in 1962. "There's no doubt that he would rather embarrass them—perhaps unseat them—than any other AFL-CIO officials."

The opening for the Teamsters incursion was provided by disgruntled Western Electric installers. The 1953 dissolution of installers District 10 still rankled and though the installers enjoyed a feisty reputation they were among the lowest paid craftsmen within the Bell System. Installers worked on a progression schedule up to a certain mark, and then, as one once described the system before it was finally eliminated by CWA in 1970, "it was merit, solely at the discretion of the company" which "caused an installer to work against another. The term 'brown-noser' got into the act, 'carrot dangling,' and that sort of thing, where you had to outshine your buddy to get a raise. It was a horrible arrangement." Constant travel, too, became an irritant. "When we went out of town years ago, they had manual telephone offices, and they all had telephone operators in them. So actually the Western Electric installer looked forward to going to this little town in western Pennsylvania with forty girls all in one room. A date every night with a different one. Many of the guys married telephone operators. But that's gone now. When you go out of town now, you're working on automatic equipment. The girls are gone. That inducement, that little fringe benefit, is gone." And, too, "as a man develops and grows older and marries, purchases a home, has children, then he has less desire to be on the road." Still, the work was attractive. "It's *very* diversified. There's no such thing as routine work. You're doing something different every day, and the guys like that diversification. They don't care about some travel but they do care about constant travel."

The Installation National Bargaining Unit, however, was so torn apart by internal dissension that the seventeen local union presidents could not agree as to how best get rid of the invidious merit pay system nor ease the irritant of constant travel. Kenneth A. Silvers, a "Hoosier with a lot of selling ability" and president of the Ohio-Indiana local, repeatedly challenged Joe Dunne, Ernie Weaver's successor as installation director. Silver finally won out after Dunne bowed out of the 1961 contest in favor of Richard Hackler. Silvers immediately brought the installers' grievances against the CWA national leadership to a boil. He campaigned against acceptance of a wage re-opener fourteen-cents-an-hour package negotiated in 1962 by CWA. When he lost, 4,610 to 6,152, Silvers turned to the Teamsters. He—and others—met in Chicago on June 15 with Teamsters' vice president Harold J. Gibbons. Along with twenty other local officers, Silvers was charged in July with "dual unionism" and expelled after a trial unique in trade union annals. The week-long trial—August 5 to 11, 1962 —was open to newsmen, members of the union and the "interested public." CWA paid for "necessary and reasonable" expenses of the accused. Three members of the union sat as judges—W. Robert Hansen, Myrtle Robertson and George Kobayashi. Neither side was allowed lawyers though both could call witnesses. Glenn Watts conducted the prosecution. Of the twenty-one defendants, only eleven showed (Silvers, already on the Teamsters payroll, did not appear). As *Business Week* later reported, the eleven "appeared more interested in making a case against Beirne than in defending themselves. At times in the early stages of the proceedings, it was hard to decide whether the Beirne administration was on trial for 'company unionism,' a charge frequently hurled at CWA by the rebels, or the rebels for dealing with Hoffa."

During the trial, Watts elicited from witnesses the extent of Teamster subornation. John J. Bowen, president of Local 2590 in Philadelphia, testified that the Teamsters were paying Silvers $25,000 a year to work against CWA. Frank Wescott, president of New Jersey Local 1090, revealed that Silvers had told him, as he had others, that the Teamsters were willing to spend $500,000 in a drive to take over the 17,000 installers from CWA. Wescott also said that Silvers offered him a Teamsters' job at $100 a week with $150 in "expense money." Despite provocations, the trial proceeded smoothly, the judges remained unruffled. "The individual choice of the individual member for one union or another is not in question," Watts declared. "What these trials are all about is the question of conspiracy, of assisting and supporting a Teamsters grab at an entire bargaining unit."

"Hoffa's raid on CWA," *Business Week* informed its readers, "was a test of a strategy of taking over, intact, an integral part of a major industrial union in a campaign to seize a union jurisdiction piece-meal." And, for a time, it appeared that it might work. The so-called rebels claimed that they had eighty percent of the support needed to switch the WE Installation locals from CWA to the Teamsters through a National Labor Relations Board conducted election. The southeastern local, based in Atlanta, voted 1,275 to 195 to join the truck union. Patrick Morgan, appointed to fill the vacancy as national director created by the expulsion of Silvers, traveled extensively in the fall of 1962 to find out what shape CWA was in among the installers. "I didn't go into a friendly meeting in almost a year," he later recalled. "There was no physical abuse outside of some jostling and pushing and some shoving, and throwing match books and that sort of a thing." But, "I was booed down many, many places, never given an opportunity to really tell my case." And, "there were threatening calls made to my wife, including one kidnapping threat involving Morgan's youngest daughter.

Though the Teamsters charged CWA with "poor representation" and promised "a bargaining agent able to match the strength of the biggest monopoly in the world," their attack was increasingly centered on Beirne as a "labor statesman". But "Teamster power" was double-edged and CWA was quick to capitalize on its threatening aspects. The contest, said CWA leaflets and spokesmen, was between a "clean" union and a "dirty" one. In this fight, CWA had the unanimous backing of the AFL-CIO, which condemned the raid as "reckless, divisive and ruthless." According to newsmen, one of CWA's "most telling" pieces of campaign material was a *Teamsters' Coloring Book,* featuring cartoons of Teamsters and of Hoffa. One showed a stocky Hoffa with his pockets bulging with money with the caption: "My name is James R. Hoffa. The R is for Riddle. Guess whether I will do as much for you as you do for me. Color my pockets green." Another showed an exhausted floor-scrubbing housewife, "I'm a Teamster's wife. My husband had an accident, but he gets no accident benefits through the Teamster contract with the company. Color my hands and knees red."

CWA acknowledged the installers' legitimate beefs, citing "unequal and unfair distribution of wages through company-controlled merit increases" and "unequal advancement opportunity through a company planned and controlled labor grading system." National director Morgan appointed a committee to find "a reasonable substitute" for merit and reminded the members that a start had been made towards the elimination of merit. CWA frankness—and its past achievements—turned the installers around. The vote was heavy; some 16,084 installers mailed in valid ballots over December 5 to 28, 1962, and CWA won handily, 11,388 to 4,000 votes. (There were 696 no-union votes cast.) The margin of victory was greater than CWA leaders expected, and the loss jolted the Teamsters.

Then the Teamsters concentrated on the New York City plant, considered CWA's most vulnerable spot. Though Local 1101 was only three years old, its leadership had already engaged in "empire building," merging the Brooklyn and Bronx locals into the Manhattan organization. Then began what Morton Bahr, now District 1 vice president and then New York area director, termed "a kind of struggle for power. The New York plant unit then represented approximately fifty percent of the members within the district. There was disenchantment among them with the then district director, Mary Hanscom. I don't know just what; you couldn't pinpoint it other than she was a woman; they just didn't want a woman. She was an old guard from way back, recognizing she was one who helped to build this union, but, 'Time passed her by,' was their view. 'She didn't know anything about the plant department,' and things of that nature." When she retired in 1963 and was replaced by her assistant of eleven years, George Miller, he was attacked as a "southerner." (Miller came out of Knoxville, Tennessee.) By then, secretly, some of the Local 1101 officials were on the Teamsters' payroll. Hank Habel, then president of the local, apparently believed he could "use" the Teamsters to wring concessions from the company. As Bahr later put it, Habel thought "he could lead the people down to the river and then turn them around without letting them take a drink." But, in the event, Habel took the jump, and announced for the Teamsters. On January 30, 1964, Habel called a meeting of the local to consider secession. That meeting, Lester Velie of the *Reader's Digest* later reported, "was something new to CWA rank-and-filers accustomed to free discussion and democratic decorum. Dangling effigies of Joe Beirne and AT&T board chairman Frederick R. Kappel greeted members as they arrived. Banners proclaimed, "We're for the Teamsters." When CWA members rose to defend their union, they couldn't get the floor. Scattered through the hall were muscular gents wearing something red—a tie, a shirt, a boutonniere. Only these— pro-Teamsters all—were recognized. With perhaps half of the local's members present, the meeting voted to leave the CWA." Though it was technically an "uncommitted disaffiliation vote," Habel announced a few days later that the 8,000-member local would affiliate with the Teamsters.

The coup, however, lacked *d'etat* for disaffiliation could not take place by law without a poll conducted by the NLRB of the entire 24,000-member New York state plant unit. CWA counter attacked by expelling the ringleaders of the secession move on charges of dual unionism. As George Miller later acknowledged, "it was a rough fight . . . We played the Teamsters' history to the people." The character of that history received startling confirmation on the eve of the NLRB election, held in February 1964, when Manhattan District Attorney Frank Hogan announced the Grand Jury indictment of six men, including Habel and Teamsters' organizer William Griffin, on charges of conspiracy to wage "a campaign of terror and intimidation in connection with union organizing activities." The defendants, according to Hogan, "agreed to have a number of persons beaten, injured and threatened with injury." Once again, the AFL-CIO aligned itself with the embattled CWA. In a letter to New York telephone workers, expressing the hope that they would vote CWA, AFL-CIO president George Meany pointed out that "A national union like CWA is best able to cope with a big telephone company like the Bell System . . . in bargaining, in handling of grievances, in general union know-how." CWA defeated the Teamsters on February 18, 1964, in the representation election conducted by the NLRB among 23,000 New York Telephone Company plant workers throughout New York State, 12,558 to 8,751. (The independent Brotherhood of Telephone Workers received 574 votes.)

"We had hoped to do better than that," George Miller later said. "We thought we had at least now cleared the way to start building a unit in New York Tel, hopefully to use that unit to organize the traffic, commercial, and accounting, which were and still are (as of 1970) independent units." But New York remained faction ridden throughout the rest of the decade. This was particularly so in Manhattan where out of a potential of 8,000 members, CWA held the loyalties of barely 2,000 dues-paying members. "We lost," Morton Bahr estimated, "ninety percent, or darn close to it, of those leaders that we developed in 1959 to 1961." CWA developed a new leadership but did not entirely ease the tensions within New York plant. The

Teamsters made another try in 1967—and again in 1970—under the guise of an independent organization, the Technical Electronic and Communications Union headed by Habel. (The Teamsters as Teamsters were unable to make headway among telephone workers and were defeated in Pennsylvania plant and Illinois accounting as well as in New York.) CWA defeated TECU by 2,000 votes in 1967, and finally routed the Teamsters by two-to-one in 1970.

The struggle with the Teamsters occupied much of CWA's available energies, entailed great risks and grave consequences for collective bargaining and organization. As *Business Week* noted in a story about the long-running California General Telephone strike, "Neither side appeared anxious this week to settle before a vote is tallied this month in a Teamsters challenge of CWA at the New York Telephone Company. *CWA will be stronger—or weaker—afterwards.*" (My italics.) The California strike was itself a consequence of CWA's growing collective-bargaining strength. General of California, considered a pace-setter in the General System, balked at CWA's insistence on improvements comparable to those achieved in the pattern negotiated earlier in 1963 with Michigan Bell. Some 9,000 CWA members employed by General carried out tasks identical with those performed by fellow CWA members employed by Pacific Tel. & Tel. As Richard Hackler graphically described it, "On one side of LaCienega Boulevard there'd be a lineman up a pole working for PT&T. On the other side of the boulevard would be a lineman working for General, with the wages and related benefits being entirely different. And so the issue at General was, 'For Christ's sake bring General up to the same line of scratch.'"

General management, however, took the view that the Bell System was not going to negotiate for them. (In addition to the 9,000 at General of California, the wages and working conditions of some 5,000 other CWA members in five other General units were at stake.) As Frank A. Lennberg of Southwest General put it, "Gains [in the Bell System] were made in pensions, vacations, and health insurance that . . . amount to a breakthrough . . . CWA, having tasted an appreciable degree of success, is attempting to make it our problem." Lennberg defined this "problem" as the "rat race set up by CWA international for its 1963 bargaining strategy." The strike, the third largest in CWA history, began in mid October 1963, and ran for 150 days. District 9 director Louis Knecht assigned Richard Hackler to serve as strike director. The company was clearly prepared for a long strike. Supervisors were promptly transferred from other General locations to carry on telephone service. Some 400 "rent-a-cops" and security guards were hired and posted in front of all central offices, garage locations and field operating centers in southern California. And the company began immediately to hire "replacements;" mid-strike, *Business Week* reported that the company had hired 3,000 replacements and that the company maintained "normal" service for its 1.3 million or so subscribers. CWA started the strike with a ninety-six percent turnout, but as the strike dragged on support slowly eroded, down to eighty percent, to seventy-five percent. General claimed that sixty-five percent of its normal workforce was on the job; CWA estimated that what with "replacements" and supervision, roughly 4,500, or about one-half of the old work-force number were "at work" towards the end. Actually, few strikers returned. Hackler pointed out later, "the majority [of 3,000 claimed by the company as having returned] found other employment and just never returned to General . . . I guess *they* didn't want to go through that again."

General fired some 187 during the strike for alleged violence and sabotage. (CWA won jobs back for eighty percent in arbitration after the strike was settled.) Picketing was, at first, enjoined but CWA won what director Knecht termed an "important victory" in the struggle against company harrassment. The CWA secured a court order that permitted double pickets walking two abreast and allowed "perimeter picketing." CWA imaginatively exploited the new situation. A young lady on a jackass informed the press that she preferred it "to the one that scabs for the company." Strike captains maintained contact with roving pickets with walkie-talkies, proof of CWA's keeping atop of the new electronic age. On Halloween, members appeared in costume on picket lines, dramatizing high morale and company "horrors." All picketing was suspended for a day of mourning when President John F. Kennedy was murdered in Dallas.

Five thousand strikers turned out for CWA president Beirne at a rally kicking off a four-day tour of picket sites and regional meetings. Strikers were relieved of picket duty to attend the February rally by brothers and sisters from neighboring non-striking Bell System locals. "For those Casandras inside and outside the labor movement spreading the word of trade unionism doom," Beirne told his audience, "let them come to California and see our people on the picket line. Then let them dare talk about the decline of unionism." As for the "zero progress" negotiations, Beirne scornfully declared, "This company doesn't want to waste time bargaining— they'd rather spend their time counting scabs." When General Telephone boasted that it was saving money while its employees were out on the picket line, CWA suggested that the California public utility commission cut rates to pass the savings on to the consumer.

As for the strikers, CWA's strike fund, in Hackler's revealing phrase, was "cutting in, picking up the *needs.*" Food, rents and insurance coverage— basic costs of living—were somehow sustained. At the close of the strike, when all the bills were in, including arbitration costs, the strike Fund expenditures amounted to about $7.5 million. The Community Services Committee, which dispensed defense fund monies under the direction of CWA staffer Ken Ferguson "never faltered" and "always came through in the pinch," according to striking rank-and-filers. Finally, with an assist from California Governor Pat Brown and chairman of the state Public Utilities Commission William Bennett, state and federal mediators were able to bring about a settlement. General Telephone of California agreed to the return to work of *all* strikers, a 3.54 percent wage increase, a reduction in social security deductions from pensions, as well as improvements in vacations, extraordinary medical expense coverage and disability pensions. The California settlement broke the log-jam for the rest of the independent system with contracts following the pattern set by CWA.

The resolution of the California struggle and the driving out of the Teamster incubus set the stage for the next phase in CWA's development. Vice president James Massey reported that CWA's national membership surged past the eighty percent mark in 1963, rising to 291,648 dues payers out of a potential of 363,379 within CWA units. "Since the increases are scattered throughout the international," Massey declared, "we know this is not merely a one-shot sectional development but rather a matter of everyone having put their shoulder to the wheel to bring non-members into the union." A massive internal organizing effort thrust CWA membership over 300,000 by the 1965 June convention and prepared the groundwork for a major external organization drive. Suddenly, or so it seemed, CWA was everywhere—organizing electrical firms in Texas and meter maids in New York City, civil service administrators as well as radio operators, cable television installers, construction workers and dairy employees. By the end of the decade, CWA was the fourteenth largest union in the country with a total membership of 422,000.

XIV

All This, and More . . .

Though CWA grew rapidly at the close of the 1960s, energetically organizing everywhere in communications and in related industries, national bargaining with the Bell system remained an elusive goal. Bell management stubbornly stuck to the fiction of "autonomy" in the face of the evolution of "pattern bargaining" toward uniform contract terms on wages and other benefits. Still, the pressures inherent in a collective bargaining relationship built up over twenty years could not forever be denied. Each strike, each set of negotiations made a national agreement all the more inevitable. However, its achievement was no sure thing and its accomplishment took place within a society undergoing dramatic change.

When President John F. Kennedy sent military advisors to Vietnam as a step in a continuing effort to prevent a communist takeover, he could not possibly have foreseen all of the consequences. While President Lyndon B. Johnson intensified that effort by sending combat troops to engage the enemy, he also tried to maintain a precarious balance—and succeeded for most of his administration—between more guns and more butter in an expanding economy. American workers carried the burden of maintaining that balance, producing the necessary goods and sending their sons to fight in Vietnam, while the affluent caviled at doing their share, and their children escaped by going to college.

The country was deeply divided and that division ultimately surfaced in collective bargaining. Twice in living memory—during World War II and the Korean War—the government intervened in labor-management relations. Wage and price controls were imposed. Tripartite boards comprised of government, union and employer representatives were setup to determine and administer wage increase and benefit formulas. But as our involvement in Vietnam deepened, President Johnson was unable to gain the same measure of governmental control over prices. Taking a leaf from President Kennedy's attempts to "hold-the-line" voluntarily on wage-price increases, President Johnson sought a policy of restraint. But without price controls there could be no equity of sacrifice and by the end of the 1960s American workers were pressing for relief against an escalating cost-of-living.

This was the immediate background for CWA's 1968 negotiations on a

227

wage-re-opener midway in its three-year contracts with Bell System associated companies. Ostensibly in an effort to adhere to governmental guidelines set down by the president's Council of Economic Advisors, AT&T companies thumbed down CWA's request for a seven percent wage increase to meet the rise in living cost. AT&T demands for an eight percent rate of return were up for consideration by the Federal Communications Commision, and the telephone-industry giant would only offer 5.6 percent more in wages. Bell family employment had peaked at 697,000. The system owned ninety-one million telephones, forty percent of the world's total, and its assets in 1968 were a staggering $46 billion. In 1967, it grossed $13 billion, a sum greater than ten percent of the United States Government's administrative budget. It declared $1.2 billion in dividends out of a net income of $2.1 billion. With average earnings at $2.76 an hour, telephone workers had to cope with a rapid rise in prices, a jump in the annual average rise of consumer prices from 2.9 percent in 1967 to 4.2 percent in 1968 (and to 5.4 percent in 1969). In the spring of 1968, they authorized a strike by a vote of seventeen to one. The walkout of 200,000 began on April 18.

The first national strike against the Bell System in 21 years lasted eighteen days. The 200,000 strikers remained firm, patiently walking picket lines all over the nation. Unhappily, in terms of direct economic pressure on the Bell companies, telephones kept on ringing. During the last national strike in 1947, there was a fair amount of disruption, especially of manually-operated telephones and of long-distance calls. At that time only 59.8 percent of Bell System telephones were direct dial and there was no long-distance dialing. Twenty-one years later, 99.8 percent of the System's telephones were dial and ninety-one percent of long distance calls could be direct dialed. CWA president Beirne acknowledged this, but he cautioned the complaisant: "The $30 billion computer they call the Bell Telephone System is just about the most spectacular achievement in the whole world of automation—but without the skill of our members who repair it and keep it running, that computer will eventually become an enormous pile of junk."

Initially the negotiations were limited to wages under the terms of the old agreement. But when CWA president Beirne met on Easter Sunday with AT&T representatives, at the suggestion of the Federal Mediation Services, he brought up a range of additional issues for resolution. Soon the talks encompassed the full range of a new contract and finally the parties agreed to an increase of nearly twenty percent in wages and benefits over a three-year period. The average of 6.5 percent a year was well above comparable settlements then being made in other industries, roughly at 5.6 percent on the average. AT&T president Ben S. Gilmer acknowledged the system's need to keep up with the movement of wages and fringe benefits in other major industries "in order to attract and keep good people." CWA president Beirne called the settlement "big—in every sense." The three-year contract provided wage increases of $34 a week for skilled installers, $24 for top-scale plant craftsmen, and $16 for switchboard operators and clerks. Under the previous contract, wages averaged about $154 weekly for installers and craftsmen, $83 for operators and $103 for clerks. Minimum pensions were raised, as of June 1, 1969, to $125 a month from $115 and deductions equivalent to twenty-five percent of social security pay were eliminated. New vesting rights permitted an employee with fifteen years of service to take his personal investment in the pension with him on leaving. Night differentials were increased and holiday pay was boosted to two-and-one-half times the normal rate. Employees with twenty-five years or more service got five weeks vacation and eight holidays were assured for all Bell System employees.

The 1968 negotiations attained the content but not the form of true national bargaining. Although fourteen Bell telephone units accepted the terms of the new agreement, the rest settled in piecemeal fashion. Michigan remained out on strike another two weeks and a second ratification vote proved necessary among Western Electric employees. Southern Bell, the Mountain States, New York Telephone and AT&T Long Lines finally settled on roughly the same "pattern," but separate negotiations took place in each instance. Nonetheless, as Louis Knecht later pointed out, "we had real national bargaining." The overall terms of all the Bell System contracts were worked out nationally between representatives of the union and representatives of AT&T. This would again hold true in 1971.

There was some dissatisfaction with the 1968 settlement, notably among the installers. It surfaced in a mild way at the 1969 CWA convention in Kansas City. The top officers of the union, with the exception of George E. Gill, who, however, won handily with 77 percent of the votes, had been re-elected without opposition at the 1967 convention. Two years later, Beirne and Executive Vice-President James M. Massey faced opposition as a consequence of the grumbling over the 1968 terms. They defeated their opponents with ease, however. Bill Smallwood had retired as secretary-treasurer and Glenn Watts was elected to fill the vacancy without opposition. Gus Cramer filled the executive vice-presidency formerly held by Watts. Executive vice-presidents Cramer and Gill were elected without opposition. Two years later, in 1971, all the top officers were elected without opposition with Louis B. Knecht replacing James M. Massey who had retired as an executive vice-president. As usual there were several contests within the districts over vice-presidencies and among the bargaining units over directorships.* Overall, throughout the period, CWA continued to

---

*The following individuals were elected on June 15, 1971, in Kansas City, Missouri:

President   J.A. Beirne**
Executive vice-president   Louis B. Knecht**

exhibit a stability of leadership coupled with a lively, democratic internal life.

The leaders of the union ensured stability by paying attention to the changing needs of the members and by assuring that those needs were met by the appropriate changes in the structure of the union. The care exercised illustrates the character of CWA leadership and its interaction with the membership. Toward the end of the 1960s, it became clear to CWA's officers that some changes were needed in the structure of the union. The union was changing and while the Bell System remained a major component it was felt that the union's structure should no longer simply reflect that of Ma Bell. An outside consultant firm, the Arthur D. Little Organization, was called in to examine the union's operation. Its report was widely studied along with numerous suggestions from various CWA locals. In 1970, CWA convention delegates elected a Structure Review Committee consisting of members from each district, representatives of the staff, the executive board and the national bargaining units. After much deliberation, it was decided to call the first special convention in CWA's history to consider the report and recommendations of the review committee. The convention met in Denver, Colorado, in March, 1971.

"Our job this day," CWA president Beirne said in his opening remarks, "is to finally plot the course the CWA will take in its structure into our

Executive vice-president	Gus Cramer**
Executive vice-president	George E. Gill**
Secretary-treasurer	Glenn E. Watts**
Vice-presidents	
District #1	Morton Bahr**
District #2	William Edwards**
District #3	Ben Porch**
District #4	Walter Schaar**
District #5	Ray Stevens
District #6	D.L. McCowen**
District #7	D.K. Gordon**
District #8	John C. Carroll
District #9	James Booe**
District #10	Willard Brown**
National bargaining unit directors:	
Long Lines	George Myerscough**
Western Electric Sales	Frank J. Novotny
Western Electric Installation	P.J. Morgan**
Independent Telephone	Rudy Mendoza

**Indicates no contest. George E. Gill died on May 6, 1976. Richard W. Hackler, Assistant to the President since 1970, was named by the Executive Board to fill the vacancy left by the death of Gill. He was elected as Executive Vice-President by the 1976 convention. James B. Booe, the former head of District 9, was named by CWA president Watts to replace Hackler. Avelino Montes, Booe's assistant, was named Vice-President of District 9 by the Executive Board. He was elected to the post at the 1976 convention by the District 9 delegates.

uncertain future." But, as he also indicated, there were differences. A resolution calling for the organization of thirteen districts as opposed to the existing twelve was defeated as was a proposal to establish dues on a percentage of income basis. The terms of office at both the international and local level, however, were extended to three years as were the terms for members of the Bargaining Councils and Trial Courts. Delegates, by constitutional amendment, created CWA Retired Members' Clubs and established a 65-year-old mandatory retirement for all elected officers. Most important, however, were the setting of standards for the local unions. The locals, in effect, were constitutionally bound to establish and maintain "actively functioning" organizing, education, legislative, community services, and other such committees to effectuate the policies of the union. The minimum standards adopted called for all local unions to participate actively in a wide-ranging series of programs and meetings aimed at keeping CWA officers and members in-tune with one another. Vehicles were provided for carrying out union policies in the areas of political and legislative activities, the training of officers and stewards, internal and external organizing and for streamlined grievance handling.

At the regular June, 1971 convention, CWA president Beirne stressed the importance of the work done at the special March meeting. "These changes," he declared, "envision the strengthening of our legislative work as well as strengthening the work of all our locals. I foresee further development and upgrading of our local leaders and the more active involvement of our members. The band between all groups and all levels within the union will be made stronger."

Politics within a union, as within most major democratic institutions, involve differences over issues, questions of ideology, the clash of personalities and the quest for power. Within a union, however, as important as such matters are, all must ultimately center about collective bargaining, for, though unions enhance workers' lives in many ways, they begin and end at the workplace. CWA's remarkable stability of leadership, which goes back to its very beginning, rests not only on the political abilities of the union's officers but on their ability to shape and deliver contracts acceptable to the great majority of CWA members. A good illustration of this was 1968, for there was a tension between a responsive leadership, not entirely convinced of the wisdom of a strike at that time, and the rank and file, ready and willing to take on the Bell System. The outcome was a good contract and another step toward national bargaining.

By 1971, an inflation-stoked economy had built up an irresistible head of steam. "Our members are hurting," CWA president Beirne declared at the start of bargaining. "We must recoup our lost buying power—costs are up 17.7 percent since 1968—and secure additional improvements in recognition of our members' work and increased productivity." (Productivity had been rising at 5.5 percent a year.) AT&T continued to insist on separate negotiations even though the associated company wage offers and demands for work rule changes were, as a union spokesman ironically put it, "pretty consistent" and "inadequate" propositions. And once again, the government was a third party in negotiations, admonishing the parties that settlements as high as nine percent were unacceptable. The new administration of Richard Milhous Nixon was on the verge of a reversal in Nixonian economic strategy, a startling switch from *laissez-faire,* non-interventionist economics, to direct economic controls *via* a wage-price freeze. Shrewdly, Beirne called on CWA members working for the Bell System to tighten ranks for the needed "unity and strength [to] offset that third party at bargaining tables."

To effectively mobilize the membership, CWA's spokesmen took to television, an appropriately modern medium for communication with the rank and file. The union bought thirty minutes on sixty-five television stations and also on about fifty-five radio stations in areas not reached by television. Notice of the program was relayed to the members by a 50,000 member task force mobilized within the locals. All the officers and executive board members appeared on the televised "union meeting." Contracts were running out in a dozen or more Bell companies. Negotiators reported "no progress" in key "pattern" talks with Western Electric and the Chesapeake & Potomac Telephone Company, as well as with all the others. President Beirne branded company "offers" as "largely unacceptable" and urged a strike-authorization vote. And on July 14, 1971, over 400,000 CWA members struck the Bell System.

The strike lasted a week and the 33.5 percent settlement package was ratified in a mail ballot of the members two weeks later. Marathon talks over the last weekend of the strike with top echelon Bell officials produced an immediate 12.8 percent wage hike along with a rise in average wages and fringe benefits over the term of the three-year agreement from $4.62 an hour to $6.18 an hour. The new contract also included a clause providing additional pay for each increase in the Consumer Price Index without any ceiling. The union also won a modified agency shop requiring all Bell employees, after thirty days employment, to join the union or pay union dues. (The agency shop agreement, however, contained a "grandfather clause," allowing long-time non-union employees to continue freeloading.)* Wage inequities between male and female workers were reduced; pensions, health insurance, holidays and work schedules were all improved. Extra pay of $5 to $9 a week was secured for workers in major cities such as New York, Chicago and San Francisco to compensate for the higher costs of living in metropolitan areas. It was a good settlement for an inflationary

---

*Now ended in the last CWA-Bell contract.

time, especially so since the settlement was negotiated just before President Nixon imposed a wage-price freeze. "We beat the freeze by thirty-three hours," Beirne later said.

But New York State's 38,500 installers, repairmen, switchmen, linemen, cable splicers and clerks rejected the national settlement against the advice of the national leadership. Beirne met with the local leadership and repeatedly told them, "Look, you can't get anything for ninety days. There's only one possible way we can get it for you, and that's *join* us. The rest of us have gotten all the money of the 1971 contract on the basis of our vote preceeding President Nixon's freeze. So join with us now and accept this national [agreement], and you can get that money in your pocket and you won't have to wait ninety days." But, as Beirne later put it, "They are too hot up there. There are too many problems in New York for them to see what I think is a reasonable, rational way to act today in the light of a freeze."

Although New York's telephone workers acted against the best advice their national leaders could give, they also got the best support that the national union could give during a strike. The strike lasted seven months and cost the union $11 million in strike benefits. The vote of acceptance was 13,769 to 9,193 for a settlement essentially in line with the national agreement, along with some local issue gains. Despite company-inspired hopes of a back-to-work movement, it never materialized and New York Telephone finally had to bargain. It also had to grant the agency shop without the notorious "grandfather clause." The strike, moreover, reinforced CWA's determination to finally achieve national bargaining.

As the Bell System Bargaining Council declared on September 14, 1972, "We must continue to express our discontent with having to bargain with the Bell System in twenty-one operating companies under the pretense that these companies operate as separate and distinct entities. These companies do in fact constitute a system—a system subject to the final and absolute control of the American Telephone & Telegraph Company. This is common knowledge, and in point of fact these twenty-one companies are essentially mirror images of one another in the vital areas of pensions, vacations, health and life insurance, and disability benefits, to name but a few. And yet, we are supposed to embrace this facade and bargain with each individual company as though each were separate from one another. To continue this farce, the Western Electric Company and Bell Laboratories also maintain they, too, are separate entities unrelated to the operating companies or to each other—a relative of no one."

What Joe Beirne once termed "the charade" would, however, soon be over. Quietly, company and union leaders sat down to discuss and thrash out the question. "We kept working on them to be honest," Beirne later told a Bell System bargaining council meeting, "to face up to what is actually going on, to legitimize it." In a poignant speech to the council on January 16, 1974, Beirne, who had undergone operations to remove two malignant tumors, declared, "We made our breakthrough: The Bell System has agreed to national bargaining with the Communications Workers of America.

"That was one of the privileges I wanted to reserve to myself, even if they had to take me down here in a wheelchair. I would want to be the one to say we got national bargaining. Of course they kept dilly-dallying, you know, for a couple years. And if they had waited five or six years and finally agreed to it, I'd die a bitter man. I'd be cursing them into hell and out of hell, 'Why didn't they do it while I was there?' "

CWA president Beirne and AT&T vice-president Rex R. Reed jointly announced to the public on January 16, 1974, the terms of the new agreement to bargain nationally. Representatives of the union, under the direction of the CWA international, and representatives of the Bell telephone companies under the direction of AT&T, were to negotiate all national issues. Local issues were to be bargained on a unit-by-unit or company-by-company basis. Agreement on a settlement of the national issues was to be subject to ratification by a national referendum of the membership involved and separate from any ratification required on local issues. The parties defined national issues as including but not limited to such matters as basic wages, pensions, health insurance and length of contract. Local issues had to do primarily with local unit working conditions. Beirne and Reed described the change to national bargaining as "a logical outgrowth of past bargaining experience" and one that "serves the best interests of both parties."

When CWA contracts with the Bell System ran out in July of 1974, CWA's Bell System membership authorized a strike. As negotiations came down to the line, a strike date set for August 4, both sides imposed a news blackout on talks. Talks were intensified, and at the eleventh hour the union and AT&T reached an agreement on a three-year pact calling for wage and benefit improvements amounting to 35.82 percent. The total value of the package was estimated at more than $3.119 billion, making it by far the largest labor settlement since the lifting of federal wage-price controls. The thirty-four local bargaining teams took another week to wrap up town and job upgrades, the correction of wage inequities and other local issues. CWA won an immediate wage increase of 10.7 percent, with the total of wage and wage-related items—including an additional $5 on the maximum rate for service representatives—calculated at about twelve percent. On the first and second anniversary dates, wage increases for productivity amounted to 3.3 percent on maximum rates with an average of three percent throughout the system. (Salaries of telephone workers under the old contract ranged from $108 to $166 weekly for operators and $148 to $260 for craftsmen.) The pact established a dental plan, fully paid for by the company and available to dependents as well as employees. Medical insurance benefits were improved with the company agreeing to pay ninety percent of usual and customary fees for benefits covered instead of eighty percent. Pension gains amounted to thirty-three percent over past benefits during the life of the agreement.

"All of us can take credit for [the settlement]," the Bell bargaining committee noted in its report to the members, "for it was only with the strong and united support of the rank-and-file members and local officers across the country—demonstrated by your seven to one strike authorization—which enabled national negotiators to stand firm to the very end in a year which the company clearly was testing our mettle and the government urging restraint." The pact was approved by a 210,000-to-103,000 vote in a national referendum.

The imperceptible changes always underway within any democratic institution seemed to gather additional momentum in 1974 for the CWA. Gravely ill with cancer, CWA president Beirne resigned in the spring. He died at 63, on September 2, after more than thirty years of dedicated service to the labor movement. At the funeral service, where trade unionists from around the country came to pay tribute to Beirne, Monsignor George C. Higgins delivered a moving eulogy. He recalled that Beirne once said, "When you're the head of a union, you've got to be a sociologist, marriage counselor, father confessor, psychiatrist, economist, legal expert, all wrapped into one. You must have the desire to help people help themselves. . . . Labor unionism is a movement of the people, not just a legal structure. A union leader who lacks feeling ought to be doing something else." Monsignor Higgins added, "It would not do justice to the man to think of him primarily as a public figure concerned impersonally with important public issues and involved as a celebrated VIP in all sorts of public events. He was that, of course, but, first and foremost, he was interested in people—ordinary people, the so-called rank and file. In his opinion, they were the salt of the earth."

Joseph A. Beirne's passing marked the end of one era and a new beginning for CWA. Prediction, at best, is a chancy business: all that a historian can do is point up the forces already at work changing society and its institutions. Leadership, for example, is a major factor in both continuity and change. As the great economist Joseph A. Schumpeter correctly pointed out, "The social necessary functions that succeed one another in historical time are related in important respects—administrative skill, resoluteness, and the ability to command are vital in any leading position." Since, as Schumpeter adds, "both the attainment and the practice of leadership are aided by a tradition of leadership." One can argue that a test of leadership for a democratic organization is likely to occur at the death of an outstanding figure, during the passing of a generation of leadership, or at a critical juncture of a deep and divisive crisis. While our economy during the mid-seventies appears to be teetering on the edge of the latter, there are no signs of such a crisis within CWA. In the death of Beirne, however, the union experienced the passing of a strong, dominant, if not domineering, figure as well as a symbol of the passage of generations. Considering that the yeast of change is always at work, the transition of leadership within CWA was remarkably smooth. Of the five top officers, three—Watts, Gill and Miller—were district directors in 1965; Knecht and Cramer were highly placed staff members. But of the twelve vice-presidents, only one, D.L. McCowen, was on the executive board in 1965. McCowen goes all the way back to the beginnings of CWA, which makes the change all the more marked.

Indeed, few unions have undergone so thorough a change in their leadership within a decade. Few have undergone so great a change without intense factionalism. Beirne's decision to step aside in the spring of 1974 effectively transferred leadership from those who created a militant union out of the cluster of telephone-company unions of the late 1930s to those who came out of World War II and whose unionism is shaped by the nationwide strike of 1947. When Glenn E. Watts was elected to succeed Beirne at the 1974 Kansas City convention, he faced only a token opposition, winning by 458,665 votes to 12,148. Two executive vice-presidents were elected without opposition; the third, George M. Miller, defeated three opponents (one, a serious threat), but the contest was not a challenge of the overall leadership. Miller's opponents, for example, as they might in a more divisive situation, did not team up in caucus to contest other officers. Clara Allen, CWA New Jersey Area Director, ran against Louis B. Knecht, then an executive vice president, for the secretary-treasurership. She based her campaign on the slogan, "The Time Is Now" (presumably for a woman as a top officer). No other issue was raised, nor any major criticism leveled at the administration (or at Knecht). Knecht won handily, 299,561 votes to Allen's 160,034 and 11,422 for a third candidate. Clearly, the convention delegates—and by extension, the membership—were solidly behind the new administration as they were behind the old.

That was so because within change there has been continuity aptly symbolized by the career of the new CWA president. Glenn Ellis Watts, born and raised in North Carolina until the age of eleven when the Watts family moved to Washington, D.C., went to work for the Chesapeake and Potomac Telephone Company as an installer in 1941. Within a year, he transferred to the Commercial Department as a service engineer and was elected job steward, the first step on the elective rise to his present post. Where the founding generation of CWA leaders, so to speak, started at the top, Watts came up through the ranks of a growing, ever-changing union. After holding several offices while still working for the telephone company, he was elected local president in 1948 and became a full-time union officer. In a time of considerable ferment within the union, Watts evidenced qualities of leadership that made him a natural choice as Director of CWA's District 2. He was elected in 1951 to serve a region encompassing the states of Virginia, West Virginia, Maryland, Pennsylvania, Delaware and the District of Columbia. In 1956, CWA president Beirne asked Watts to serve as Assistant to the President, a position Watts held until his election as CWA executive vice-president in 1965.

Watts, a candid, soft-spoken man with a broad forehead and a warm smile that breaks up a seriousness of face accented by gold-rimmed glasses, epitomizes the best in modern, progressive trade union leadership. While not a flamboyant speaker, he holds the attention of his audiences and as the chairman of CWA's convention guides the delegates through a complex range of business with a fair but firm hand. He is a capable administrator, is resolute in carrying out the policies of the union and commands the respect of his peers. He reads widely and has a keen interest in international affairs. As a consequence of his concern about social and economic progress, he is a volunteer in many community programs and organizations. He was the first union leader to head a United Fund Campaign, directing the 1968 drive for the United Way of the National Capital Area. He is a vice-chairman of the Board of Governors and chairman of the Executive Committee of the United Way of America; a member of the Governing Board of Common Cause; Treasurer of the National Urban Coalition; and a trustee of the Ford Foundation. He and his wife, Bernice, have three children and seven grandchildren. Though he does not spend as much time as he would like puttering around his Chevy Chase backyard, Watts is an avid gardener. "If I have a hobby, that's it," he once remarked. As for photography, "that's an absolute pleasure" so "I really don't consider it a hobby."

That sheer enjoyment of something well done infuses nearly everything Watts does, especially his work for the union. He makes a point of getting around the country to visit CWA districts, taking the opportunities afforded to have discussion with rank-and-file members. Such exchanges, not solely limited to Watts but embracing all the other leaders of the union, have an impact on leadership thinking and on the ordering of priorities for change and improvements. But it is also a way of ensuring continuity as a core for change and progress. This keeps the question of leadership—as well as program—a very lively one within the union. When asked what advice he would give young people embarking on a union career, Watts replied, "Work about twenty-four hours a day as a volunteer for the Union to begin with. Get elected to every office and the highest office that you can within your local. Work hard to do a good job. To the extent that your formal education is limited, as often ours is collectively as workers, and go do something about it. If you haven't finished high school, go to a night school and do that. Go pick up some college credits somehow or other, at night school or otherwise, and get that piece of paper. You can peddle it and it's a pretty good thing to have around. And while doing that, develop the good habits of a successful politician. That means getting around so that you get to know people and they get to know you. And if you've got it on the ball, you'll make it—but you've got to work at it."

As any observer of recent CWA conventions will confirm, there is a much younger group of workers coming up behind the current generation of leaders eager to take part in union life. Clara Allen, in 1974, made a respectable showing for a first try and for a union, as one delegate put it, "not ready for a woman president" (the secretary-treasurer being perceived by the delegates as the apparent line of succession). Her supporters, judging from those passing out leaflets and caucusing on her behalf, tended to be young, ardent about women's liberation, and many were black and Latinos. Today, in sharp contrast to ten or fifteen years ago, CWA membership reflects the national averages for minority participation in the work force, roughly twenty percent black and six-to-seven percent Latino. There is a greater concentration of minorities in the big cities, especially of the North, though increasingly so in the South and West, than in the smaller towns and cities. Their presence within the union has only recently been felt in an active way. A black caucus was formed several years ago and there has been an increase in the number of black and minority local officers.

Women have always played a greater role within CWA than in most unions with a substantial female membership. Of CWA's 507,428 members, approximately fifty-two percent are women. Automation, however, has reduced the proportion of operators, heretofore a woman's job. In 1950, 43.4 percent of the Bell System work force were operators; by 1970, that proportion had dropped to 25.7 percent. This affected the concentration of women within the union and, in part, explains the recent absence of women at the very top level of leadership. Women today are more widely dispersed within the union. Equal opportunity developments have opened traditional male jobs, especially in the plant, to women and, along with the union's success at making an operator's pay and working conditions more attractive, opened operator positions to men. The movement of men into telephone operating and of women into installation, plant and maintenance work has been fractional, but it is sure to increase. In the future, women are not so likely to be concentrated in all-female locals as in the past. This will affect participation. Over a third of the local union officers today are women. Dina Beaumont, who brought back to the union after an absence of nearly thirty years a bloc of southern California operators, was elected vice-president of a new district, District 11, created in part to assure women a voice in the national leadership.

CWA leaders are aware of the need for affirmative action in the industry and within the union. To assure fair and equitable treatment and representation for minorities, the executive board has encouraged the formation of active equity committees within each local union. In preparation for voter registration drives and political education for the 1976 campaign, black CWA members participated in training conferences organized by the A. Philip Randolph Institute. Executive Vice-President George M. Miller is on the Randolph Institute's executive board. CWA Latinos are active in the Labor Council for Latin American Advancement. Independent Telephone Director Rudy Mendoza is on the council's administrative committee. Avelino B. Montes, vice president, District 9, and Norma Garza, Local 12137, are elected members of the council's executive board. CWA is active in the ratification of the Equal Rights amendment, and the CWA Executive Board endorsed the Coalition of Labor Union Women. Assistant to the President Patsy L. Fryman was elected Recording Secretary at CLUW's 1975 convention, CWA vice president Dina Beaumont, a regional vice president, and CWA members Christine Hodgson, Donna McClain and Carmen Hernandez are CLUW executive board members. Within CWA, Vice President Beaumont chairs the Concerned Women's Advancement Committee which consists of two representatives from each of the twelve CWA districts. The committee is studying the roles women play at all levels of the union and seeks to stimulate more participation of women at the grass roots level.

Few, if any, of the thousands of delegates who have attended recent CWA conventions to discuss and to shape union policy on a wide range of issues remember those first conventions when a bare handful of people met, hardly daring to speak of anything but of their immediate concern, the formation of a telephone workers organization, for fear of controversy. Today, CWA resolutions range widely and the union speaks out resolutely on matters of domestic and international concern. As CWA president Watts reminded delegates at the 1975 convention, "All of us are affected by events and actions in other parts of the world, and we cannot overlook them." And CWA deeds have given life to CWA words in a way that is unique among unions. CWA has been committed to the assistance of free trade unionists the world over ever since telephone workers decided on the momentous step of affiliation to the CIO. It has been active in the Postal, Telegraph and Telephone International (PTTI), a trade union secretariat representing tele communications workers in all parts of the free world, as other American unions are active in the international bodies of their own trades. In 1959, however, CWA developed a unique program to give substance to its commitment to free trade unionism. CWA president Beirne, vice-president Ray Hackney and Louis B. Knecht, then director of District 9, initiated a project to provide direct voluntary assistance from CWA District 9 locals to communications workers unionization efforts in Ecuador. Eighty locals pledged two dollars a month, which allowed José M. (Pepe) Larco, now the general secretary of the Ecuadorean Federation of Telecommunications Workers, to work full time as a union organizer in his country. Since then, CWA's Operation South America has grown, sustaining union activities in thirteen different Latin-American and Caribbean countries with all of CWA's twelve districts involved.

In cooperation with PTTI, CWA also established a school for Latin-American unionists at Front Royal, Virginia. At the first graduation ceremony, AFL-CIO president George Meany, CWA president Beirne and a few others gathered around the same table and had an idea which became the American Institute for Free Labor Development organized under the aegis of the AFL-CIO. Now in its fifteenth year, AIFLD graduates approximately 150 students a year who return to their countries with invaluable know-how about union organizing and union operations. CWA's Operation South America, its involvement with PTTI, its support of Soviet dissidents, commitment to Israel and other democratic forces opposed to Soviet aggression and totalitarianism in all its forms is rooted in a concern, perhaps best stated by AFL-CIO president Meany when he declared, "We feel that unless there is a free-trade union movement, there's always a danger of people losing their freedom—of people becoming chattels or becoming slaves or becoming colonial assets, as it were, of imperialist countries."

When the National Federation of Telephone Workers rather hesitatingly endorsed President Franklin D. Roosevelt for reelection in 1944, few of the founders would have even dared dream of the kind of political involvement now commonplace within CWA. The union today can count among its members half a dozen mayors, scores of city councilmen and members of state legislatures. The union has created a growing number of state-level legislative political-action committees. It endorsed Hubert Humphrey in 1968 and George S. McGovern in 1972. In 1974, it was involved in nineteen senate races, helping to win fifteen; in 195 House of Representative contests, scoring 146 victories; and in twenty gubernatorial campaigns, winning fifteen. Working closely with others in the labor movement and with women, blacks and other minorities, CWA helped ensure rights of participation to all within the Democratic Party processes. Beirne had served on the Democratic Party National Committee, and CWA president Watts succeeded him in 1974. Vice president Martin J. Hughes of District 5 and Norma Sublett of Local 9241, Sacramento, California, were elected delegates-at-large to the DNC, giving CWA three members, more than any other labor organization. The lifeblood of participation in politics for labor is the flow of voluntary membership contributions. CWA's record is outstanding: $397,000 in 1974; $468,000 in 1975, the highest ever in sixteen years of fund-raising history. According to Al Barkan, AFL-CIO Committee on Political Education (COPE) director, on a percentage of membership basis, "it's just about the best record in the federation."

CWA was among the first unions to endorse Jimmy Carter for the presidential nomination and CWA members worked hard for the election of the Carter–Mondale ticket. Carter addressed the 1975 San Diego convention and won the endorsement of the 1976 convention in June before the Democrats convened. CWA joined nine other unions to form the Labor Coalition Clearing House to develop a coordinated effort to elect delegates to the Democratic Party convention. It fielded more than 400 delegates and alternates. Together with an additional 150 labor delegates, the trade unionists at the convention were able to help draw up a party platform that strongly reflected labor's goals for America. By mid-October, CWA–COPE provided funds for some 150 rank-and-file members to take leave from their jobs to work in voter registration and education programs. Staff members in many districts were assigned full-time to organize and supervise telephone banks and other election activities. Hundreds of CWA volunteers worked the phone banks and hundreds more went to work directly for Carter–Mondale campaign committees. CWA–COPE spent over a quarter of a million dollars in the final campaign effort, with the bulk of the money going to local and district level operations. Some fifty CWA members worked full-time exclusively in congressional campaigns. Altogether, CWA–COPE supported—either with campaign contributions or volunteer efforts—278 House candidates (with 221 victorious), 27 Senatorial candidates (19 victories), and nine gubernatorial candidates (7 winners). It was an impressive performance.

CWA is not only an active participant in AFL-CIO-COPE and in federation legislative activities, but it is also active at every level within labor's mainstream. CWA president Watts serves on the AFL-CIO executive council as a federation vice president. Secretary-treasurer Knecht represents the union in the councils of the AFL-CIO Industrial Union Department. Executive vice president George E. Gill, served a term as president of the Council of Professional Employees, AFL-CIO, and, until his death in May, 1976, served as a vice-president. Executive vice-president George M. Miller is a vice-president of the newly created AFL-CIO Public Employee Department. While CWA president Watts has put this participation in largely political terms, the overall thrust of commitment is unmistakable. "The new emphasis we are putting on legislative and political action is one of the most significant things that is happening in CWA in terms of our future well-being." Shoring up CWA legislatively, he adds, "is our major new thrust to help our friends in Congress and to defeat those who oppose us. Members are becoming increasingly active at the grass roots and at all other levels of politics. In the Washington headquarters we have combined the CWA–COPE activities with our legislative program in the President's office. We are continuing to urge all locals to affiliate with AFL–CIO state and local central bodies. We want our people to have a stronger voice in the decision-making process in those bodies, particularly in the selection of candidates who will have labor support."

Within a huge and lively institution such as CWA, the passing of a major figure or a marked generational change in leadership and significant changes in the make-up of the membership, may mark the end of an era, but that is not a full stop. The achievement of national bargaining with the Bell System, for example, is the culmination of three decades of struggle, but the effort to improve the bargaining relationship, to build on the gains of the past and to extend those gains to all of the communications industry continues unabated. Overall, CWA's achievements are truly impressive. Using wages as a yardstick, there has been a steady increase over the past twenty years. The actual or monetary increase from 1950 to 1970 for all Bell employees, except officials and managerial assistants, was 154.4 percent. In real earnings, allowing for the rapid rise in living costs, Bell workers are still better off in 1970 than they were in 1950 because wage increases won by the union have kept ahead of increases in the Consumer Price Index. In real wage terms, the percentage increase for all employees, excepting officials and managerial assistants, was 57.6 percent. For production and nonsupervisory workers on private nonagricultural payrolls throughout the nation the comparable gains were 124.8 percent for the monetary jump and 39.3 percent for real earnings. In sum, CWA-represented employees have consistently exceeded the national averages. Nonetheless, as demonstrated in 1974, union negotiators continue to press for wage gains commensurate with worker gains in productivity, with rises in the Consumer Price Index and in keeping with the American worker's desire to improve his lot.

Recent CWA bargaining with the independent telephone companies has been considerably rougher than with Ma Bell, even though gains over 1974, averaging from nine to ten percent, are approximately in line with those experienced in other industries. A trend toward shorter contracts, or, at union insistence, on wage reopeners reflects the mid-1970s economic uncertainties. The managements of the independent companies have rejected the union's claim that a wage parity should exist throughout the industry. They have insisted on acting independently from bargaining policies established by other companies in the telephone industry. As a CWA statement acknowledged, "our ability to continue to negotiate effectively will depend upon more intimate knowledge of each independent company rather than to rely on our historic insistence that what is accomplished in one group must, therefore, be accomplished in another." This strategy in historic terms is, of course, an illustration of the union's flexibility as well as of its powers of adaptation to given economic circumstances. Changes in conditions, obviously, will bring about changes in strategy.

There have been, as a consequence, a rash of hard-fought strikes among the independents. Mid-Texas telephone workers walked picket lines for eight bitter months to win a basic package in a three-year agreement, effective September 1, 1974. The Alabama division of the Southeast General Telephone Company was struck for four months over a wage reopener, netting a 9.2 percent wage increase at the "go down," with another 2.77 percent and 2.89 percent due at subsequent four-month intervals. Several other strikes—Carolina Telephone and Telegraph (United System), Virginia-West Virginia General Telephone and Continental's Western Carolina—won comparable gains for the workers involved. But not all the independent strikes were over wages. Workers at the Rochester Telephone Corporation struck for twenty-eight weeks when management insisted on the right to lay off, transfer and assign work without regard to seniority or craft lines. A similar strike lasted twelve weeks at the Mid-Continent Eastern Illinois Telephone Corporation. Fringe benefits and work rules were at issue during the 200-day Kentucky General Telephone Company walkout in 1976.

CWA continues to grow in membership despite the mid-1970s economic downturn. CWA remains the dominant union within the Bell System, the largest of thirty-odd employee organizations, representing seventy percent of the system's eligible workers. This includes some or all nonmanagement employees in all Bell System companies, except the Pennsylvania, Diamond State (Delaware) and Southern New England companies. The union continues to make inroads among the dwindling number of independent associations. They have won over, to give some recent examples, commercial and marketing and directory sales employees in Indiana Bell, Mountain Bell accounting employees, and won back not only the Federation of Women Telephone Workers of Southern California but also Maryland Traffic— groups that left the National Federation of Telephone Workers during the formative years. Growth, however, has been greatest most recently in the public-and service-employees sectors. The Bureau of National Affairs reported that CWA had organized more potential members in the white-collar field during 1974 than any other union, winning thirty out of fifty-one elections conducted by the NLRB in this field. (Overall, the union won 154 elections in 234 organizing projects for the year).

As of 1975, CWA represented more than 32,000 employees in nontelephone categories under approximately 400 contracts covering workers in public and service employment, communications manufacturing, construction, other nontelephone communications, inter-connect, sound and electronics, cable television, gas and electric utilities, professional and semi-professional employees, and in a number of other miscellaneous categories. In the public sector, active campaigns were under way in 1975 in the states of California, Colorado, Florida, New Jersey, New York, Ohio and Texas.

What strikes the observer is the way CWA adapts, changes, and meets new challenges. In organizing, as an instance, the present thrust of the union is outside its traditional arena. "It is moving in the direction of finding the unorganized and organizing," as CWA president Watts phrased it. But in reaching out, the union has not relied on its staff. According to Watts, "There is no possibility of the full-time staff of the Union organizing the unorganized. It takes more people than there are staff to do it. And so, if it's to be done at all, the local leadership has got to recognize that, and use themselves as well as their membership to accomplish the objective." And this participation marks the union's efforts in other areas of concern. During the 1974 negotiations there were complaints that a news blackout left the members in the dark about developments that concerned them. The 1975 convention authorized a rank-and-file committee to look into "problems associated with collective bargaining" and its report was adopted at the following convention with amendments that barred blackouts during negotiations and provided for "brief daily reports . . . made by tape" by both national and local bargaining committees.

Great care is taken to involve CWA members in the development of collective bargaining policy. In early 1977 bargaining appeared to be moving along traditional lines with the union insisting on increases to improve living standards and for a "catch-up" to cover losses through inflation. Beyond that primary concern, however, there is a new interest in job security and job content. In particular, Bell System workers rebelled against "monitoring," a system of "absentee control" and observation of job performance that smacks of spying. The union understands the need for productivity, observations of work that measure the quality of service, efficiency and for guidance for further training. But the union objects to monitoring being used for disciplinary purposes and seeks to limit its use to legitimate purposes. To cope with the problem of job content, the union formed a study group composed of selected staff and professionals. The study group, the Job Value Analysis Committee, met with a resource group of two rank-and-file members from each CWA district to assure participation and a flow of information both ways.

Only by looking back can we see how far CWA has come, how much it has changed, and how involved it has become in our country. CWA president Watts, after his first year in office, reported the great awe he felt on fully realizing "how many people turn to CWA for help of all kinds, ranging from help on a piece of social legislation to our moral support for Soviet Jews," on coming to appreciate "the vast amount of prestige and influence that you [union members] have built for yourselves and this organization," and on understanding "in a way I never did before how closely a democratic CWA parallels a democratic United States of America."

Philip Murray, the late beloved president of the Congress of Industrial Organizations, once described the goals of unionism as "a rug on the floor, a picture on the wall, music in the home, food on the table, clothes and education for our children." All this—and more—CWA has accomplished for its members. Through their union communications workers have enriched their lives, enhancing the quality of life as well as achieving straightforward gains in wages and fringe benefits. They have also enlarged the lives of all of us through their participation in community activities, in political action, and by building a better union, a better country and a better world.

BIBLIOGRAPHY

Most of my sources are indicated in the text. *The Telephone Worker,* the monthly publication of the National Federation of Telephone Workers, *The CWA News,* and Federation and CWA convention proceedings were invaluable as were the oral history interviews conducted by John N. Schacht on behalf of the Communications Workers of America–University of Iowa Oral History Project. For those curious readers who may want to dig on their own into various aspects of CWA history, I suggest the following:

Barbash, Jack. *Unions and Telephones: The Story of the Communications Workers of America.* New York: Harper & Brothers, 1952.

Beirne, Joseph A. *New Horizons for American Labor.* Washington Public Affairs Press, 1962.

———. *Challenge to Labor: New Roles for American Trade Unions.* Englewood Cliffs, N. J.: Prentice-Hall, Inc., 1969.

CWA–University of Iowa Oral History Project. Washington: Communications Workers of America, AFL–CIO Headquarters, n.d.

Curry, Nelle B. *Report: Investigation of the Wages and Conditions of Telephone Operating.* Washington: United States Commission on Industrial Relations, 1915.

Danielian, N. R. *A. T. & T.: The Story of Industrial Conquest.* New York: Vanguard Press, 1939.

Diebold Group. *Automation: Impact and Implications.* Washington: Communications Workers of America, AFL–CIO, n.d.

U. S. Senate. *Labor-Management Relations in the Bell Telephone System.* Hearings before the Subcommittee on Labor-Management Relations of the Committee on Labor and Public Welfare. U. S. Senate. 81st Congress, 2nd Session. Washington: Government Printing Office, 1950.

INDEX